HV

1973

Search and Destroy

Search and Destroy

A Report by the Commission of Inquiry
into the Black Panthers and the Police

Roy Wilkins and Ramsey Clark,
Chairmen

METROPOLITAN APPLIED RESEARCH CENTER, INC.
NEW YORK

14368

FIRST EDITION

ISBN: 06–010828–2

LIBRARY OF CONGRESS CATALOG CARD NUMBER: 73–7068

Contents

PREFACE

Those of us who want to love our country are not anxious to ask whether our police are capable of murder. So we do not ask. We do not dare concede the possibility.

But we live here, and we are aware, however dimly, that hundreds of us are killed every year by police. We assume the victims are mad killers and that the officers fired in self-defense or to save lives.

Then came Orangeburg, the Algiers Motel incident, the Kent State killings, and reasonable persons were put on notice. Official conduct bears investigation. In a free society the police must be accountable to the people. Often, instead of seeking facts, we tend, largely in ignorance, to polarize, with ardent emotional commitment to the state and order on the one side and, equally passionately, to the oppressed and justice on the other.

Does the truth matter? If not, we are in an eternal contest of raw power. If it makes a difference, if it changes minds and hearts, can we find it?

This report pursues the truth of an episode that occurred early on December 4, 1969, at 2337 West Monroe Street in Chicago, Illinois. It was a time of darkness, cold, rage, fear, and violence. Facts are not easily found in such company.

The early dawn stillness had been broken at about 4:45 A.M. by heavy gunfire, eighty rounds or more, which lasted over a period of ten minutes. When it stopped, two young men, Fred Hampton and Mark Clark, were dead. Four other occupants of the premises, the Illinois Black Panther Party headquarters, were seriously wounded. Two police officers were injured, one by glass, the other by a bullet in the leg.

Of the total of perhaps one hundred shots fired that fatal night, probably one bullet was discharged by a Panther. It is possible that no Panther fired a shot, or that two or even three shots were fired by them. But it is highly unlikely that any Panther fired more than a single shot. The physical evidence does indicate that one shot was fired by them; and bullets fired inside a house make their mark.

Fred Hampton may or may not have been drugged or asleep throughout the episode; one can never be sure. Still, the probability is that he was unconscious at the time of his death. Nor can we be positive whether he was shot in the head by a policeman standing in full view of his prostrate body or by blind police gunfire from another room. But we must not weight the probabilities with our wishes. If Hampton never awakened, if he was murdered, it is better to know it. It tells us something we need to know.

The accounts—including those of the police and survivors, the coroner's report, the ballistics and autopsy reports—are not entirely clear or consistent. Nor are the press reports, or the federal grand jury *Report,* or, indeed, this study. Clarity and consistency may occur principally in fiction.

Some conclusions about the episode are reasonably clear, however.

1. Whatever their purpose, those officials responsible for planning the police action and some who directly participated acted with wanton disregard of human life and the legal rights of American citizens.

2. The search warrant for the premises, assuming it was legally supportable, could have been executed in a lawful manner with no significant risk to life.

3. The hour of the raid, the failure to give reasonable warning to the occupants, the overarming of the police, the wildly excessive use of gunfire, all were more suited to a wartime military commando raid than the service of a search warrant.

4. There can be no possible legal or factual justification for this police use of firearms. There was no "shoot-out." The police did virtually all, if not all, of the shooting and most of it blindly. If the one shot that can be attributed to a Panther was fired, and was fired first, it could not justify the more than eighty shots that were fired by the police. If any of these shots were fired in the mistaken belief that

they were being fired in response to fire from the Panthers, that such a belief was entertained by police officers would evidence the inadequacy and consequent irresponsibility in planning and control of an operation involving the use of lethal force.

5. It is not safe to entrust enforcement of the laws to authorities who permit the use of a machine gun the way the Chicago police did during the episode.

6. Many statements made after the episode by participating police officers, such as that of Sergeant Groth that "Our men had no choice but to return their fire," are not credible.

7. State's Attorney Edward V. Hanrahan's statements that the police acting under his authority "exercised good judgment, considerable restraint, and professional discipline," and that "The immediate, violent criminal reaction of the occupants in shooting at announced police officers emphasizes the extreme viciousness of the Black Panther Party," render him unworthy of public trust.

8. The failure of the Chicago police and other state and local officials to employ basic investigative practices such as fingerprinting, preserving evidence, examining all firearms, sealing the premises, and examining and photographing the bodies before removing them, as well as gross errors on the part of these officials in ballistics, autopsy, and other examinations, are professionally inexcusable and can only undermine confidence in the competence and integrity of the police and the legal system.

9. The "exclusive" account of the police action given by State's Attorney Hanrahan's office to the Chicago *Tribune,* and the filmed re-enactment of the episode by police for CBS-TV, demeaned public office, misinformed and prejudiced the public, and violated professional ethics.

10. Systems of justice—federal, state, and local—failed to do their duty to protect the lives and rights of citizens.

There is no chance that needed reforms will be made until the people have the opportunity and the will to understand the facts about official violence. Many may simply refuse to believe officials are capable of unlawful violence. Others will believe such violence and support it. But surely most Americans will not knowingly accept police lawlessness. If official violence is to be renounced, the truth must finally overcome our natural reluctance to incriminate government. It is our hope that this report will serve that end.

Of all violence, official violence is the most destructive. It not only takes life, but it does so in the name of the people and as the agent of the society. It says, therefore, this is our way, this is what we believe, we stand for nothing better. Official violence practices violence and teaches those who resist it that there is no alternative, that those who seek change must use violence. Violence, the ultimate human degradation, destroys our faith in ourselves and our purposes. When society permits its official use, we are back in the jungle.

There is a common thread that runs through the violence of B-52 raids in Indochina, police shooting students at Jackson State College in Mississippi, and the slaughter of prisoners and guards at Attica State Penitentiary in New York. We do not value others' lives as we do our own. The Vietnamese, the black students, the convicts and their guards are expendable. Until we understand that George Jackson and Mark Clark and Fred Hampton, as well as the victims of Kent State and the nameless and faceless victims of Jackson State and on all sides in the Indochina war, are human beings equal in every way to our children and ourselves, we will see no wrong in using violence to control or destroy them.

Fred Hampton and Mark Clark were valuable young men. They could have enriched our lives. If they spoke of violence, suffered it, or used it, we should not be surprised. It was not foreign to their environment, nor did their government eschew it. And talented or not, violent or nonviolent, they were human beings whose lives and legal rights must be cherished by a just society.

Our Commission was formed in December 1969 to make a searching inquiry and to report on confrontations between police and the Black Panther Party. It sought, as a major purpose, to stimulate government investigation and a faithful performance of duty. It recognized from the beginning the great difficulty official efforts have in finding truth, even with their vast resources, including investigatory and subpoena powers.

The Commission's task has not been easy. Early on it found that few Americans with power are prepared to consider objectively po-lice-Panther confrontations. Money was hard to find, tentative in its commitment, and slow to be paid. Government was uncooperative, if not hostile. The federal government through then Assistant Attorney General Jerris Leonard asked the Commission to delay its investiga-tion in Chicago, implying federal indictments were forthcoming. Long delays were made necessary by grand jury investigations of the Chicago episode and finally by the trial of various officials involved in the episode on the charge of conspiracy to obstruct justice. This trial resulted from the efforts of Special Prosecutor Barnabas Sears to see truth found, justice done; the Commission was concerned that premature release of any report might prejudice the right of potential or actual defendants to a fair trial.

Finding and keeping an objective professional staff was hard. The Commission itself, large and unwieldy, was made up of busy people scattered over the country, and soon evolved into a steering commit-tee. Its members are Marion Wright Edelman, Sam Brown, Kenneth Clark, George Lindsay, John Morsell, and Ramsey Clark. This com-mittee is finally responsible for the work of the Commission and for its report.

This report, as is the case with most Commission efforts, is largely the work of the staff, which has performed under extremely adverse conditions. An enormous amount of time and energy went into its wide-ranging investigation and hard analysis. A massive amount of material has been collected on police-Panther confrontations around the country. The report reflects the most comprehensive investigation made of a single incident by the Commission, and for it we are indebted to the staff. The original director, Norman Amaker, served on loan from the NAACP Legal Defense Fund, Inc. His successor, Herbert O. Reid of the Howard University Law School faculty, com-pleted the assignment. All Commission staff members are listed in the appendix.

Steven P. Dolberg, Deborah B. Morse, and Allan R. Abravanel, associates at Paul, Weiss, Rifkind, Wharton & Garrison, also made substantial contributions to the report by editing the staff's manu-script and preparing it for publication.

It is the hope of both Commission and staff that this report will help us recognize our common humanity, understand the need and joy of living together, lay aside our violent ways, and walk in the paths of justice.

May 1973

ROY WILKINS
RAMSEY CLARK
Chairmen

SEARCH AND DESTROY

INTRODUCTION

The Chicago Incident
on December 4, 1969

At approximately 4:45 A.M. on the morning of December 4, 1969, a detail of Chicago police officers assigned to the Cook County State's Attorney's Office went to an apartment at 2337 West Monroe Street on Chicago's South Side with the stated purpose of executing a search for illegal weapons.

The first-floor apartment was occupied by nine members of the Illinois chapter of the Black Panther Party, including its chairman, Fred Hampton. Approximately ten minutes later, two young men were dead and four other persons were seriously wounded. Their ages ranged from seventeen to twenty-two.

Mark Clark, twenty-two, who was in the front living room when the police entered, and Fred Hampton, twenty-one, who was in the rear bedroom, were killed. Hampton was shot four times, twice in the head; Clark, twice in the arm, and through the heart and lungs. Both were dead on arrival at the hospital.

Four other occupants of the apartment were wounded: Ronald Satchel, eighteen—one of three occupants of a middle bedroom—received five gunshot wounds from a machine gun, two in the lower right abdomen, one in the left long finger, one in the right thumb, and one in the right thigh. (He underwent general surgery that day—including a hemicolectomy—and remained in the hospital for one month.) Verlina Brewer, seventeen, suffered two gunshot wounds from the machine gun, one in the left buttock and one in the left knee, with fracture of the tibia. Blair Anderson, eighteen, had three gunshot wounds from the machine gun, in the left thigh, at the base of the penis, and in the right thigh; the last bullet was not removed. Brenda

3

Harris, nineteen—who, like Clark, was in the living room—was shot twice, once in the right thigh and once in the left hand, with a fracture of the third metacarpal. Two Chicago policemen, Officers John Ciszewski and Edward Carmody, suffered minor injuries.

The four wounded occupants and three others who were in the apartment—Deborah Johnson, eighteen, Harold Bell, twenty-two, and Louis Truelock, thirty-two—were arrested and held on a variety of charges, including attempted murder.

Some public officials were quick to praise the conduct of the police, contrasting it with what one called "the vicious, animal, criminal" nature of the Black Panthers.

Within hours of the incident, Cook County State's Attorney Edward V. Hanrahan held a press conference. He castigated the actions of the Panthers and charged that they had made a vicious, unprovoked attack on police attempting to carry out a legitimate search of the apartment. Cook County State's Attorney Hanrahan praised his police officers for "good judgment, considerable restraint, and professional discipline." A series of vivid, if contradictory, accounts of the raid were given by members of the police raiding party to the press and were widely circulated.

United States Senator John McClellan of Arkansas had called Fred Hampton a "Red Communist" before the Senate Permanent Subcommittee on Investigations. Police described him as a "known felon" and "a convicted felon under indictment for a violent crime"; he had, in fact, been sentenced to from two to five years in the penitentiary for allegedly helping black youths steal seventy-one dollars' worth of ice cream from a street vendor the previous summer.

But many in the black community and a number of white residents of Chicago condemned the actions of the police and called the deaths of Hampton and Clark "murder" or "assassination." Fred Hampton had held a position of some respect in Chicago's black community. He was known as a top student and star athlete in suburban Maywood, where he grew up. In 1966, after graduation from high school, he prepared to enter Triton Junior College as a prelaw student, and became president of the Youth Council of the West Suburban Branch of the NAACP. He led a movement for recreational facilities and better school conditions for black youths in Maywood. The white mayor of that city was among the first to call for an investigation of his death.

From the time he left Maywood until his death, Fred Hampton grew increasingly militant, often reported as working among and organizing the black ghetto residents of Chicago. The Panthers' free breakfast program, free medical clinic, and other community services projects were credited to him. The interracial alliances he forged among the Panthers, black youth gangs, and Puerto Rican and Appalachian white youths and students testified to his leadership and organizational ability.

Five thousand people attended Fred Hampton's funeral service in Chicago. The Reverend Jesse Jackson in eulogy said, "When Fred was shot in Chicago, black people in particular, and decent people in general, bled everywhere."[1] The Reverend Ralph Abernathy, Martin Luther King, Jr.'s heir as head of the Southern Christian Leadership Conference, spoke also:

> If they can do this to the Black Panthers today, who will they do it to tomorrow? If they succeed in repressing the Black Panthers, it won't be long before they crush any party in sight—maybe your party, maybe my party.
>
> I want to tell you this, Fred—You did not die in vain. We're going to see to it that you didn't die in vain. But I don't think you will rest in peace, Fred, because there isn't going to be any peace.
>
> We're going to take up your torch, Fred. Though my fight will be nonviolent, it will be militant. There will be no peace in this land.[2]

Mark Clark was the ninth of seventeen children. His father, William Clark, was pastor of Holy Temple Church of God in Christ, and had worked for twenty-eight years, until his death in May 1969, in the foundry at the Caterpillar Company. Mark's mother, Mrs. Fannie Clark, had worked at St. Francis Hospital and occasionally as a domestic. Clark went to Roosevelt Junior High School and Manual High School, apparently only a fair student, but with talent in art, drama, and speech. He did not finish Manual. There were disciplinary problems, including an alleged assault upon a teacher. He later attended some classes at Illinois Central Junior College in Peoria.

1. Chicago *Daily News,* Red Flash Edition, December 10, 1969, p. 5.
2. Chicago *Sun-Times,* 4 Star Final, December 10, 1969, p. 5.

Mark Clark became active in civil rights in his mid-teens and, with his brothers and sisters, joined demonstrations in Peoria under the sponsorship of the local branch of the NAACP. John Gwyn, president of the local and state NAACP chapters, said that by the time Clark was thirteen years old he was "demonstrating against discrimination in employment, housing, and education."

He had had contacts with the law. Peoria police records show that he was fined twenty-five dollars in February 1965 for carrying a concealed weapon; sentenced to four months in jail in October 1965 on a charge of aggravated battery; fined fifty dollars in February 1967 for curfew violation and one hundred dollars for carrying a concealed weapon. In most instances he served out the fines in the Peoria county jail at the rate of five dollars a day.

Miss Donna Cummings, a Peoria policewoman for twenty-seven years and former juvenile officer who had known Clark since his childhood, said, "He was one of my children, but no one in the world is perfect. The path he chose in life was his destiny. What he was doing, in his heart he felt he was doing for his people. He gave his life for the thing he believed in most."

According to his sister Eleanor, he became interested in the Black Panther Party about a year before his death. He and another Panther from Peoria, Anthony Harris, twenty-one, had come to Chicago on November 20, 1969, to confer with Party leaders there. Harris was arrested after a gun battle with police, and charged with attempted murder and aggravated battery, on December 2, two days before Mark Clark was himself killed by police.

Of those who survived the raid, Ronald Satchel had attended the University of Illinois for two quarters after high school graduation the previous year. Brenda Harris attended the University of Illinois for one year. She later enrolled at Malcolm X College in Chicago. Harold Bell had completed high school studies in the army after dropping out of school in Memphis. He had been discharged after three years' service in June 1968 and attended a junior college in Rockford, Illinois, for a year. Deborah Johnson, who graduated from high school in 1968, had attended Wright City College for one year. At the time of the raid she was eight and one-half months pregnant with her son, Frederick Ted Nathaniel Jake.

Charges and countercharges filled the pages of the newspapers in the days that followed the incident. Pressure grew for an investigation into the actions of the police and the State's Attorney's Office. The drama was heightened as hundreds of visitors were led by Black Panther Party "guides" through the bullet-scarred rooms of the unsealed apartment.

After touring the apartment, the vice president of the Afro-American Patrolmen's League, a pioneer black police officers association, said he believed the shootings were "an obvious political assassination," and the president of the League was quoted as saying, "We found no evidence that anyone had fired from inside the apartment." The League announced its own investigation of the case, saying it appeared that the men were killed "for no reason" in a "deliberate police set-up."[3]

Typical of the troubled response of many in the community at large was a statement issued by Roman Catholic priests representing ten parishes in the Lawndale–Garfield Park area of Chicago, as reprinted in the Chicago *Sun-Times* on December 10, 1969:

We Catholic priests of Lawndale and Garfield are prompted by the recent death of a prominent black citizen, Fred Hampton, to speak to the people of Chicago. We have often watched with appreciation and respect the professional work of many fine men and officers of our Chicago Police Department.

FRUSTRATION AND RAGE
Those efforts, however, cannot dispel our feelings of frustration and rage over the general failure and mistrust of police service in our communities. We also stand ready to accept our share of responsibility in that failure. We have tried for years to deal rationally with the many incidents of harassing arrests and of unprovoked station beatings.

With rising anger we have watched police action which provokes violence in the interest of retaliation, rather than promoting understanding and cooperation in the interest of peace.

MUST SPEAK OUT
Now, with the deaths of Panther leaders Fred Hampton and Mark Clark, we must speak loudly and clearly.

The purpose of a police department and a state's attorney's office is to bring citizens before the bar of justice. Its purpose cannot be punitive or retaliatory. It must be one of protection and service.

Our police agencies have vast resources and manpower at their disposal. Yet, time after time, those agencies have failed in their efforts to bring members of the black community, particularly members of the Black Panther

3. "Blacks Launch Probe," Chicago *Daily News*, December 6, 1969.

Party, and so-called "gang" members, before a court of law when the law apparently has been trespassed.

EXECUTION WITHOUT TRIAL

Further, that failure too often has resulted in execution without trial. We regard that as unacceptable police work, while we also deplore any killing of a police officer in the line of his duty. Other alternatives must be found. We are especially angered when our nation's cherished judicial system becomes thwarted and the police department takes on the role of a punitive agency.

PLEA TO STATE'S ATTORNEY

We must demand the highest professional excellence from our law officers. It is only such excellence which offers the hope of helping heal some of the sicknesses of our society.

We submit that there are serious illegal situations which are the root causes of poverty and frustration in our community. We urge the state's attorney to address his efforts to their redressment. In that way he will help heal some of the problems which lie beneath last week's violence.

We proudly live and work in Lawndale and Garfield Park. We dare not speak for the black community but stand ready, with the combined clergy of our area, to meet with the state's attorney and others to work toward the proper and responsible solution of the vital problems of our community.

Since the raid had been planned and executed by the State's Attorney's Office and its Special Prosecutions Unit, questions were raised by many about the ability of that office to investigate the incident without prejudice. The State's Attorney's Office, the principal state agency charged with the responsibility of investigating any allegations of wrongdoing growing out of the December 4 incident, was in effect inquiring into a case in which its own agents had been the principal participants.

State's Attorney Hanrahan made clear that he believed that his office was entitled to the public's trust.

I would have thought our office is entitled to expect to be believed in by the public. Our officers wouldn't lie about the act. I'm talking about the credibility of our officers here and myself.

On December 15 newspapers reported that the Federal Bureau of Investigation had been ordered into the case to inquire into possible violations of federal law. At the time, Marlin W. Johnson, head of the Chicago FBI office, said only that "Attorney General John N. Mitchell has asked us to make a preliminary investigation, compile evidence and make a report."

Shortly after the FBI investigation was announced, FBI Director J. Edgar Hoover issued his annual report, in which he blamed the Panthers and other groups for recent attacks on policemen and an increasing number of violent acts.

On December 16 the Internal Inspections Division (IID) of the Chicago Police Department announced that it had conducted an investigation of the incident. It found that the police were innocent of any wrongdoing and that their actions were justified.

In its interviews with citizens of Chicago, including members of the bar, the working press, and prominent businessmen, Commission of Inquiry investigators heard numerous bitter criticisms of the police department's Internal Inspections Division. The IID, responsible for investigating allegations of police misconduct, was accused by many of bias in favor of the police. There seemed to be little, if any, confidence that citizens' complaints against policemen would be investigated and resolved impartially. Representatives of the black community reported long-standing grievances against the IID for lack of responsiveness and objectivity in dealing with instances of alleged police misconduct against blacks. There was considerable skepticism about the fairness in an IID investigation of the December 4 raid.

The Cook County Coroner's Office, which also had investigatory responsibilities, shared the lack of credibility in most of the black community. Coroner's inquests into so many cases of citizens shot by police had resulted in verdicts of "justifiable" or "accidental" homicide that a number of blacks interviewed by the Commission of Inquiry said they considered the Coroner's Office to be virtually an arm of the State's Attorney's Office and not an independent and objective agency.

Shortly after the two deaths on December 4, a controversy had arisen over the coroner's autopsy on Fred Hampton's body. Under pressure, the city announced that a special "Blue-Ribbon Coroner's Inquest" composed of prominent citizens, black and white, would be constituted to inquire into the deaths of Hampton and Clark. The inquest, headed by a specially appointed deputy coroner, Martin S. Gerber, convened on January 6, 1970. After twelve days of testimony the special deputy coroner ruled the inquest closed, and a verdict of "justifiable homicide" was returned.

The verdict of the coroner's inquest did not diminish agitation for further investigation. For many, the police testimony before the corner's jury had, instead, raised new questions about the nature of the evidence recovered from the apartment, the credibility of the police accounts, and the justification for the police actions.

As a result of letters, telegrams, delegations, and editorials calling upon the United States Department of Justice to initiate an objective investigation, Attorney General John N. Mitchell, on December 19, 1969, appointed Assistant Attorney General Jerris Leonard to head a Justice Department team "to collect all the facts relating to the incident and present them to an inquisitorial Federal Grand Jury."

On January 30, 1970, a Cook County grand jury indicted the seven surviving occupants of the apartment on charges ranging from attempted murder to illegal possession of firearms. No indictment was brought against the police. On February 11 the survivors pleaded not guilty.

As the state and local authorities failed to indict the police or other officials, public attention turned to the federal grand jury. Interviews by Commission investigators indicate, however, that the black community of Chicago and many others were skeptical as to the objectivity of an investigation conducted under the U.S. Department of Justice. Shortly after he had assumed office, Attorney General Mitchell had labeled the Panthers a subversive threat to the national security. This laid the groundwork for the application by the Department of Justice of its expanded claim of wiretapping authority. During the late summer of 1969 the Justice Department set up a special task force on the Panthers. This task force was staffed with high-level personnel drawn from the three major divisions of the department: Criminal, Internal Security, and Civil Rights.

The American Civil Liberties Union, in a press release dated December 24, 1969, (PR 51–69) announced that its surveys had not proved a directed national campaign to "get" the Panthers, but that, if high national officials were not actually conducting a concerted program of harassment, they had, by their statements and actions, helped to create a climate of oppression and encouraged local police to initiate crackdowns. The release cited as examples: Vice President Spiro Agnew had called the Panthers "a completely irresponsible, anarchistic group of criminals"; Assistant Attorney General Jerris

Leonard had said, "The Black Panthers are nothing but hoodlums and we've got to get them"; FBI Director J. Edgar Hoover, a few months prior to the December 4 raid, had said that "The Black Panther Party without question represents the greatest threat to the internal security of the country [among] violence-prone black-extremist groups"; and, as noted above, Attorney General Mitchell had ruled that the Panthers are a threat to the national security and thus subject to Federal Bureau of Investigation surveillance by wiretapping.[4]

On March 8, 1970, the Illinois chapter of the Black Panther Party sponsored a "People's Inquest" at the First Congregational Church on Chicago's West Side. Dr. Charles G. Hurst, president of Malcolm X College in Chicago, presided over the "inquest" as "coroner." Jewel Cook, a member of the Black Panther Party, acted as "people's attorney," and Illinois Panther Deputy Minister of Defense Bobby Rush participated in the public hearing.

Six of the seven survivors testified: Brenda Harris, Ronald Satchel, Verlina Brewer, Blair Anderson, Harold Bell, and Deborah Johnson. Louis Truelock was also to testify, but, according to members of the sponsoring groups, a personal emergency arose about twenty-five minutes before he was scheduled to appear causing him to miss the proceedings.[5]

4. The nation's first black United States Attorney, Cecil F. Poole, resigned effective January 31, 1970, from the federal prosecutor's post in San Francisco he had held since 1961. Poole had an interview with the press on January 14, 1970, on the eve of the resumption of the federal grand jury investigation of Panther activities on the West Coast, directed by the Justice Department. Poole had not been consulted about the grand jury investigation in his district. Two Justice Department attorneys, Victor Woerheide and Jerome Heilbron, comprised the second two-man team assigned since the probe was launched in May 1969. This special grand jury probe, under the direction of the Criminal Division of the Department of Justice, was focusing on possible violations of the federal riot conspiracy law, and the Smith Act—which prohibits advocating violent overthrow of the government. The press reported that during this interview Poole said: "Whatever they *say* they're doing, they're out to get the Black Panthers" (San Francisco *Examiner,* January 14, 1970).

5. The People's Inquest was modeled after a regular coroner's inquest, with the major difference that the "officers of the court" and the "jurors" were selected as "representative" of the survivors' "peers"—the black community of Chicago. Witnesses were sworn in by Rush, and questions about the raid were put to the survivors by Jewel Cook, Dr. Hurst, and the various jurors. Photographs of the apartment and other exhibits of evidence were shown to the persons assembled. The testimony of the six survivors participating in the People's Inquest was recorded by a certified court reporter and later transcribed.

The "jury," having heard the testimony and reviewed the evidence, pronounced the fourteen policemen in the raiding party guilty of premeditated murder.

On May 8, 1970, a week before the federal grand jury released its report on the case, but after the state had been informed that FBI ballistics reports would not support the charges that the Panthers took part in a shoot-out, the state dropped all charges against the seven survivors.

On May 15, 1970, the federal grand jury released the results of its inquiry. A public report on the proceedings was issued, but no indictments were brought. The published report was unique in federal jurisprudence; it was believed by many to be unauthorized and unlawful since the business of grand juries is to indict or absolve, not to publicize. Its hearings are secret. The report, prepared by Justice Department attorneys, criticized all parties to the incident to some degree.[6] However, it concluded: "The physical evidence and the discrepancies in the officers' accounts are insufficient to establish probable cause to charge the officers with a willful violation of the occupants' civil rights."[7]

The criticisms which the federal grand jury report leveled against the local agencies charged with a full investigation of the raid stilled some of the discontent with previous investigations, but numerous questions remained unresolved.

As of this writing, the only public documentation and explanation of the federal government's intervention into this incident and its resultant investigation is contained in the *Report* of the January 1970 grand jury. The minutes of the federal grand jury remain sealed.

Petitions were filed for the establishment of a special state grand jury, headed by an independent prosecutor, to inquire into the events of December 4 and into the conduct of the public officials connected with the case. Representatives of the survivors and several organizations in the black community presented lists of names that would be

6. In particular, the ineffectiveness of the Coroner's Office and serious incompetence in the Internal Inspections Divison were described. The FBI was singled out for praise for the conduct of its June 4, 1969, Panther raid.

7. *Report of the January 1970 Grand Jury,* United States District Court, Northern District of Illinois, Eastern Divison, p. 113.

acceptable to the black community in directing the special investigation.

On June 26, 1970, a prominent Chicago corporation attorney, Barnabas Sears, was appointed by the chief judge of the Cook County Criminal Court, Joseph A. Power, to direct a new probe into the raid. Sears appointed four assistants, two of whom were black lawyers, to aid in the investigation. Despite continued criticism that the appointment of Sears, a white man, had ignored the interests of the black community, a December 1970 special county grand jury[8] began its deliberations one year after the raid. In the summer of 1971, after months of pressure against this county grand jury and amid rumors that indictments might be pending, the police filed suit to prohibit release of any grand jury indictments on grounds of improper prosecution. After one of the most incredible power struggles in our judicial history, involving two reviews by the Supreme Court of Illinois and denial by the United States Supreme Court on May 15, 1972, of State's Attorney Hanrahan's petition for a writ of certiorari, a handful of officials involved in the episode were tried, not for homicide but for obstruction of justice. After a lengthy trial, which raised more questions than it answered, the charges against the officials were dismissed.

The central questions addressed in this report are thus left unanswered by official action. Was the raid legal? Was its purpose the execution of a search warrant on a Black Panther? Were the deaths of the two Panthers justifiable homicides or murder? Were the injuries inflicted on the four wounded Panthers the result of excessive force or lawful police action? Was there evidence of criminal conduct on the part of those occupants who survived the raid, or of the police and other public officials involved in the raid or subsequent proceedings? These are questions of the greatest significance. They are the reason for the work of the Commission of Inquiry.

8. Case No. 70, Special Grand Jury 3.

CHAPTER 1

Police-Community Relations
in Chicago at the Time of the Raid

In studying the background of the deaths of Hampton and Clark, the Commission staff attempted to determine whether the predawn police raid on December 4, 1969, was an isolated event or was related, generally, to the state of police-community relations or, specifically, to previous police-Panther confrontations. To this end, it conducted numerous interviews with members of Chicago's black community and with many civic leaders, black and white. It also studied a large body of other evidence and analyses—news stories and commentaries, special reports, and official documents—related to the background against which the deaths occurred. The product of the investigation is a story of increasing tension and distrust between blacks and police in Chicago through the ten years preceding the police raid.

Police-Community Relations, 1960-1968

In the early 1960s, Chicago's Police Department, under the direction of Superintendent Orlando W. Wilson, was widely considered a national model of modern professional police adminstration. At a time when police officials across the country were beginning to be subjected to public criticism because of the police treatment of civil rights demonstrators, Wilson was singled out for special praise for the sensitive and professional conduct of the Chicago Police Department. During the middle of the decade, however, a marked change in the operations of the Chicago Police Department occurred.

In 1966 and 1967 Chicago's black neighborhoods, like those of many other cities, were hit with sporadic instances of civil disorder, looting, and arson. The city responded by developing new procedures and methods of policing, including a special two-stage "riot control" program. The first phase of this program consisted of saturating an area with a large number of police (as many as 1,500 in a few square blocks), who were divided into roving "tactical units" and who engaged in massive "sweep arrests" to clear the streets. The second phase, carried out with the active assistance of judges and prosecutors, involved setting consistently high bail for all those arrested in the course of a disturbance, in order to detain them for a month or more in prison and thereby temporarily keep the streets "clean."

This "mass-arrest and high-bail" policy drew particular criticism from the black community and members of the legal profession. Hostility toward police actions grew in the black community, and police in turn began to intensify their patrol and surveillance of black neighborhoods. Allegations of harassment, verbal abuse, beatings, shootings, and other forms of police misconduct toward black citizens filled the pages of the *Daily Defender,* Chicago's major black newspaper.

In the fall of 1966 Albert Reiss, of the University of Michigan, undertook a detailed study of police-community relations in several cities, including Chicago.[1] In surveying one white and one black police precinct in Chicago, Reiss found significant differences in the attitudes about the police held by residents of the two communities. Asked whether being a Negro made any difference in the way a person is treated by police, 44 percent of the respondents living in the predominantly black district said it did make a difference, while only 14 percent of the respondents from the white precinct felt that there was any disparity in treatment. One out of four respondents in the black district felt that blacks were treated unjustly by police, while only one out of ten people surveyed in the white district had that opinion. Twice as many respondents from the white precinct as from the black district felt that police were doing "a very good job," and while one out of every five surveyed in the black district felt that blacks were special targets for poor treatment by the police, only one out of fifty

1. His findings were later published as a supplementary report to the President's Commission on Law Enforcement and Administration of Justice, 1967, entitled *Studies in Crime and Law Enforcement in Major Metropolitan Areas* (Washington, D.C.: Government Printing Office), vol. 1.

in the white police district felt that blacks were singled out for mistreatment.

On April 4, 1968, Dr. Martin Luther King, Jr., who had led a campaign to combat racism in Chicago, was assassinated in Memphis, Tennessee. Chicago's black communities, like many in the nation, expressed their grief and anger in an outburst of violence. Police actions in attempting to control and halt the three days of burning and looting which ensued led to general praise for the Chicago Police Department's restraint and regard for the lives of those engaged in the disturbances. But Mayor Richard Daley of Chicago openly criticized the police for failing to act more harshly, and issued his much-publicized edict to policemen: "Shoot to kill arsonists, shoot to maim looters." Soon afterward, Chicago police began to patrol the black communities of the city armed with loaded shotguns.

Although the mayor's order was eventually softened, and although the shotguns were ultimately relegated to the trunks of police patrol cars, the consequences of this attitude were unmistakable and irrevocable. Ironically, the immediate effect of Daley's words was dramatized not by an incident involving the black community, but by police actions at a peace march in Chicago's Loop on April 27, 1968, the participants in which were predominantly young whites. The march was disbanded when police moved in suddenly to clear the streets, beating demonstrators, bystanders, and newsmen alike. In the police sweep, sixty-three persons were arrested, many were beaten by police who had removed their badges and more than half were reportedly sprayed with chemical mace after they had been arrested.[2]

The "Walker Report" of the Violence Commission later characterized police action in the peace march as a prelude to the "police riot" that occurred at the Democratic National Convention later that year.[3] The Walker Report further concluded that the April 1968 incidents and the mayor's public espousal of violent police action resulted in "the conditioning of Chicago police to expect that violence against

2. See Joseph L. Sander, "Chicago: A Study in Law and Order," *Nation* (May 20, 1968).

3. Daniel Walker, *Rights in Conflict, the Violent Confrontation of Chicago During the Week of the Democratic National Convention: A Report to the National Commission on the Causes and Prevention of Violence* (New York: Bantam Books, 1968).

demonstrators, as against rioters, would be condoned by city officials."

Black Legislators' Investigative Committee on Black Police

By the summer of 1968 concern over the relationship of the police to the black community began to be shared by black officers on the force. The Afro-American Patrolmen's League (AAPL), formed in the spring of that year, began to exert pressure within and without the department to alter the existing relationships between the police and the community. The AAPL represented far more than a black version of one of the many traditional police associations. A founder of the organization, Renault Robinson, described its formation as follows: "The League wanted the public to know that they formed to improve the relationship between the black community and the black policemen. Also, the League wanted to change the relationship between the white policemen and the black community." More significantly, Robinson said:

A group of black policemen wanted to fracture the traditional relationship that existed between themselves and the police administration and the black community. This relationship is, of course, a colonial police type relationship. The white police administration has used the black police against black people. This is the only reason black police make it impossible to integrate the police force, or deploy black police in sufficient numbers in the white community. Therefore black police have only one function and that function is "pawns" of the white man to be used against black people.

The Commission's staff found, among the blacks interviewed, virtually unanimous support for the AAPL, which in 1970 had a membership of 800 to 1,000 of the 2,100 black policemen on Chicago's 13,000-man force.

Allegations of harassment of the members of the AAPL by the Chicago Police Department led black Illinois state legislators to form a special investigative committee in the fall of 1969. In the five weeks of hearings that followed, a number of officers testified that after taking an active part in the activities of the AAPL, they had been subjected to harassment from white officers, given "poor" assignments regardless of their previous experience and qualifications, repeatedly called before the Internal Inspections Division on complaints filed by white officers, and in some cases suspended from active duty. At the same hearings, residents of the black community, representatives of established black community organizations, gang leaders, militant young blacks, attorneys, and black civic leaders praised the work of the Afro-American Patrolmen's League, and condemned the general practices of the Chicago Police Department. These witnesses also told of instances of police brutality in the black community, reciting cases of alleged beatings, shootings, and homicides of blacks by white police. Their testimony was supported by several black policemen and former officers who also testified.

In December 1970 Officer Renault Robinson, quoted above, with more than fifty citations for outstanding police work, was suspended for a year from the police department on an accumulation of minor charges filed by his superiors.

Police and Black Youth Groups

Ethnic youth gangs in Chicago, as in many large urban areas, have had a long history of violence that has led, understandably, to considerable friction and conflict between the gangs and the police. During the mid-1960s, however, certain of Chicago's black gangs shifted their attention, to greater or lesser extents, from combating other gangs (and police) to combating poverty, discrimination, and violent disturbances. The official—i.e., police—image of the gangs remained, nonetheless, unchanged, which had the effect of maintaining, and perhaps even increasing, the mutual hostility between police and the gangs.

The altered role of the black youth gangs, and the continued existence of the hostility between the gangs and the police, are illustrated by the following examples.

Funds for a federal antipoverty project were granted to The Woodlawn Organization (TWO), a community action group, to be used to support community activities to be carried out by the Blackstone Rangers, a black youth gang on Chicago's South Side. The direct grant to TWO bypassed all the regular city agencies, was made without city approval, and was for a program to be conducted without city control. Subsequently, a congressional investigation of the grant was commenced, in part, at least, at the behest of Mayor Daley. Witnesses at the congressional hearings included officers from the Gang Intelligence Unit (GIU) of the Chicago Police Department, who testified about "pot and sex parties" allegedly held with the knowledge of TWO personnel. The TWO grant was withdrawn.

By the summer of 1968 the police, led by the GIU, were involved in a series of confrontations involving black youth gangs. The Blackstone Rangers, who had reportedly cooperated with police in averting potential racial disturbances in the previous two summers, had by 1968 become a target of the GIU and "gang busting."

During the fall of 1968 the Black P. Stone Nation, an amalgamation of several youth gangs, ran a "no-vote" campaign on the black South Side to take black votes away from the Democratic machine in the city. In 1969 members of black gangs provided the bulk of the demonstrators who closed down Chicago's construction industry over demands for more black jobs in the building trades.

It was in this context that the Illinois chapter of the Black Panther Party was chartered in November 1968. The Panthers began an active recruitment campaign and by early 1969 had developed a close rapport with the major black street gangs, as well as alliances with other militant groups including the Young Lords (formerly a Puerto Rican gang), the Young Patriots (an organization of young Appalachian whites on Chicago's North Side), and the Students for a Democratic Society. The Panthers, like their allies, attracted heavy police surveillance and were subject to frequent arrests.

In the spring of 1969 Mayor Daley and Cook County State's Attorney Edward V. Hanrahan announced a "War on Gangs." The mayor brought major city officials together in a highly publicized meeting to plan strategy for the "war." Superintendent of Schools James Redmond, Police Superintendent James Conlisk, Fire Commissioner Robert Quinn, and Human Resources Director Deton Brooks were named as a top-level committee to coordinate the city's actions, and State's Attorney Hanrahan, under whose auspices the raid of December 4, 1969, was later conducted, took public leadership of the effort.

The gangs became a highly visible target of police attention. City officials released special reports of statistics on youth crime in black neighborhoods. A special county grand jury was impaneled to consider indictments against gang leaders, and the State's Attorney's Office announced a daily account of the number of resulting indictments against reputed gang members. These indictments, on charges such as extortion, robbery, intimidation, assault, and murder, rose rapidly as the summer months of 1969 passed, eventually totaling more than two hundred.

State's Attorney Hanrahan additionally supported the War on Gangs in speeches and radio broadcasts. On June 20, 1969, addressing several hundred young black women, members of the Neighborhood Youth Corps, Hanrahan described gang members as "animals unfit for society," and went on to say:

> I'm trying to take the romance out of gangs and let the brutality show through. It's one thing to call gangs "Mad Latins" or "Maniac Africans," but when you see their conduct is like that of a vicious animal there is nothing desirable about that.
>
> Nobody in their right mind would appove that kind of conduct and they shouldn't approve the name.
>
> I wish you had an opportunity to see a dead body, some young boy shot or stabbed or clubbed. When you see a young person dead in a pool of blood, and realize the grief this means to a mother, then you know what gang warfare is all about.

He was booed by his audience.

Hanrahan's "Special Prosecutions Unit"

Shortly after Hanrahan took office in January 1969 he formed an elite nine-man state's attorney's unit for dealing with the gangs. Known as the Special Prosecutions Unit, it closely paralleled the regular police Gang Intelligence Unit, and in fact drew some of its members from the GIU, as well as from the Anti-Subversive Unit of the Intelligence Division (the "Red Squad") of the Chicago Police Department. The Special Prosecutions Unit under Assistant State's Attorney Richard Jalovec (who was to assume direct supervision of the December 4 raid), rapidly emerged as the major "gang buster" in the city. Unlike the GIU, which functioned through ordinary police channels, the Special Prosecutions Unit operated directly out of the

State's Attorney's Office. A close relationship evidently continued between the two units, however; information, equipment, and men were shared on a regular basis.

A second team of nine men was added to the Special Prosecutions Unit in June 1969 as a result of screening and selection by Jalovec. This additional team of officers, under the command of Sergeant Daniel Groth (who was to lead the raid on December 4), was not part of the regular state's attorney's police contingent subject to the direction of the state's attorney's police chief, Charles G. Ward. Rather, it reported, together with the other team in the Special Prosecutions Unit, directly—and exclusively—to Jalovec and State's Attorney Hanrahan. The selection of Sergeant Groth's team of officers was described in the federal grand jury *Report* on the December 4 raid:

Assistant State's Attorney Jalovec stated that he had personally supervised the selection process of Sgt. Groth's team of officers after soliciting suggested names from a number of other attorneys in the office. The group was designed to provide a cross section of experience and expertise, and includes officers from the Gang Intelligence Unit, Robbery, Homicide, Youth Division. In the course of the selection, Jalovec requested the disciplinary records of each officer from the Internal Inspections Division (IID), and was advised that only one, James Davis, had a rather minor charge against him sustained. He neither sought nor received the records of all charges filed against the officers which had been classed by IID as unfounded or not sustained.[4]

The grand jury's footnote at this point (footnote 23) explained that although subpoenaed records of the IID showed that the personnel files of the officers on Groth's team contained records of commendations, they also showed that each of the officers had previously had complaints filed against him at the IID, and that charges had been sustained against two of them.

The Special Prosecutions Unit represented an expansion of the traditional function of the prosecutor's office—prosecution, presentation of evidence, and investigation of crime—to include extensive surveillance, infiltration, and arrest activities. While this extension of the prosecutor's role was not without precedent, it aroused increasing

4. U.S. District Court, Northern District of Illinois, Eastern Division, *Report of the January 1970 Grand Jury* (Washington, D.C.: Government Printing Office), p. 28 (hereafter cited as *Report*).

controversy as the activities of the SPU began to receive public attention.

Although general public opinion about the War on Gangs was favorable at first, and although the program received extensive newspaper support, public interest began to lag as the indictments against alleged gang leaders mounted, and criticism of the policy increased. John Kifner of the *New York Times* wrote in *Scanlan's* magazine, in June 1970:

> Unquestionably, many of the gang members were still delinquents, and many youths affiliated with gangs committed a number of crimes. But there were indications that, contrary to official pronouncements, violent gang activity was decreasing and to many the campaign seemed questionable; in fact, one Justice Department official privately called it "a racist purge."

The Deaths of Black Youths

In the seven months preceding the deaths of Fred Hampton and Mark Clark, at least eleven young blacks in the same neighborhood were killed in altercations involving the police. The circumstances surrounding their deaths, and the deaths themselves, were rarely reported in the Chicago press. There is no indication that these youths were gang members or known felons. They were not killed in riots or mass disorders or organized "shoot-outs," but in isolated instances on the streets of their community or in their homes.

In most cases the police offered explanations of the deaths. In most cases residents of the community and families of the dead youths claimed that these explanations were false or inadequate. The Commission learned that complaints were lodged in many of the cases; in each instance the police IID exonerated the officers involved or failed to investigate the case in more than a cursory manner. Coroner's inquests regularly returned verdicts of "justifiable" or "accidental" homicide.

Among the cases were the following:

On April 30, 1969, Charles Cox, twenty, was found dead in a cell in the 11th District Police Station. A medical examination determined that Cox had died from two blows on the head. Homicide detectives determined that young Cox had died "accidentally" while being held in jail for a court appearance on charges of disturbing the peace. Officers reported that there had been no apparent sign that the youth was injured in any way when brought into the station house. Eugene Moore, who had been with Cox when he was arrested, stated that he and Cox had been walking down the street on the evening of April 30 when they were stopped by a cruising police car. According to Moore two officers jumped out and began "slapping Cox in the face with an open hand." Cox was taken to the station, where his body was found in a cell the next morning. Dr. Earl Caldwell of the Veterans Administration Hospital, a pathologist who examined Cox's skull during an autopsy, found that Cox had been struck at least twice on the head with a blunt instrument. No action was taken on Cox's death.

In May 1969 Mr. C. Green was killed when police, purportedly searching for street-fighting suspects, entered his home with a shot-gun. Patrolman John Kemp of the Marquette District reported that he thought he saw Green with a weapon trying to attack his partner. Kemp said he shouted a warning and his partner, Patrolman W. G. Bixby, whirled around and shot Green in the abdomen. Members of Green's family reported that Green was shot by the police without provocation after they had entered his house. The police Internal Inspections Division judged the case "justifiable homicide."

Also in May 1969 Pedro Medina, seventeen years old, was stopped as a burglary suspect by three plainclothes policemen in an unmarked car. The officers told newsmen that they had seen a bulge in Medina's pocket which they thought was a gun, and had called him to the car. Police alleged that when they opened the car door, Medina bolted and ran several blocks while they pursued him. When the officers were about six yards behind, Medina tripped and fell. Police said that a struggle ensued and that during the struggle Medina was accidentally shot in the stomach with a policeman's revolver. Witnesses stated that the youth neither reached toward his pocket nor drew a gun. According to them, an officer turned Medina over, put one knee on his chest, and deliberately shot him in the stomach. Police who searched Medina's body after the shooting found only a pen and twenty cents. No action was taken on the death.

The deaths of John and Michael Soto were significant not only as isolated incidents, but also in the context of the community activity during which the deaths occured. Teen-agers had been petitioning for over a year for installation of a traffic light at the corner of the Henry Horner housing project on Chicago's all-black West Side, where residents had to cross a heavily traveled road leading to one of Chicago's suburbs in order to go to the local health center or to neighborhood schools. Several previous accidents had occurred at the crossing, and in September 1969 two small children were killed on different days when crossing the street. When the city still refused to install a traffic light, seventeen-year-old John Soto emerged as the leader of a community protest urging that a traffic light be placed at the intersection. His brother, Michael, a twenty-year-old army sergeant home on leave, participated in a subsequent protest on September 16, 1969, and was one of several youths arrested at that time.

On October 5, 1969, three weeks after the first September protest, John Soto was killed by police near the Henry Horner project. Police reported that two Task Force patrolmen stopped a group of three youths who were "acting suspiciously," passing a brown paper bag back and forth among them. The police alleged that one of the young men, John Soto, fought with one of the patrolmen, and was killed when the officer's revolver "accidentally" discharged and fired a shot into the back of his head. Several black witnesses insisted that the youth had not fought with any of the officers, but rather had been shot down deliberately, without provocation.

Anger over John Soto's death grew in the community in the ensuing days, and came to a violent and tragic climax on October 10, 1969. On that day Michael Soto attended his brother's funeral. A few hours later, Sergeant Michael Soto, holder of numerous combat decorations —including the Bronze Star and the Vietnamese Gallantry Cross with Palm—was also dead, also shot by the Chicago police.

The police versions of Michael Soto's death were variously that Michael was robbing a nearby grocery store or beating up a white man in an alley. Officers said they pursued him into the Henry Horner project, where he pulled a gun on them. Police fired, and Michael Soto

after all charges against them were dropped. It was this raid that the grand jury *Report* on the December 4 affair later recommended as a "model raid."[5] No one was injured, there was minimal property damage, and the raid took place in the daytime.

Following the June 4 FBI raid, encounters between law enforcement officials and members of the Black Panther Party became increasingly frequent and violent. Raids on Panther offices and residences, and confrontations between individual Panthers and policemen, resulted in numerous arrests and the deaths of two police officers and two Panthers.

An altercation reported by the police as a shoot-out between two Panthers and two policemen on July 16, 1969, resulted in the death of one of the Panthers, Larry Roberson, and the arrest of the other, Grady Moore. Moore was charged with attempted murder and interfering with an officer; these charges were later dropped.

On July 31, 1969, police reported a "gun battle" with Panthers at the headquarters of the Party. The Panthers and witnesses on the street said police had arrived at the building and opened fire. Five policemen were wounded and three Panthers were arrested; eventually all charges against the latter were dropped.

A third police raid on Chicago Panther headquarters occurred early on the morning of October 4, 1969, when, police said, they responded to "reports of sniper fire." Six Panthers were arrested on charges of attempted murder. The Panthers contended that the police had destroyed their office, stolen money, set a fire, and ruined food and medical supplies; police denied the charges. The charges against the six Panthers were dropped on November 10.

On November 13, 1969, a shoot-out between a group of police and two Panther members resulted in three deaths: Panther Spurgeon Winters and Chicago police officers Gilhooly and Rappaport. A second Panther was wounded and charged in connection with the police officers' deaths.

5. In commenting on the procedures of the state's attorney's police in the December raid, the *Report* stated: "The Grand Jury believes that a professional police department would not have adopted such an approach but would have used a system similar to the one used by the FBI in June 1969, evacuating the entire Panther Headquarters and effecting eight arrests without firing a single shot" (p. 117).

Commission Discussion of Police-Community Relationships

The foregoing accounts illustrate some of the kinds of events that underlay the atmosphere of anger, fear, and mutual hostility which the Commission found to exist between black Chicagoans and the police. That such an atmosphere existed could come as no surprise to anyone even casually familiar with the state of police-community relations in black areas of American cities at that time. Chicago's experience during the late 1960s may have been especially violent and tense, but it was fundamentally no different from the situation that prevailed in almost every major urban center in the country.

The documentation on the situation is well known. From the report of the Chicago Commission on Race Relations[6] on the Chicago race riot of 1919, through the investigation by the Governor's Commission on the Los Angeles (Watts) Riots of 1965 to the McCone Commission, to the 1968 report of the National Advisory Commission on Civil Disorder (the Kerner Commission), and the report of the President's Commission on the Causes and Prevention of Violence issued in 1969, at least one thread of consistency is established: the critical impact of distrust of the police by large numbers of blacks juxtaposed against the fear and outrage of the police at the resistance they encounter.

As the McCone Report put it:

> The bitter criticism we have heard evidences a deep and longstanding schism between a substantial portion of the Negro community and the Police Department. . . . The reasons for the feeling that law enforcement officers are the enemy of the Negro are manifold and it is well to reflect on them before they are accepted. An examination of seven riots in northern cities of the United States in 1964 reveals that each one was started over a police incident, just as the Los Angeles riot started with the arrest of Marquette Frye.[7]

Neither the McCone Commission nor the other investigative bodies were concerned with the *validity* of popular conceptions about the

6. *The Negro in Chicago* (University of Chicago Press: Chicago, 1922).
7. Calif., Governor's Commission on the Los Angeles Riots, *Violence in the City— An End or a Beginning?*, Report by the McCone Commission (Los Angeles: 1965).

role of the police. For diagnostic purposes, it was sufficient to ascertain that the suspicion, distrust, and hostility existed and to assess the intensity of their contribution to explosive events. Similarly, this Commission's approach was initially directed not so much to whether the black community's attitude was justified as to the fact that such an attitude existed.

The Commission found little awareness in the larger Chicago community, or across the nation, of the incidents described in this chapter, but they bore heavily on the minds of black Chicagoans. This concern was further evidenced by the fact that virtually every major black organization in Chicago held the improvement of police-community relations high on its list of priorities. Indeed, one organization founded in response to community anger at the police named itself "The Committee to End the Murder of Black People."

A number of black residents of Chicago expressed to the Commission their own experience of witnessing a series of ill-explained or unexplained deaths, beatings, and other police actions, most of which had not received wide public attention, and some of which had brought high praise to the police for exemplary conduct in the line of duty. Prominent black citizens and responsible black community groups in Chicago presented testimony to this Commission which likened the situation of many black Chicagoans to life under a military regime. They regarded their community as patrolled twenty-four hours a day by the "troops" of the Chicago Police Department, and as the prime focus of the "elite" police units: the state's attorney's Task Force, the Red Squad, and the Gang Intelligence Unit. Similar testimony was given in the previously described hearings of the Ad Hoc Investigative Committee of Black Legislators.

Many ghetto inhabitants said they no longer looked to the police for assistance in even the most harrowing circumstances because of fear of personal abuse at the hands of the police. The frustrations of this tragic state of affairs were summed up for the Commission by a Chicago social worker:

Of course, the people here don't usually call the police. Response is so infrequent when they *are* called—and often so disastrous—that most people wouldn't dream of calling them for any kind of help. Maybe the gangs are the only answer here—I don't know. But a lot of people are beginning to feel that at least the gangs *want* to make things better.

It is not necessary to believe all, or even most, of the reports of police misconduct described in this chapter in order to arrive at the conclusion that by the end of 1969 police-community relationships in Chicago had reached crisis stage. Every charge of police misconduct is countered by a police denial, and, in the absence of determinations by a body the good faith of which is acknowledged by both sides, it is often impossible to know where culpability lies. The unquestionable conclusion, however, from the sheer volume of the charges, counter-charges, and denials, is the existence of a basic mistrust and hostility.

CHAPTER 2

The Plan for and Purposes of the Police Raid

The raid at 2337 West Monroe Street on December 4, 1969, was planned in an atmosphere that involved two critical elements. The first was the mutual animosity between the Chicago police and the black community—and particularly the Panthers. The second was the extensive use by the police, State's Attorney's Office, and FBI of surveillance and informants concerning Panther members and their activities.

Numerous violent confrontations between the Chicago police and black youths, some of which have been discussed earlier, had led to fear, distrust, and hostility between the Chicago police and the black community. Those emotions and the tensions they generated were aggravated on November 13 when two Chicago police officers and one Panther died in a gunfight.

FBI and Other Informants

Eight days later, on November 21, 1969, the FBI began a series of communications to the Chicago Police Department and the Cook County State's Attorney's Office concerning the presence of weapons at 2337 West Monroe Street. In the first such message an FBI informant stated that there was a "stockpile" of weapons and ammunition at the apartment. The information indicated, however, that the weapons had been purchased by persons who had no criminal records, and did not indicate any violation of federal gun laws.[1] The informant

1. *Report*, pp. 28–30.

further stated that the persons most frequently present at the apartment included Fred Hampton, Ronald Satchel, Louis Truelock, and Deborah Johnson.

Based on the informant's allegations, and notwithstanding the fact that the FBI communication had not indicated any violations of law, the Chicago Police Department planned a raid on the premises at 2337 West Monroe. Two days later, however, on November 23, the FBI agent in charge called the director of the Chicago police Intelligence Division and informed him that the weapons had been removed from the apartment, allegedly because the Panthers anticipated a police raid set for November 25. The Chicago police canceled the planned raid.[2]

From November 21 until the time of the raid, the FBI's informant system generated a flow of information about the presence or absence of weapons in the Panther apartment and the individuals who resided or were frequently seen there. On December 1 the FBI again contacted the Chicago police and the State's Attorney's Office, this time to inform them that some of the weapons reported to have been removed from the apartment at the end of November had been returned. An FBI agent reconfirmed this information with Assistant State's Attorney Richard Jalovec early in the day of December 2, and reviewed with him the types of weapons. The agent also reconfirmed that Hampton, Satchel, Truelock, and Johnson were frequently seen at the apartment, and told Jalovec that the occupants would be away from the apartment at 8:00 P.M. on Monday, Wednesday, and Friday nights attending political education classes.[3]

Later on December 2 Sergeant Daniel Groth—who commanded one of the teams of the state's attorney's Special Prosecutions Unit which reported exclusively to Jalovec and State's Attorney Hanrahan—received a telephone call from an informant. Groth's contact, contrary to previous FBI informants, indicated that there were weapons in the apartment the possession of which might constitute violations of the law. The informant, who had been in the apartment on December 1, reportedly told Groth that the weapons at 2337 West Monroe

2. Ibid.
3. Ibid; Groth, coroner's inquest, January 7 and 9, 1970; Chicago *Tribune,* "Exclusive," December 11, 1969.

consisted of three sawed-off shotguns with barrels about twelve inches long, three stolen Chicago Police Department riot shotguns, an unspecified number of rifles and handguns, and forty-five or fifty thousand rounds of ammunition.[4]

Plans for the Raid

On the following morning, Sergeant Groth drove to the neighborhood of 2337 West Monroe and inspected the area for about twenty minutes from his automobile. He then met and exchanged information with Jalovec. Neither informed the Chicago police of the information Groth had received the previous night.

Sergeant Groth then began to plan a raid on the premises.[5] At noon on December 3 Groth discussed the subject with Officers James Davis and Bill Kelly, and dispatched them in unmarked cars to obtain a description and sketches of the building at 2337 West Monroe and of the neighborhood. Before Kelly and Davis left, Groth discussed with them the timing of the raid; they agreed that it should not be made at 8:00 P.M. (as suggested by the FBI communication on December 1), but at an early-morning hour, so as to achieve the maximum surprise and minimal "neighborhood interference." The time for the raid was then set at shortly before 5:00 A.M., December 4. "Our object was to avoid an incident," Sergeant Groth later said.[6]

Later in the afternoon of December 3 Groth determined that he would need several men for the raid in addition to those under his immediate command. He contacted Sergeant Cagney, who commanded another unit of the state' attorney's police, and without informing Cagney why he needed the men, obtained five officers (Broderick, Gorman, Hughes, Harris, and Corbett) from Cagney's command to supplement his own team of officers (Davis, Jones, Howard, Carmody, Ciszewski, Joseph, Kelly, and Marusich). According to Groth, the thirteen men were "volunteers."[7]

4. *Report*, p. 29.
5. Ibid.
6. *Report*, pp. 30–35; Groth, coroner's inquest, January 9, 1970; Chicago *Tribune*, "Exclusive," December 11, 1969.
7. *Report*, pp. 30–35; Groth, Howard, and Harris, coroner's inquest, January 7–12, 1970; Chicago *Tribune*, "Exclusive," December 11, 1969.

Meanwhile, Assistant State's Attorney Jalovec prepared a complaint for a search warrant, based on some of the information which he and Sergeant Groth had received. The only possible legal basis for the warrant, however, was the asserted statement by Sergeant Groth's informant that stolen police weapons and illegal sawed-off shotguns were in the apartment at 2337 West Monroe; Jalovec's own information from the FBI did not indicate any violation of laws. Moreover, of the two categories of illegal weapons allegedly known to Groth, only one—the sawed-off shotguns—was specifically listed in the warrant. It was only after police reported that they had seized a stolen police weapon from the apartment in the raid that Sergeant Groth testified as to his "information" about stolen weapons.[8]

The complaint provides as follows:

COMPLAINT FOR SEARCH WARRANT

Daniel Groth, Complainant, now appears before the undersigned judge of the Circuit Court of Cook County and requests issuance of a search warrant to search the premises located at 2337 W. Monroe, Chicago, Illinois, 1st floor apartment and seize the following instruments, articles and things:

Sawed-off shotguns and other illegal weapons which have been used in the commission of, or which constitute evidence of the offense of Unlawful Use of Weapons.

Complainant says that he has probable cause to believe, based upon the following facts, that the above listed things to be seized are now located upon the (person and) premises set forth above:

A reliable informant, who has furnished reliable information to affiant on several past occasions which has led to the confiscation of 2 sawed-off shotguns in two separate raids, and has provided information that has led to several convictions, informed the affiant DANIEL GROTH that on December 2, 1969 he had occasion to enter the above described premises at 2337 W. Monroe, 1st floor apartment. During this visit, he observed numerous weapons, including three sawed-off shotguns, whose barrels appeared to be approximately 12 inches in length. Along with these weapons he observed numerous rounds of ammunition. When he left the premises the above described sawed-off shotguns were still there. Independently of this above information, DANIEL GROTH was informed by ASA Richard S. Jalovec that on December 2, 1969, Jalovec had a conversation with a reliable informant who also stated that sawed-off shotguns and other weapons were being stored in the first floor apartment at 2337 W. Monroe, Chicago, Illinois. This infor-

8. *Report,* pp. 30–31, 106–107; Groth, coroner's inquest, January 7, 1970.

mant, according to Jalovec, has provided information in the past which has led to the arrest and indictment of numerous individuals.

(signature) DANIEL R. GROTH
Complainant

At 4:45 P.M. on December 3, Circuit Judge Robert J. Collins issued the search warrant based upon Groth's complaint.

SEARCH WARRANT

On this day DANIEL GROTH, Complainant, has subscribed and sworn to a complaint for search warrant before me. Upon examination of the Complaint, I find that it states facts sufficient to show probable cause.

I therefore command that you search the premises located at 2337 W. Monroe, Chicago, Illinois, 1st floor apartment, and seize sawed-off shotguns and other illegal weapons which constitute evidence of the offense of Unlawful Use of Weapons.

I further command that a return of anything so seized shall be made without unnecessary delay before me, or before any court of competent jurisdiction.

(Signature) ROBERT J. COLLINS
Judge

Groth then began to draw up a plan for the thirteen officers who were to accompany him on the raid, with their respective assignments for entering and covering the front and rear doors.[9] In the course of the planning the men discussed the possibility that the apartment was a "warehouse" for Panther weapons. Asked about the purpose of that discussion, Sergeant Groth said later, "Because of the danger factor—the possibility of people being fired on—to avoid a confrontation."[10]

The initial planning having been completed, the officers armed themselves for the raid. From the state's attorney's police arsenal, the officers drew heavy weapons: a Thompson submachine gun with 110 rounds of ammunition, and three shotguns. Three officers decided to bring heavy personal weapons—two shotguns and a carbine. Altogether, the fourteen officers were ultimately equipped for use on the mission with nineteen or twenty .38-caliber pistols, one .357-caliber

9. Chicago *Tribune*, "Exclusive," December 11, 1969.
10. Groth, coroner's inquest, January 7, 1970.

pistol, and the heavy weapons listed above.[11] Groth then instructed his men to assemble for the mission at 4:00 A.M. the following day; he advised them that the early-morning hour for the raid had been chosen to avoid "a trap." Groth said later, "It was the ideal time to lessen the chance of injury to others and to catch any occupants of the apartment unaware."[12]

Following the briefing of the raiding party, Groth met again with Assistant State's Attorney Jalovec and reviewed the basic plan. Jalovec suggested that Groth should use more than fourteen men, because "you never know what is going to happen."[13] Despite the fact that the Chicago Police Department generally used fifty to one hundred men in situations where armed confrontations are anticipated, Groth disagreed with Jalovec's suggestion; Jalovec has agreed in retrospect that fourteen men was a sufficient complement.[14]

Jalovec met with State's Attorney Hanrahan at 5:00 P.M. on December 3, after his meeting with Groth, and informed him that police officers from the State's Attorney's Office would be serving a warrant for Panther weapons in the morning. Jalovec later testified that he considered the raid "a normal thing," and probably would not have informed Hanrahan of it had it not been for "other matters" which he had to discuss with the state's attorney.[15]

Groth then drew up a detailed plan for the raid at his home on the evening of December 3. The plan set out specific assignments for the officers, including the stationing of men outside the apartment and entry at both the front and rear of the house.[16] The plan did not include the use of portable sound or lighting equipment, the use of tear gas, or surveillance to determine whether the apartment was occupied. Nor did Sergeant Groth approve of a device used previously by FBI agents—surrounding the premises, then advising the occupants by megaphone that they were surrounded; he strongly believed

11. *Report*, pp. 30–35; Chicago *Tribune*, "Exclusive," December 11, 1969; Harris and Corbett, coroner's inquest, January 13–15, 1970.
12. Groth, coroner's inquest, January 7, 1970; Howard, Ibid., January 13, 1970; *Report*, pp. 30–35.
13. *Report*, p. 32.
14. Ibid.
15. Ibid. p. 33.
16. Ibid., pp. 32–33, 117.

that this approach was "a bad idea."[17] Groth had no special plan "for dealing with the possibility of resistance."[18]

At 4:00 A.M. on December 4 Groth and the thirteen other members of the raiding party assembled at the State's Attorney's Office. Groth briefed the officers on his plan for the raid, which called for five men to enter the front door of the apartment, four to enter the rear door, and five to remain outside to cover the two exits. Groth had no objection to the heavy armament and personal weapons which his men had brought for the raid, but said he advised them to avoid gunfire if possible:[19] "This has been my criteria ever since I have been a sergeant, don't shoot, don't shoot, don't shoot."[20] Groth later stated that he had never before been on a raid where a machine gun was carried.[21]

The Raid Begins

The briefing over, the fourteen heavily armed officers left the State's Attorney's Office and drove to 2337 West Monroe Street in three cars and an unmarked panel truck.[22] As the vehicles approached the area of the apartment, Sergeant Groth made a radio call to the 13th District of the Chicago Police Department for backup cars to cover the front and rear of the apartment. This was the first time since planning for the raid had begun that the regular police department had been informed that the State's Attorney's Office was going to conduct a raid.[23]

Commission Discussion of the Plan

The planning for the mission—the purported purpose of which was the search for and (if found) seizure of weapons the possession of which might violate local and state statutes—was characterized by

17. Ibid., pp. 32–35, 117.
18. Ibid., pp. 35, 117.
19. *Report,* pp. 34–35; Groth and Harris, coroner's inquest, January 12–13, 1970.
20. *Report,* p. 35.
21. Ibid., p. 32.
22. Ibid., p. 35.
23. Ibid. p. 91.

unusual secrecy. Until the last possible moment Groth and Jalovec kept the nature, purpose, and fact of the raid secret. Only State's Attorney Hanrahan and the men engaged in the mission were briefed. Until the raid had virtually begun the Chicago police were kept uninformed.

The extent of the preparations was also unusual for the execution of a search warrant. State's Attorney Hanrahan was notified of the raid in advance. The Panthers' apartment and the surrounding neighborhood were reconnoitered at least twice by Groth or his men before the plans for the raid were finalized. The fourteen men executing the search warrant carried twenty-seven firearms, including a Thompson submachine gun, five shotguns, and a carbine. And Jalovec, who termed the raid a "normal thing," suggested before the raid that such manpower and firepower were insufficient—that it might be better to use fifty to one hundred men.

In addition to the unusual nature of the preparations, the planning for the mission seems curiously inconsistent with the objective of executing a search warrant. A raid at 8:00 P.M. when there was reason to believe that the apartment would be unoccupied, was rejected, and a daytime raid was apparently never considered. Instead, a predawn raid was planned for maximum surprise. The only benefit of surprise could have been to avoid violence; the weapons that were the object of the search warrant could not have been disposed of by the Panthers once the raid had begun. But the easiest way to avoid violence would have been to conduct the raid at 8:00 P.M. when the apartment was empty. Alternatively, if violence on the part of the Panthers was anticipated, the police could well have followed the established procedure of using sound equipment, portable lighting, and tear gas to force the Panthers out of the apartment and then search it.

The federal grand jury *Report* described the raid as "ill-conceived":

The whole concept of going on a raid in a high crime density area to obtain weapons from known militants—led by a convicted felon believed to be dangerous—with only fourteen men, in plainclothes, in the dead of night, with no sound equipment, no lighting equipment, no tear gas and no plan for dealing with potential resistance, seems ill-conceived. [P. 117.]

The small, select group of men chosen, the officials' knowledge that Panthers were involved, the police information that Fred Hampton was a likely occupant of the apartment, and the timing of and planning for the raid do not coincide logically with the contention that it was considered a routine police mission. The testimony of Assistant State's Attorney Jalovec and Sergeant Groth indicate quite the contrary: preparations for this raid were extraordinary by all standards. Indeed, if the object of the mission, as stated, was to search for and seize illegal weapons, the grand jury's characterization of the planning as "ill-conceived" is a considerable understatement.

CHAPTER 3

The Opening Moments of the Raid—
The Issue of the First Shot

The most important and most controversial aspect of the beginning moments of the raid at 2337 West Monroe Street is the issue of who fired the first shot: a member of the police raiding party or one of the occupants of the apartment. Woven into this issue at every point is the manner of entry by the police into the apartment. The police and state officials alleged that the members of the raiding party fired only in response to hostile gunfire which met them at some point in their entry into the building. These statements differ, however, as to who fired the alleged first shot and where the shot (or shots) originated.

The state's attorney's police and members of the State's Attorney's Office (including State's Attorney Edward V. Hanrahan and Assistant State's Attorney Richard Jalovec) asserted, in public statements and in testimony before investigatory bodies, that the police in the raiding party entered the apartment only after properly announcing their presence and fired only in response to hostile gunfire which broke out as they entered.

In statements made by officials and attorneys of the Black Panther Party and, subsequently, through testimony by some of the surviving occupants at ad hoc investigative hearings, the opposite assertion was made: The police did not sufficiently announce their presence and it was the police who initiated fire as they crashed into the apartment.

This chapter will present the statements, first of the police and then of the survivors, made with respect to the events that occurred during the opening moments of the raid. The Commission has examined these reports for internal consistency, both on an individual basis and in the aggregate, on the basis of the general version of the raid as each group depicts it; its conclusions are summarized below. Finally, this chapter will discuss various examinations of the physical evidence relating to the beginning of the raid, the conflicting evaluations of that evidence, and the Commission's conclusions about the bearing of the physical evidence on the questions at issue.

Accounts by Police and State Officials

The Positioning of the State's Attorney's Police

An official description of the positioning of the state's attorney's police as the raid was about to begin was not made available to the public until December 11, 1969, at which time an "Exclusive" statement to the Chicago *Tribune* was issued by State's Attorney Edward V. Hanrahan.[1] In the seven days between the raid and the issuance of Hanrahan's statement, however, a number of somewhat contradictory versions of the positioning of men were expressed unofficially by police participants in the raid and by state officials.

Assistant State's Attorney Richard Jalovec: On December 4, immediately after the raid, Assistant State's Attorney Richard Jalovec related to reporters what he claimed members of the raiding party had told him. Five state's attorney's police, he stated, had surrounded the building at 2337 West Monroe Street, with other police stationed on the roof of that building and the roofs of certain nearby structures. Regular Chicago police officers from the Wood Street Station had cordoned off the block. Sergeant Daniel Groth, commander of the state's attorney's police raiding group, approached the back door of the apartment with Detectives Edward Carmody and John Ciszewski, while other officers went to the front of the apartment. It was reported in the same news story that state's attorney's investigator James "Duke" Davis led the police through the front door.[2]

In an article appearing later the same day Jalovec altered his account in some respects, but he still maintained that Sergeant Groth and other officers had approached the back door of the apartment.[3]

1. Designated as Composite Version 1.
2. *Chicago Today,* 5 Star Final, December 4, 1969, p. 1.
3. *Chicago Today,* 7 Star Final, December 4, 1969, p. 1.

Officers Edward Carmody and John Ciszewski: Officers Edward Carmody and John Ciszewski, members of the raiding group, spoke to reporters on the morning of December 4, 1969, shortly after being treated for wounds received during the raid (Carmody was cut by glass and Ciszewski was wounded by gunshot). The two officers told newsmen that thirteen state's attorney's police had surrounded the building and that the two of them had approached the back door.[4]

In another story which appeared the same day Officers Carmody and Ciszewski gave a more detailed account of the positioning of officers for the raid, explaining that "five or six" officers covered the rear, while another "six or seven" officers approached the front.[5]

Sergeant Daniel Groth: The first account of the raid by Sergeant Daniel Groth appeared in the newspapers on December 4.[6] Groth asserted that he was positioned at the *front door* of the apartment; he maintained this assertion in all his later accounts. At the coroner's inquest called in January 1970 to investigate the deaths of Mark Clark and Fred Hampton, Groth also stated that Officer Davis was with him at the front door.[7]

Officer Joseph Gorman: Officer Joseph Gorman testified at the coroner's inquest that he was positioned at the front of the apartment with Officers Groth and Davis.[8]

Officers Philip Joseph, Raymond Broderick, and William Kelly: Officers Philip Joseph, Raymond Broderick, and William Kelly[9] testified at the coroner's inquest that they were stationed at the rear of the apartment. They also placed Officer Carmody at the rear.

Composite Version 1: In the official "Exclusive" released to the Chicago *Tribune* by State's Attorney Hanrahan on December 11, 1969, detailed information as to the positioning of the police was made available. According to this version fourteen officers participated in the raid on the apartment, and were stationed as follows:

4. *Chicago Today,* Green Streak Edition, December 4, 1969, p. 16.
5. Chicago *Daily News,* Red Flash Edition, December 4, 1969, p. 6.
6. *Chicago Today,* Green Streak Edition, December 4, 1969, p. 1.
7. Coroner's inquest, January 7–13, 1970.
8. Ibid., January 15, 1970.
9. Ibid., 1970; Joseph on January 14, Broderick on January 16, Kelly on January 13.

Approaching the front door:	Davis
	Gorman
	Groth
	Hughes
	Jones
Covering the front yard:	Marusich
	Howard
	Harris
Approaching the back door:	Carmody
	Ciszewski
	Joseph
	Kelly
Covering the back door:	Corbett
	Broderick

This official description of the deployment of the officers was maintained by Hanrahan and by police officers in all later statements.

Announcements by the Police and Responses by the Occupants:

Police and state officials claim uniformly that repeated and clearly audible announcements were made by the raiding party prior to their entering the apartment. Statements by the police and those officials differ, however, as to how and by whom the announcements were made and how the occupants responded.

Assistant State's Attorney Jalovec: In his statements to the press on the day of the raid, Assistant State's Attorney Jalovec asserted that the police had announced their presence to the occupants by knocking on the door and stating the purpose of the raid.[10] Jalovec said that Sergeant Groth (supposedly with Officers Carmody and Ciszewski at the rear of the apartment) announced: "Police—police, we have a search warrant!" Jalovec said that Sergeant Groth told him that both male and female voices from within the apartment called out, "Who? Who?" Groth then repeated the announcement and received the same response; this exchange seemed to last for "several minutes."

10. *Chicago Today*, 5 Star Final, December 4, 1969, p. 1.

In a later version released on the same day,[11] Jalovec focused on the activities of Officers Davis and Jones at the front door of the apartment. Jalovec stated that those officers had gone to the front of the apartment and "were seeking peaceful entrance by proclaiming their identity and the fact that they had the search warrants." Davis reportedly heard "scuffling or shuffling" inside the front door, followed almost instantly by "blasts of gunfire."

Officer John Ciszewski: Ciszewski, who had been at the rear door, was quoted on the day of the raid as saying, "As soon as we announced that we were State's Attorney police, a burst of shotgun fire came through the back door."[12]

Officer Edward Carmody: In another of the numerous reports that appeared on December 4, 1969, Carmody was quoted as saying that when the police first arrived at the rear of the apartment, he heard "other policemen" knocking on the *front door*, followed by a voice that asked, "Who's there?" This question was followed by shooting.[13]

At the coroner's inquest on January 16, 1970, Officer Carmody testified that he approached the kitchen door and heard the following verbal exchange from the front of the apartment: "Who's there?" "Police." The exchange was followed by a "loud blast."[14]

Sergeant Daniel Groth: In his first account of the raid, Sergeant Groth described the opening moments as follows:

I knocked on the front door, and someone asked, "Who's there?" I identified myself as a police officer and said I had a warrant to search the premises. I got no response. I repeatedly demanded entry for several minutes.[15]

In an interview conducted later on December 4, Groth did not mention hearing any response from the occupants after he had identified himself at the front door. After several minutes had passed with no response, he said, Groth put his shoulder to the outer door and forced it open.[16]

On the evening of December 11, 1969, WBBM-TV (CBS) in

11. Ibid., 7 Star Final, December 4, 1969, p. 1.
12. Ibid., Green Streak Edition, December 4, 1969, p. 16.
13. Chicago *Daily News,* Red Flash Edition, December 4, 1969, p. 6.
14. Coroner's inquest, January 16, 1970.
15. *Chicago Today*, Green Streak Edition, December 4, 1969, p. 1.
16. Chicago *Sun-Times,* 5 Star Final, December 5, 1969. p. 1.

Chicago, at the request of State's Attorney Hanrahan, presented a filmed "re-enactment" of the raid.[17] The re-enactment was performed by the officers who had participated in the raid, with each officer describing his own actions. In this presentation Sergeant Groth repeated his previous description of the initial police activity. He knocked about ten times on the front door, but received no response from within. Taking his revolver in hand, he pounded on the door with it approximately five times, and a male voice called from inside, "Who's there?" Groth responded, "Police officers. I have a search warrant. Open the door." He waited several seconds, and hearing no reply pounded on the door again, waited, and a voice responded, "Just a minute." He again waited and then told Officer Davis, "O.K., Duke." Officer Davis then crashed through the door.

Sergeant Groth described his announcement again at the coroner's inquest. According to this account, he had arrived at the front of the apartment with several other police officers. He knocked on the outside door to the building with his left hand, and then with his gun butt. After a male voice from inside the apartment responded, "Who's there?" Groth announced that police officers were present with a warrant to search the premises. He waited ten, twelve, or fifteen seconds for an answer, knocked loudly several more times with his revolver, and waited another fifteen seconds. Groth then ordered Davis to force open the outer door.[18]

State's Attorney Edward V. Hanrahan: On December 8, 1969, State's Attorney Hanrahan met with reporters to answer questions about the raid. Hanrahan said that the police knocked on the door and announced themselves several times before entering the apartment, and that police did not use their guns until after the occupants resisted and fired.[19]

In the "Exclusive" story given to the Chicago *Tribune*, Hanrahan said that Groth and Davis entered the front door of the building, followed by Gorman, Jones, and Hughes. As they stood on either side of the *inside* door leading to the apartment, Groth knocked on the

17. Referred to as Composite Version 2.
18. Coroner's inquest, January 7–13, 1970.
19. Chicago *Tribune*, 4 Star Sports Final, December 9, 1969, p. 1; and Chicago *Sun-Times*, 5 Star Turf Final, December 9, 1969, p. 5.

door with his left hand. When there was no response, he pounded again, this time with the butt of his gun. According to the story a voice from the inside called out, "Who's there?" Groth answered: "This is the police. I have a warrant to search the premises." When there was no response, Groth pounded on the door again, shouting, "Police! Open up!" A voice answered, "Just a minute." Suspicious of the delay, Groth ordered Davis to break down the door.

Statements by Assistant Deputy Police Superintendent Merle Nygren: On January 7, 1970, Assistant Deputy Police Superintendent Merle Nygren testified before the coroner's inquest that he had arrived on the scene shortly after the shooting. He stated that Sergeant Groth told him at that time that the police approached the front door of the apartment, rapped on the door, and announced their identity as policemen. Sergeant Groth reportedly said that they had a warrant to search the premises. The only response was a shot through the door.

The Federal Grand Jury Report: The federal grand jury *Report*[20] contains an attempt by the grand jury to construct a "most consistent version" of the facts based on the testimony of the police officers. According to this version, Groth proceeded through the outer front door of the apartment to the inner door. He knocked and received no response. He waited several seconds, rapped agan, this time with his revolver butt, and heard a male voice from the apartment call out, "Who's there?" Groth responded, "Police officers; I have a warrant to search the premises." Groth waited again for about ten or twelve seconds, then pounded on the door with his fist. A voice from inside called out, "Just a minute." Groth waited another ten or fifteen seconds, and then told Davis to enter the apartment.

Entry into the Apartment and Initial Firing—Action at the Rear

Assistant State's Attorney Jalovec: Jalovec first stated on the day of the raid that the officers in the *rear* decided to break down the back (kitchen) door, and "were met by a blast of shotgun fire as they smashed inside." At that moment, Jalovec reported, Carmody was struck by a pellet or wood fragment in the right hand, and Ciszewski was grazed on the left leg.[21] Jalovec added that when the raiding party

20. Referred to as Composite Version 3.
21. *Chicago Today*, 5 Star Final, December 4, 1969, p. 1.

came through the back door into the kitchen, they fell to the floor, while a woman fired a shotgun at them. More blasts of gunfire came at them from other parts of the room; Sergeant Groth reportedly explained to him that "The firing must have gone on 10 or 12 minutes. If 200 shots were exchanged, that would have been nothing."[22]

In an account reported later the same day Jalovec said that as the police were waiting for responses to their announcements, "blasts of gunfire roared through the front and rear doors." Police then "blasted back through both doors" and "crashed them down."[23]

Officer Edward Carmody: Carmody, who was at the rear of the apartment, reported on December 4, 1969, that he had heard policemen at the front door knocking, followed by a voice asking, "Who's there?" He claimed this sound was followed by shooting. At that point, he "kicked in the back door and went to the rear window. Two other policemen were covering the door with me. Shots were fired through the back window. Flying glass hit my right hand."[24]

Carmody also described his entry into the rear of the apartment one week later in the WBBM-TV filmed re-enactment. He said he had come up on the porch close to the back door, whereupon he heard voices in the front of the apartment. After hearing a loud shot "like a shotgun," he kicked open the door and started into the kitchen. Before he could "get past the threshold," however, three shots were fired toward him from the back bedroom. Carmody backed out, went over to the kitchen window and smashed it: "I dont know why, I was going to go in, into the kitchen through this window, but I don't know why I didn't."

Testifying on January 16, 1970, at the coroner's inquest, Carmody's story was somewhat different. He described the problem the officers at the rear had in deciding which apartment to enter, since there were two stairways in the rear, each leading to a different apartment (one above, one below). He chose the first-floor apartment "because the light was on in the kitchen." Carmody heard the announcements by the police in front of the building and a loud blast, after which he kicked the door in. "Before I could even cross the threshold," he

22. *Chicago Today,* 5 Star Final, December 4, 1969, p. 1.
23. Ibid., 7 Star Final, December 4, 1969, p. 1.
24. Chicago *Daily News,* Red Flash Edition, December 4, 1969, p. 6.

continued, "I saw three other shots fired in my direction from a handgun.'" He also heard three corresponding reports. Noticing a hand holding a handgun pointed directly at him from the area where the dining room, the back bedroom entrance, and the inner kitchen entrance met, he backed out of the doorway and moved against the outside wall. He crossed the doorway to break open a window with his revolver, but returned to the kitchen door to dive into the kitchen. Carmody was unable to explain this apparently useless movement to the window, saying:

I don't know why I—the reason I went to this window was to go in, figuring, well they wouldn't feel that we are going to come in this window.

For some reason or another I stopped and I went back to the door, and just dove right in on my hands and my stomach in the middle of the kitchen floor.

There was no mention in this version of being wounded by flying glass caused by shots fired through the window from within the apartment.

Officer John Ciszewski: Ciszewski, on the day of the raid, also described the first few moments of the raid from his vantage point at the rear:

As soon as we announced that we were State's Attorney police, a burst of shotgun fire came through the back door. We [Ciszewski and Carmody] were both wounded then, but we broke down the door and started firing. Once we got inside the kitchen we could see firing coming from the hallway and a back bedroom. . . . By this time, other police had broken down the front door and shots were being fired at them, some through the door of another bedroom. It was as if all hell had broken loose. . . . It couldn't have lasted more than five minutes from the time the first shot came through the back door of the apartment, but it seemed like five hours.[25]

In a second account which appeared on December 4, 1969, of the entry into the rear of the apartment, Ciszewski established that the exchange of gunfire began in the front of the apartment:

I heard one of the officers in the front yell, "We're shooting. Watch yourself." My partner [Carmody] tried to get through the window and was cut

25. *Chicago Today*, Green Streak Edition, December 4, 1969, p. 16.

with flying glass. We finally got into the rear room. . . . I saw flashes coming from the middle and back bedroom to my right.[26]

At the coroner's inquest on January 16, 1970, Ciszewski testified that he heard a loud blast, followed by two or three "poplike" shots from inside the apartment. He saw Carmody kick open the door, and heard "three rapid pops" from the rear. He saw Carmody back away from the door, smash the kitchen window, and then re-enter the apartment through the door.

Officer Philip Joseph: Joseph testified at the coroner's inquest on January 14, 1970, that as the raid began he was standing at the rear of the building, a few steps below the porch, with several other officers, "trying to figure out which was the right apartment." He then heard "a loud shot, followed by sporadic fire, sounded like small arms, I could not tell." The officers proceeded up the stairs toward the back door, where they heard a voice from inside shouting, "Come on in, come on in." At this point, Officer Carmody kicked the rear door open. Through the open door Joseph observed two flashes (indicating small arms fire) and the tip of a gun in the area of the rear bedroom. Carmody then moved out of the doorway and broke the kitchen window, after which he returned to the doorway with other officers and dived inside.

Officer Raymond Broderick: Broderick testified before the coroner's inquest on January 16, 1970, that from his post at the rear of the apartment he heard a shotgun blast from inside the apartment, followed almost immediately by what sounded like a second shotgun blast. He then heard what appeared to be small arms fire. Carmody kicked open the door, Broderick said, but he jerked back at the sound of firing, which Broderick believed came from the rear of the apartment. Broderick then saw Carmody retreat, smash the kitchen window, and return to the doorway and dive into the kitchen. Carmody's entrance was followed by the sounds of shooting.

Officer William Kelly: Kelly testified before the coroner's inquest on January 13, 1970. He described the confusion of the officers when they approached the rear of the building as to which apartment to enter:

26. Chicago *Daily News*, Red Flash Edition, December 4, 1969, p. 6.

And I don't recall who, but one of the officers went up—we didn't know which set of stairs to go up. And, Officer Carmody went up one set and somebody else went up the other set, four or five stairs up.

Kelly said he saw Carmody listen at the kitchen door, kick it open and start to enter. Several shots sounded and Carmody ran to the kichen window. After smashing the window, Carmody returned to the door and dived into the kitchen. Kelly jumped up the second set of stairs, peered through the broken window and poked his shotgun through the opening. He saw Carmody lying on the kitchen floor, while beneath the window he saw a stove with lit burners. Kelly continued:

And, shots were—explosions were going on all over. I took my shotgun and knocked out the rest—not all of it, most of the upper portion of the window to get a wider range of coverage. And, then it was a cease fire.

The Federal Grand Jury Report: In the "most consistent version" of the police testimony constructed by the federal grand jury, the assumption was made that the police at the rear of the apartment entered just as the first shot was fired in the front of the apartment. Officer Carmody, upon hearing a loud bang which he believed to be a shotgun blast at the front of the apartment, kicked open the kitchen door. As he entered, he saw three gun flashes and a hand holding a gun protruding around the corner of a doorway between the kitchen and dining room. Carmody quickly backed out of the apartment. Ciszewski, waiting outside the back door, heard three "poplike" shots, then saw Carmody retreat from the apartment. Carmody went over to the kitchen window and smashed it with the butt of his gun, cutting his hand in the process. Since the burners were lit on a stove just below the window, however, Carmody decided not to enter that way. He began to re-enter the apartment with Ciszewski through the kitchen door and was followed by Broderick.

Entry into the Apartment and Initial Firing—Action at the Front

The entry by the police into the front of the apartment is one of the crucial aspects of the raid, for, although contrary statements are presented, most of the police participants in the raid agree that the first shot was fired by the occupants at the front of the apartment.

Rear view of Panther apartment, 2337 West Monroe Street, Chicago.

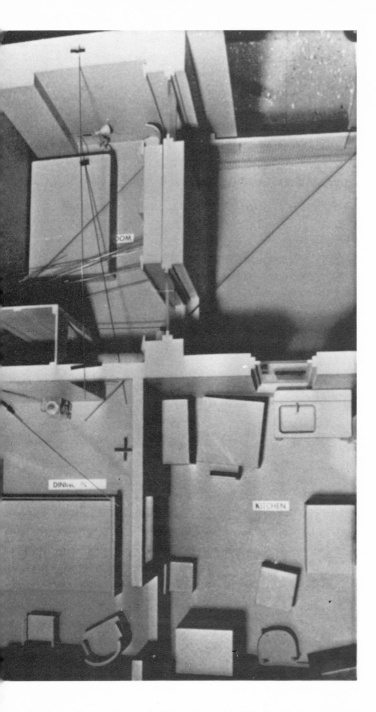

The federal grand jury used this scale model of the Panther apartment
in its deliberations.

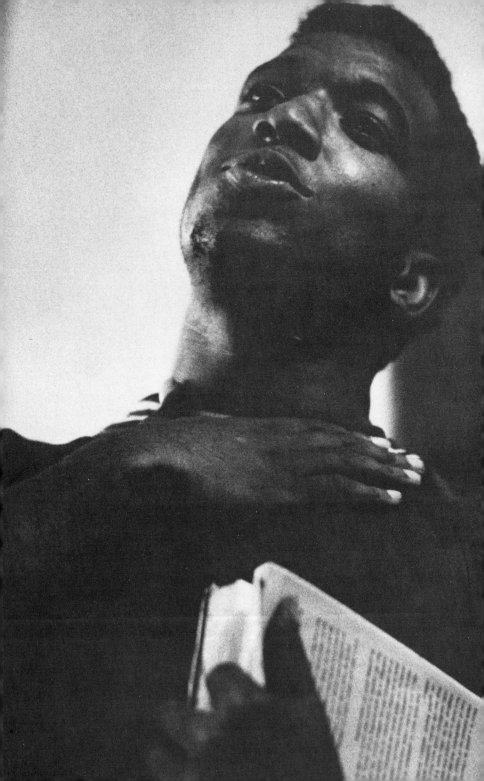

Fred Hampton's blood-stained bed as photographed after the police
raid on the Panther apartment, December 4, 1969.

Fred Hampton (left) shortly after his release from Menard Prison in the
summer of 1969.

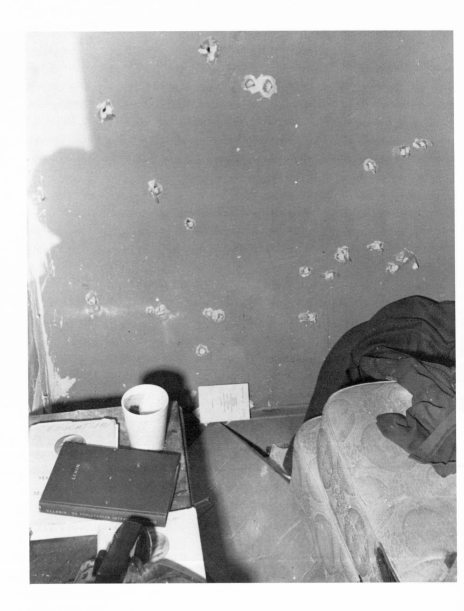

Bullet-riddled wall of Fred Hampton's room.

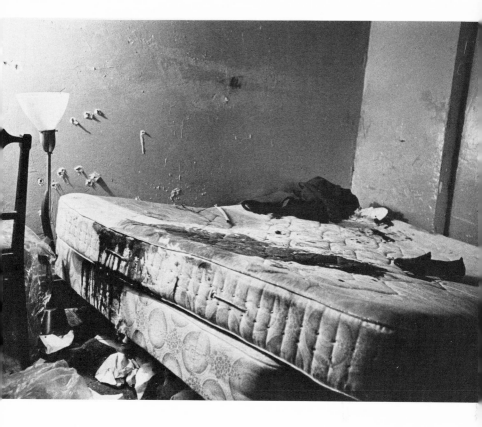

Another view of Fred Hampton's blood-stained bed.

Chicago police removing Fred Hampton's body.

Contradictions exist in the police reports, however, on the way in which entry was made, on who fired the first shot, and on the immediate reactions of the police.

Assistant State's Attorney Richard Jalovec: In his second statement to the press on December 4, 1969, Assistant State's Attorney Jalovec focused his comments on the action at the front of the apartment. While still placing Groth at the rear door, Jalovec indicated that Officers Davis and Jones entered through the front door. The police were greeted by "blasts of gunfire," Jalovec reported, which "roared through the front and rear doors." After the police "blasted back through both doors" and "crashed them down," a young woman, Officer Davis was alleged to have said, fired a shotgun at police as they came through the front door. Police returned fire and the woman was hit.[27]

Sergeant Daniel Groth: Groth, who stated that he was positioned at the front door, did not mention any shotgun blasts occurring before the door was broken open.

Then I forced the front door with my shoulder. It was only a light touch. As I entered the darkened apartment, I saw a girl on a bed holding a shotgun. As she fired the gun, Detective Duke Davis and three others fell to the kitchen floor.

Groth said he returned the woman's fire as Davis "exchanged shots" with an unidentified man elsewhere in the apartment. Shots came from another room, and Groth ordered the officers to cease firing.[28]

A more detailed account of the entry by Groth appeared in the newspapers on December 5. Groth reported that after announcing his presence and receiving no response, he put his shoulder to the outer door and forced it open. With four other officers he entered a darkened hallway and spotted a woman with a shotgun, who held it "at about a 45 degree angle" from his position. The woman fired, he said, and Davis, who had entered with him, fell to the floor. Groth returned fire, and the flash of Groth's shot enabled Davis to see a man behind a nearby door pointing a shotgun toward Groth. Groth said that

27. *Chicago Today*, 7 Star Final, December 4, 1969, p. 1.
28. Ibid., Green Streak Edition, December 4, 1969, p. 1.

Figure 1: First-floor plan of 2337 West Monroe Street, Chicago, Illinois, identifying areas containing bullet holes, and the directions of their trajectories, following the police raid. (Plan drawn for use in the federal grand jury investigation, and identifications taken from the grand jury *Report*, pages 80-86.)

KEY

1. Impact point of #7½ or #8 shot in northeast corner of entrance hallway.
2. Hole from 12-gauge rifled slug, recovered from stair well.
3. Hole in door from rifled slug fired from living room 15 inches from door.
4. Hole from .38-caliber pistol bullet fired from hallway into living room.
5. .30-caliber bullet hole in top right drawer of chest.
6. Bullet hole in northwest corner of living room.
7. .38-caliber bullet, probably fired through living room door.
8. 42 bullet holes of shots fired through south wall of living room into north bedroom; of these, 19 passed through south wall of north bedroom into south bedroom.
9. Bullet hole in bottom drawer of chest (no bullet recovered).
10. Bullet hole in south door jamb of entrance door (probably predating raid).
11. 6 holes from bullets fired through the north bedroom doorway.
12. Impact points of 3 shotgun blasts fired through north bedroom doorway.
13. .45-caliber bullet holes from machine gun fired from north bedroom doorway into closet; some of these bullets passed through closet wall into south bedroom.
14. 8 bullet holes in chest, 3 from bullets fired through living room wall, 4 from bullets fired through bedroom doorway.
15. Bullet hole on west end of chest, made by ricochet of unknown trajectory.
16. Impact points of 2 12-gauge 00 buck shotgun blasts, fired into south bedroom from doorway.
17. Impact points of shotgun blast striking foot of bed and east wall, fired from south bedroom doorway.
18. West window broken by shot from dining room; shotgun blast impacted on shed outside house.
19. Shotgun blast fired high into east wall of dining room.

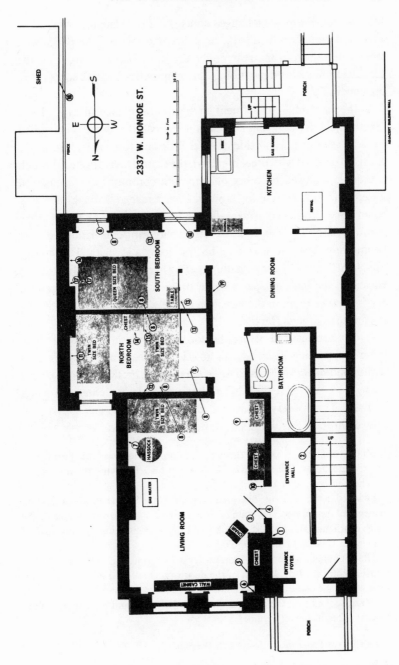

"Davis and this man exchanged shots. . . . Davis subdued the man."

At this time Groth called a cease-fire, fearing that the police who were entering from the rear might fire on police entering from the front. Groth made no mention of any gunfire from other rooms in the apartment.[29]

In the television re-enactment on the evening of December 11, 1969, Groth again asserted that he had announced his presence and waited for admission to the apartment. After hearing a few voices, Groth told Davis to proceed with breaking down the door. Davis crashed through the door, followed by other officers, and continued on through an anteroom. Still in a running crouch, Davis crashed through the living room door into the apartment, falling off to one side. As Davis broke through the living room door, a shotgun blast rang out. Groth, entering behind him, saw a woman on a bed pumping a shotgun. The woman fired in his direction, the shot illuminating her face clearly. Groth dived back into the hallway space. From the entranceway he fired several shots into the room in the direction of the woman, later identified by the police as Brenda Harris.

Groth also testified before the coroner's inquest in January 1970. After announcing his presence, he said, he heard a few voices from within and ordered Davis to force open the outer door. Davis kicked open the outer door with his right foot, and they entered a small hallway. They observed another door to their left, and Davis continued through this door. Groth described the next events:

As Officer Davis proceeded through this door, a shot was fired from within —a shotgun blast. Officer Davis fell down to his left, giving the impression that he had been shot.

I walked in the doorway, observed a female, Negro, on a bed with a shotgun in her crotch, pointed very calmly in my direction. I turned around to the other gentlemen and I yelled, "Look out! I think she is going to shoot again." And, with this, she pulled the trigger.

The illumination from the shotgun blast lit up my face—lit up her face, please. With this, I ducked out of the doorway, positioned myself in such an area where she couldn't hit me if she decided to fire again. I took my service revolver, looked into the door, on the top of my toes and high angle, I fired several shots in her direction.

29. Chicago *Sun-Times*, 5 Star Final, December 5, 1969, p. 1.

In response to a question from Special Deputy Coroner Martin Gerber, Groth said that the initial shot was fired through the inner door simultaneously with the police entry through it. He said it was not necessary to force the inner door open; the shotgun blast tore through the door at the same instant it was being opened by Davis. Groth believed that Brenda Harris had fired the first shot through the door and another shot as police came into the room.

In response to further questions at the coroner's inquest, Groth changed his story about the first shot. He said that he believed Mark Clark, rather than Brenda Harris, had fired the first shot. Groth said he had changed his mind after reviewing photographs of the apartment and conferring with Davis. Davis had told him of seeing Mark Clark sitting in a chair behind the door, pumping a shotgun as the police entered the living room.

After the first shot, Groth continued, he ducked out of the living room and fired two shots from the hallway. The next shot, Groth believed, was fired by Davis. Asked why he and his men had not retreated from the apartment after the first two shotgun blasts at them, Groth said, "I couldn't retreat. . . . I didn't know where Officer Davis was. He was in the apartment."

Officer James Davis: Davis, who entered with Groth through the front door, was initially described as the commander of the police at the front door.[30] He was, however, Groth's assistant and was the first man to enter the apartment from the front.

Davis testified at the coroner's inquest on January 19, 1970. He stated that he believed two shots had been fired simultaneously through the front door or doorway from inside the apartment as police attempted to enter the living room—one by Mark Clark and one by Brenda Harris—and a third, by Brenda Harris, as he came into the living room. Davis testified that after he had dived to the floor he fired one shot from his carbine at Brenda Harris and wounded her in the thigh. He indicated that by the light of Groth's shots he had seen Mark Clark behind the door, putting a shell into a shotgun. He fired

30. Assistant State's Attorney Jalovec in *Chicago Today,* 5 Star Final, December 4, 1969, p. 1.

two shots at Clark, he said, grappled with him, and fell on top of him onto the floor.

In the television re-enactment, Davis stated that Groth's gunfire illuminated the figure of a man, later identified as Mark Clark, who was sitting on a chair behind the living room door, pumping a shotgun. Davis fired twice at Clark, apparently hitting him. Clark stood up, and Davis, picking himself up from his position on the floor, struggled with him, falling to the floor across Clark and pinning the shotgun underneath his body.

Officer Joseph Gorman: Officer Gorman testified before the coroner's inquest on January 15, 1970. Gorman, who entered at the front of the apartment with Davis and Groth, said that Davis, after forcing the outside door to the building, dived through the inner door in a crouched position. As Davis began to open the door, Gorman recounted, "I saw a piece above Duke's arm just explode out of the door, part of the door just blew out."

State's Attorney Edward V. Hanrahan: On December 8, 1969, State's Attorney Hanrahan met with reporters to answer questions about the raid. He said that the police knocked on the door and announced themselves several times before entering the apartment, and that they did not use their guns until after the occupants resisted and fired. He concluded that "We were then [after the raid] and are still convinced that our officers used good judgment, considerable constraint, and professional discipline."[31]

On December 11, 1969, Hanrahan released the "Exclusive" story to the Chicago *Tribune*. Hanrahan claimed that because Groth was suspicious of the occupants' delay in answering the announcement by the police of their presence, he ordered Davis to break down the door. Davis kicked, and the door slammed open to reveal a small anteroom with a closed door leading to the living room of the Panthers' apartment. As the police entered the anteroom, a shotgun blast was fired through the closed living room door, narrowly missing the policemen there. Davis smashed the door open and then, followed by Groth, plunged into the living room and saw a woman in the far corner of

31. Chicago *Tribune*, 4 Star Sports Final, December 9, 1969, p. 1; and Chicago *Sun-Times*, 5 Star Turf Final, December 9, 1969, p. 5.

the living room on a mattress, "trying to pump another shell into a shotgun she held jammed against her groin." She fired at the police, who then, for the first time, returned fire.

After Groth ducked back into the hallway, Hanrahan continued, he fired two blind shots into the room and via a walkie-talkie notified the men at the rear of the building that "these people are shooting in here." Davis, who had landed on a mattress on the living room floor, fired one shot from his carbine at the woman. He was then quoted as saying:

> She slumped back against the wall with that shotgun still in her hands and I spun away and half-turned, just in time to spot a guy [Mark Clark] sitting in a chair with a shotgun in his hands. He was directly behind me, hidden behind the door I'd just broken open. Thank God, Groth fired those shots at the woman. The flash of his revolver spotted the guy for me. . . .
>
> I don't know for sure if he ever got a shot in at me or not. I fired twice and hit him. He stood up and I jumped up too, struggling with him until he fell. Then I fell across the body.

Assistant Deputy Police Superintendent Merle Nygren: Nygren testified at the coroner's inquest on January 7, 1970. He stated that Sergeant Groth told him immediately after the raid that the police raiding party at the front of the apartment was greeted by a shot through the door, which "very nearly missed two officers." According to Nygren, Groth added that this shot was fired by a woman in the front room. As the police entered, Nygren testified, the woman "was trying to pump another shell into the shotgun so that she could shoot for a second time."

Composite Version 3: In the version that the grand jury constructed, Davis kicked the outer door open with his right foot. Davis and Groth passed through this outer door into the anteroom and Davis veered to his left, striking the door leading into the living room of the apartment. As Davis broke through this entrance, a shot erupted through the door just above his arm. Davis reported seeing a flash as the shot passed over him, and Gorman, who had followed Groth and Davis in, stated he saw the wood of the door explode out as Davis plunged into the living room. Davis saw a girl inside the living room aim at him with a shotgun. She fired, and Davis, Groth, Hughes, Jones, and Gorman all saw the blast. Groth "felt something go by his left shoulder"; Gorman "observed a ball of flame come almost halfway to the officers"; Hughes felt something "brush his shoulder"; Jones "felt a sensation of a wind and felt the bottom of his coat move as a result of the blast." Davis believed this was the second shot fired by Harris; the first shot, according to his theory, was simultaneous with Clark's blast through the door.

Davis dived onto the living room floor and saw Harris braced against the east wall of the apartment in the corner. He fired at her once, as Groth was ducking out of the apartment into the hallway and firing two blind shots in Harris's direction. He immediately caught sight "out of the corner of his eye" of Mark Clark, who was sitting on a chair behind him pumping a shotgun. Davis fired two shots at Clark, who stood up, and they wrestled to the floor.[32] While Davis was firing, Sergeant Groth was turned to Officer Hughes, who was standing in the entrance hall, and said, "Put in a 10-1. They are shooting at us. Tell the fellows in the back. I think Duke is shot."

The Commission's Analysis of the Testimony by the Police and State Officials

The statements by the police and state officials, from the first informal statements of December 4, 1969, to the testimony before the federal grand jury, are inconsistent on many major and minor points. This section discusses only the testimony relating to the positions of the officers at the beginning of the raid, the manner of the announcement by the police of their presence, the occupants' responses, the method of police entry, and the initial firing—all as bearing on the central issue of the first shot.

The positions of the officers outside the apartment just prior to the raid were discussed on December 4, 1969, by Assistant State's Attorney Jalovec, who was not an actual participant in the raid. He said that Officers Groth, Carmody, and Ciszewski had approached the *back* door, while "others" went to the front. Similarly, another account the same day reported Jalovec as saying that Officers Davis and

---

32. The grand jury noted that "Despite evidence of violent bleeding by Clark, Davis found only a drop or two of blood on his clothes at the bottom of his suit coat" (p. 93).

Jones were stationed in front while Groth and others were in back. On December 4 Sergeant Groth said, however, that he had been at the front of the apartment. On December 4 Officers Carmody and Ciszewski said that police had surrounded the building, and the two of them had gone to the back door. They added that "five or six" officers had covered the rear, while "six or seven" were stationed at the front.

On December 11 in the Chicago *Tribune* "Exclusive," State's Attorney Hanrahan attempted to resolve the inconsistency by placing the officers in positions that were to remain constant in all succeeding accounts. According to Hanrahan, Officers Groth, Gorman, Jones, Hughes, and Davis approached the *front* door; Officers Carmody, Ciszewski, Joseph, and Kelly approached the *back* door; and four other officers provided cover. The fact that neither the police nor the State's Attorney's Office could agree for several days on a consistent account of where the police officers were initially stationed outside the apartment detracts somewhat from the overall credibility of their testimony and public statements, especially since confidence in other police accounts is highly dependent on accurately locating each officer during the raid.

Discrepancies in official accounts of the officers' announcement of their identity and mission is another point which casts doubt on the overall credibility of those accounts. In every official account, someone is credited with knocking on a door and announcing that police were present with a warrant to search the premises. The persons making the announcement and their respective locations, however, vary considerably. On December 4 Assistant State's Attorney Jalovec was reported to have said that Sergeant Groth made the announcement at the *back* door while Officer Davis did the same at the *front* door. That same day, Officers Carmody and Ciszewski, who were at the rear door, were quoted as saying that they heard "other policemen knocking on the *front* door." They do not mention any announcement having been made at the rear door.

Sergeant Groth told reporters on December 4 that he had knocked on the front—not the back—door and announced the presence of police with a search warrant. This report then became the "official" version, and was maintained consistently throughout subsequent press stories, the *Tribune* "Exclusive," the CBS filmed re-enactment, the coroner's inquest and the federal grand jury's *Report.*

The occupants' response to the police announcement as described in the official stories is equally subject to confusion and contradiction. Jalovec was reported in one account on December 4 to have said that male and female voices in the back of the apartment called out, "Who? Who?" to officers in the rear. But another account quoted him as saying that Officer Davis, at the front of the apartment, heard "scuffling or shuffling," followed by gunfire out of the front room. One press interview quoted Carmody and Ciszewski as saying the occupants responded to their announcement by shooting out the back of the apartment. Another reported that Officer Carmody had heard someone call out, "Who's there?" in the front of the apartment.

One story attributed to Sergeant Groth and his testimony before the coroner's inquest were to the effect that a voice in the front responded to his announcement by asking, "Who's there?," but then failed to respond to repeated requests that the police be allowed in. In a third account there was no reference to his having heard any response from within. And in the television re-enactment Groth reported that a male voice called, "Who's there?"; that Groth responded, "Police officers. I have a search warrant. Open the door"; and that after a delay the voice responded, "Just a minute." Officer Carmody's testimony corroborated Groth's first statement—he testified that he had heard the verbal exchange in front from his position at the rear of the apartment.

State's Attorney Hanrahan, on December 8, stated to the press that police had received no response except gunfire to their requests to execute the search warrant. However, in the official stories presented in the *Tribune* "Exclusive" and the filmed re-enactment, officers said they knocked repeatedly on the front door, heard a voice ask, "Who's there?," announced their identity and mission, and then heard, "Just a minute." According to the latter two accounts, there was no further response.

Finally, the federal grand jury's version of the police accounts describes a male voice which first responded, "Who's there?," and then, after the police stated their presence, shouted, "Just a minute."

The Commission does not believe that any conclusion as to the responses of the occupants can reasonably be drawn from so many contradictory statements. Again, however, the confusing testimony about events prior to the actual breaking into the apartment and prior to any gunfire casts doubt on the witnesses' overall credibility.

The police accounts of their method of entry into the apartment similarly appear in so many contradictory forms that the Commission is unable to determine with certainty what happened.

Assistant State's Attorney Jalovec apparently told reporters two completely different stories on December 4. In one account he was quoted as saying that Groth, Carmody, and Ciszewski broke down the back door and entered after the occupants failed to respond. Some time after that, he continued, Davis broke down the front door and entered. In the other account, he told how police, returning fire from inside the apartment, "blasted back through both doors" and then entered the front and rear of the apartment—the implication being that entry into the apartment was simultaneous at both the front and back doors.

Officers Carmody and Ciszewski also appear to have told inconsistent stories on December 4. According to one newspaper account, both were wounded when gunfire roared out of the back door of the apartment, but they still managed to break down the back door. By the time they entered at the back, police had already broken down the front door and entered. In another account, they described breaking down the back door and entering after they heard shooting in the front. Carmody described how he was struck by "flying glass" from shots fired through the kitchen window as he attempted to enter the kitchen window.

In the next series of accounts to appear, on December 4 and 5, Sergeant Groth told how he forced the front door open after the occupants had failed to respond, and upon entering saw a woman holding a shotgun in the front room of the apartment. On December 11 the *Tribune* "Exclusive" and the re-enactment staged by Hanrahan's office specified Officer Davis—rather than Sergeant Groth— as the man who broke in the front door and an inner door which led into the front room of the apartment. This last story finally became the version which was maintained throughout the coroner's inquest and the federal grand jury *Report*.

Finally, the Commission finds it impossible to determine from offi cial accounts who fired the first shot in the raid.

On December 4 Assistant State's Attorney Jalovec said the first shot was a "blast of shotgun fire" out of the back of the apartment which came from a woman lying on the kitchen floor. In another account on the same day he said occupants fired "blasts" simultaneously through both front and back doors.

The same day, Officers Carmody and Ciszewski told the press how a "burst of shotgun fire" or other shots were fired at them out of the rear of the apartment as they announced their office and intent. In a second account Ciszewski said "shooting in front" commenced the police action.

Sergeant Groth was quoted in the press on December 4 as saying that a woman in the living room fired as he entered the front, and he saw Officer Davis and three others fall to the kitchen floor. In two other accounts Groth told how the woman in the living room fired at him and four other officers—including Davis—as they entered the front door; this time Davis fell to the living room floor.

On December 8 Hanrahan told reporters only that the occupants fired on police as they sought entry at the front door. In the Chicago *Tribune* "Exclusive" on December 11 police described a shot fired at them through the closed door between the outside hallway and the living room. But in the filmed re-enactment that same night they seemed to believe that the shot came through the *open* living room door.

Sergeant Groth testified at the coroner's inquest, more than a month after the raid, that the first shot had been fired by a woman in the living room, through the closed living room door. A few days later, however, Groth changed his story and testified, after conferring with Davis, that he now thought a man identified as Mark Clark, and not the woman—by now identified as Brenda Harris—had fired the first shot through the living room door.

On January 19 Officer Davis told the coroner's inquest that he believed Mark Clark and Brenda Harris probably fired the first shots simultaneously through the living room door.

The composite story of police action offered by the grand jury *Report* did not confront this question directly, although it implied that Mark Clark had probably fired a shot through the living room door.

There are only three consistent themes in the official statements and testimony relating to the shooting. The officers have never wavered from their contention that one or more occupants opened fire on the police, without provocation, from inside the apartment; that the Panthers fired at police from every occupied room in the apartment; and that police fired back into those rooms. As has been seen, however, the testimony supporting those three contentions is markedly inconsistent, contradictory, or confused.

Accounts by the Survivors and Black Panther Party Officials and Attorneys

The first public accounts of the raid by persons other than the police and public officials appeared in the press during the week following the raid. These accounts were brief, secondhand statements of the incident contained in press releases issued by spokesmen of the Black Panther Party and by the survivors' attorneys.

During the trial[33] in the latter half of 1972 of State's Attorney Hanrahan and certain other officials on charges of obstructing justice arising out of their postraid conduct, Special Prosecutor Barnabas Sears delivered to defense counsel transcripts of statements purportedly made late in December 1969 by Harold Bell, Blair Anderson, Brenda Harris, and Louis Truelock to their own lawyers. (A similar statement purportedly made by Deborah Johnson was referred to at the trial but was never introduced.)[34]

In March 1970, three months after the raid,[35] six of the seven survivors (all but Louis Truelock) appeared before the county grand jury, but the proceedings of the county grand jury are not available to the Commission. The same six survivors testified before the People's Inquest sponsored by the Illinois chapter of the Black Panther Party in March 1970, and four of the six testified before hearings conducted by the Commission in October 1970.

33. See Chapter 7.
34. Only the statements attributed to Harris and Truelock have been made available to the Commission. The testimony at the trial related to the purported statements makes it difficult to determine with certainty whether they are authentic. For purposes of the report, however, the Commission will treat the statements of Harris and Truelock as authentic, and will rely on excerpts from the purported statements of Bell and Anderson, which are derived from a *voir dire* hearing at the trial, as accurate quotes from authentic statements.
35. The survivors did not testify at the coroner's inquest in January 1970 or before the federal grand jury in the winter and spring of 1970.

General Accounts of the Raid by Black Panther Party Spokesmen

To obtain a general overview of the Black Panther allegations, it is helpful to summarize the statements made by various spokesmen regarding the opening moments of the raid.

On December 5, 1969, newspapers published accounts of a press statement issued by Panther Deputy Minister of Defense for Illinois, Bobby Rush, which charged that Fred Hampton and Mark Clark had been murdered. Rush alleged in the statement that Hampton had been murdered in his sleep, and he described the opening moments of the raid. He said that police had knocked on the front door, that the occupants had asked who was at the door, and that the police had replied, "Tommy." When the occupants asked, "Tommy who?," according to Rush, police responded with gunfire through both the front and rear doors. The officers then burst through both entrances and killed Hampton and Clark.[36] Rush, who was not present at the apartment at the time of the raid, did not reveal his source of information.

Rush issued a revised account on December 12, 1969. In this slightly expanded version, he accused Officers Carmody and Ciszewski of entering at the rear and murdering Hampton, while other officers entered the front of the apartment and fatally shot Mark Clark. Rush contended that Hampton was killed while asleep in his bed and added a denial that any occupants of the apartment had called for a "shoot-out." All Chicago's major newspapers gave similar accounts of Rush's statement, though the Chicago *Tribune* quoted Rush as placing Sergeant Groth at the rear of the apartment, rather than at the front, while the other two quoted Rush as saying that Groth had entered at the front.[37] With regard to the source of his information, Rush was quoted as saying, "You'd be surprised who gives me information."

In the interval between Rush's first and second accounts, a state-

36. Chicago *Daily News,* Blue Streak Edition, December 5, 1969, p. 5.
37. Chicago *Tribune,* 1 Star Edition, December 12, 1969, page 1; Chicago *Daily News,* Red Flash Edition, December 12, 1969, p. 1; *Chicago Today,* December 12, 1969.

ment was issued by the team of attorneys representing the seven surviving occupants of the apartment. The statement appeared in the Chicago *Daily News* on December 10, 1969.[38] It was reportedly based on the statements of the survivors and on the findings of independent medical and ballistics analysts.

The attorneys' statement about the opening moments of the raid depicted police knocking on the front door of the apartment at 4:40 A.M. on December 4. After a brief exchange of words between the occupants and police, Mark Clark approached the living room door. At that moment, the statement said, police burst through the front door, fired into the living room and killed Clark.

Accounts of the Survivors

Location of the Occupants

Brenda Harris: On December 21, 1969, in a statement made to her lawyer, Harris said that she was sleeping in a bed in the front room —the living room—of the first-floor apartment when the police arrived. She said further that Truelock, Bell, and Clark were also in the living room when the police arrived, but that Truelock and Bell immediately went toward the back of the apartment. She repeated that testimony at Hanrahan's trial in August 1972. Before the People's Inquest on March 8, 1970, Harris testified that she was sleeping in the living room when the police arrived; she placed Mark Clark in the living room as well.

In her testimony before the Commission on October 29, 1970, Harris testified that she arrived at the apartment at approximately 11:30 P.M. on the night of December 3, 1969, and went to sleep in the living room at the front of the apartment between one and two and one-half hours after arriving. At the time she went to sleep, she continued, Louis Truelock, Harold Bell, and Mark Clark were also present in the living room.

Ronald Satchel: Satchel testified before the People's Inquest on March 8, 1970, that, at the time of the raid, he was sleeping in the

38. Other Chicago newspapers reported the substance of the attorneys' account on the following day.

first (the front or north) bedroom. In his testimony before the Commission on October 26, 1970, Satchel stated that he arrived at the apartment at about 8:00 P.M. on December 3. He went to sleep some time later in a bed located in the southwest corner of the front bedroom. He stated that Blair Anderson and Verlina Brewer were in this same room when he retired.

Verlina Brewer: Brewer testified at the People's Inquest on March 8, 1970, that she was sleeping in the "middle" bedroom of the apartment—apparently the middle room, which is the front bedroom—on the morning of December 4. Her testimony indicated that Ronald Satchel was in the same room, but there was no reference to Blair Anderson.

Blair Anderson: Anderson's testimony before the People's Inquest did not specify the room in the apartment in which he was located. The testimony did indicate, however, that Satchel and Brewer were in the same room with him.

Harold Bell: In his testimony before the People's Inquest on March 8, 1970, Bell did not state which room he was in when the police arrived. The testimony implied, however, that he was toward the front of the apartment.

Bell told the Commission that he arrived at the apartment at about midnight, December 3, 1969. After eating, Bell began to disassemble a shotgun on the floor of the living room. By this time Mark Clark, Fred Hampton, and several other persons had come into the living room at the front of the apartment. After working on the disassembled shotgun for a while, Bell fell asleep at a position near the center of the living room.

Deborah Johnson: Deborah Johnson testified before the People's Inquest that she had gone to the apartment after attending a Panther political orientation class and went to sleep in the back (or south) bedroom.

In her testimony before the Commission on October 26, 1970, Johnson stated that she came to the apartment shortly after midnight on the morning of December 4. When she arrived at the apartment, she saw Fred Hampton and Louis Truelock standing in the living room talking with each other. She spoke with Hampton briefly, asking why he had not picked her up to take her to his mother's house, where they had intended to go that night. After about five minutes, she went to the back bedroom, but because the bedroom was very cold she remained there only about six or seven minutes before returning to the living room. After another three or four minutes, Johnson said, she returned to the back bedroom. Shortly thereafter Hampton joined her, and the two of them received a brief telephone call.

After the first phone call, either Hampton or Johnson suggested they call Hampton's sister in Maywood to explain their absence that evening. They placed the call, and both Johnson and Hampton spoke with Hampton's family over the phone; this telephone conversation lasted approximately forty minutes, ending around 1:30 A.M. During the phone call Hampton fell asleep; Johnson attempted to wake him but was unable to do so.

Louis Truelock: Truelock, in an interview on December 22, 1969, with Donald Stang, a lawyer associated with Andrew Francis, who at the time apparently represented Truelock, stated that he had gone to bed in the front room at 4:10 A.M. on the morning of the raid. At that time, he said, Bell, Harris, and Clark were also in the living room. He stated that he had arrived at the apartment at about 8:00 P.M. on December 3, and that he was on security duty at the apartment that evening.

At Hanrahan's trial he repeated that he, Bell, Harris, and Clark were all in the living room when the raid began. He was inconsistent, however, as to certain other preraid details—for example, he stated that he had arrived at the apartment at 6:00 P.M. on December 3, rather than at 8:00 P.M.

Announcements by the Police and Occupants' Responses

Brenda Harris: In the statement that Harris gave to her lawyer on December 21, 1969, she said that she was awakened by a knocking on the door and a voice repeating twice, "Policemen, brothers, open up." She stated that Truelock left the living room for the rear of the house while she and Clark each reached for a shotgun. As the police broke through the outer door, Clark said, "Just a minute." Meanwhile, she was trying to find the safety on her gun, which was resting half on her leg and half on the bed. Harris testified at the People's

Inquest that she was awakened by knocks on the door. After several knocks a voice said, "Policemen," and told the occupants to open the door. Mark Clark, who was in the living room with Harris, replied, "Just a minute," and got up.

At the Commission's hearings Harris testified that some time after falling asleep she was suddenly awakened by the sound of two knocks on the front door and a voice saying, "Policemen, brothers, open up." She sat up, she said, as Mark Clark, also awake now, got up and called out, "Just a minute."

Harris testified at Hanrahan's trial that she was awakened by a knock at the outer door of the apartment and heard a voice say only once, "Policemen, brothers, open up." Bell and Truelock, she said, then got up and went toward the back of the apartment. Clark said, "Just a minute," and stood up; she sat up in bed. However, while acknowledging that weapons were around the apartment, she explicitly denied having handled a weapon during the raid or having seen Clark, Bell, or Truelock handle a weapon.

Ronald Satchel: At the People's Inquest Satchel said that he was awakened by "some knock on the door, and very shortly after that knock I heard shots."

Satchel repeated this story at the Commission's hearings, saying that he heard a knock at the door, followed a few seconds later by gunshots.

Verlina Brewer: Brewer testified before the People's Inquest that she was awakened by Ronald Satchel, who was shaking her and saying, "Get on the floor, the pigs are here."

Blair Anderson: Anderson testified at the People's Inquest that he was awakened by a lot of noise and Satchel telling him that the "pigs" were there. Shooting started a moment thereafter.

Harold Bell: Bell told the People's Inquest that he was awakened by sounds at the front door, which sounded like "thuds" and two shots.

At the Commission's hearings Bell said that he awoke in the living room to the sound of two "thuds" and two shots.

Deborah Johnson: At the People's Inquest Johnson testified that she was awakened by somebody shaking Hampton and saying, "Chairman, wake up, pigs are here." When she awoke, shots were being fired from both the back and the front of the apartment.

Johnson told the Commission that she was awakened by Louis Truelock, who was shaking Hampton and saying, "Chairman, wake up, the pigs are vamping." By the time she had awakened, gunfire had already commenced.

Louis Truelock: Truelock said on December 22, 1969, that he was awakened at exactly 4:15 A.M. by a knock at the door. He said that he opened the inside door and said, "Who is it?" A voice from the outer door stated, "It's Tommy." Truelock said he asked, "Tommy who?," to which the voice responded, "Tommy, motherfucker, open the door." He then said, "Fuck you," and closed the door. He said that while Clark arose, he momentarily stood by the front door, and then went toward the back of the apartment to wake Hampton.

At Hanrahan's trial in the summer of 1972 Truelock reaffirmed that portion of his statement, except that he added that before going toward the back of the apartment, he and Clark had "peeked out the window to try to detect where the voices were coming from."

Entry by the Police and Initial Firing

Brenda Harris: In Harris's statement to her lawyer, she said that right after Clark had said, "Just a minute," the police broke in the door and blinded her with their flashlights. Before she had a chance to fire her weapon, she said, the police shot her twice, shot Clark, and then began shooting in the back of the apartment. She stated that she had not fired her weapon, that she heard no shots before the police burst into the room, and that she didn't know whether she or Clark had been shot first. She did not say, nor was she asked, whether Clark had fired a weapon.

At the People's Inquest Harris described the events immediately following the police announcement of their office and Clark's response:

He [Clark] got up and the next thing I knew they had busted into the door, they came in shooting, they shot me, they shot Mark Clark; and this other pig, he came in with a machine gun and he started shooting toward the back, he sprayed the wall, he was shooting toward the back and they were yelling to each other, "There is some over there in the back, get them," and he would shoot over toward that direction and he was just shooting with the machine gun, just going crazy and what not.

She told the Commission that immediately after Clark responded to the police, she heard a loud noise, like the sound of the outer door being forced open. Approximately three armed men in plainclothes then burst into the living room:

They bursted into the door and they had flashlights and they shined the flashlight on me and then they started shooting and they shot at me and they shot at Mark Clark. . . .

I don't know how many people were shooting, and I don't know if they shined a flashlight on Mark Clark or not, but I know that me and Mark Clark got shot at about the same time, and I heard him when he fell.

Approximately four to ten shots were fired by police as they entered, Harris said. She was struck by bullets in the left hand and right thigh as she sat on her bed, and Mark Clark was also shot as he stood behind the living room door.

At Hanrahan's trial in August 1972, Harris testified that, while she sat in her bed, two to four men with flashlights and guns burst into the living room and shot her and Clark. She stated that she was shot twice, in the left hand and the right leg, and that it was after she had been shot that Clark was shot. After that, she said, a man with a machine gun began shooting toward the back of the house. She expressly denied having held a gun or having seen Clark, Truelock, or Bell hold a gun during the raid.

Ronald Satchel: Satchel told the People's Inquest that as he was awakened, bullets were coming through the room in which he had been sleeping. He tried to put on a pair of pants while waking up the other occupants of the room, he said. He continued:

Bullets were still coming in the room and we really didn't know what to do, so, I told the other people, "Let's get on the floor." So we got down on the floor, bullets were still coming.

In his statement to the Commission, Satchel related substantially the same story, although he altered the order of events somewhat:

The first thing I did was to get out of bed and I remember it was dark, I couldn't see very good. I was trying to locate my trousers or pants, so, I found my pants and I began putting them on and at the same time, I woke two other persons in the room.

At this time, Satchel said, he saw plaster coming out of the bedroom walls, and realized that bullets were being fired through the north wall of the bedroom. He warned the other two persons in the room to get on the floor, and all three dropped to the bedroom floor.

Verlina Brewer: Brewer testified before the People's Inquest that shooting had already begun as she was awakened. She and the other occupants of the front bedroom dropped to the floor between the two beds in the room. The shooting continued for a long time, and voices were interspersed with the shots, calling, "Come out, mother-fuckers."

Then they just kept on shooting and finally I didn't know how long they shot in, but it was for a pretty long time and finally, you know, we were all hurt pretty bad.

Blair Anderson: Anderson testified at the People's Inquest that shooting began a second after Satchel awakened him. He, Satchel, and Brewer all fell to the floor. Anderson described first pistol fire, then shotgun fire, and then machine gun fire. The firing continued until he, Satchel, and Brewer were all wounded.

Harold Bell: Bell told the People's Inquest that as soon as he awakened, he ran toward the back bedroom in order to awaken Fred Hampton. By the time Bell reached the doorway of the back bedroom, he saw armed men entering through the back door.

Bell repeated this story at the Commission's hearings, except that he said he heard, rather than saw, the police entering the kitchen, and only after he was in the bedroom.

Deborah Johnson: At the People's Inquest Johnson testified that as she was awakened she could see shots being fired from the back and from the front. She said she "kind of hopped on top of" Hampton and tried to move closer to the wall. Hampton apparently raised his head and laid it back down. She did not know whether he was wounded at that point, but she assumed he was.

Johnson told the Commission that as she awoke, she recognized the flashes and explosions of gunfire. She rolled over on top of Hampton's motionless body, which was lying face down and slid off to his right toward the north wall (the wall next to the front bedroom). The mattress was vibrating from bullets being fired into it. Hampton raised his head and looked at the door, and then laid his head back down. She said she could not recall whether he was breathing at this time.

Louis Truelock: On December 22, 1969, Truelock purportedly told Donald Stang that as he was heading from the living room to the rear bedroom, he heard about four shots from the front of the house. As he left the front room, he said, none of the Panthers was holding a weapon, although there were a number of weapons throughout the apartment. He could not say what kind of weapon had fired the initial shots:

It sounded like a shotgun. And it had uh . . . it was very noisy. Could have been because the room is so hollow. But it sounded more or less like a . . . a shotgun. Uh . . . it could have been a . . . .357 magnum. It was something with a very loud sound. And it was quiet and I wasn't expecting anything of this sort, so it might have just sounded like anything, thunder. It was so loud.

Before he got to the back bedroom, he reported that several police, one of them with a machine gun, had broken into the kitchen, and that they all were firing in Truelock's direction. He then crawled into the back bedroom, he said, and tried to arouse Hampton. Truelock said that Hampton appeared to have been drugged, but that he had been conscious long enough to tell Truelock to keep Deborah Johnson in between the two of them.

Later in his statement, as an apparent afterthought, and after specifically stating that as far as he knew none of the Panthers in the apartment had handled a weapon during the raid, he said that he had fired two shots from the dining room toward the kitchen with an automatic pump rifle. He said he had fired the shots to clear his way to the back bedroom, but that he hadn't hit anybody with his shots and that "I didn't want anybody hit."

At Hanrahan's trial, Truelock reaffirmed his course of action in leaving the living room for the rear bedroom. He expressly denied, however, having fired two shots during the raid or having ever said that he fired two shots.

The Commission's Analysis of the Survivors' Testimony

Arriving at one overall consistent version of the raid from the participants' various perceptions and recollections of events—a version which is also consistent with the physical evidence—is scarcely less difficult in the case of the survivors' statements and testimony than in the case of the police accounts. The statements of Harris and Truelock in December 1969 contradict in many material respects all the other accounts given by the survivors. The relatively stationary positions of the occupants limited their ability to observe what was happening in other rooms of the apartment during the raid. Moreover, the possibility exists that the People's Inquest and the Commission hearings did not uncover all the information known to the six occupants who testified. In addition, the survivors' testimony was never subjected to adequate cross-examination. Further, there were no public statements from the survivors until three months after the event, a lapse which could have given them an opportunity to discuss their statements privately and try to eliminate inconsistencies.

Despite these limitations, the testimony of the survivors is a useful source of information.

The positions of the occupants in the apartment at the time the incident began were consistently presented by all the survivors. These descriptions of the survivors' locations at the time the raid began would place Brenda Harris and Mark Clark in the living room, Ronald Satchel, Verlina Brewer, and Blair Anderson in the front bedroom, and Deborah Johnson and Fred Hampton in the rear bedroom. Harold Bell and Louis Truelock moved from the living room to the rear bedroom as the raid began. The survivors' statements further indicate that Harris, Bell, Satchel, Brewer, Anderson, Hampton, and Johnson were asleep when the raid began. Truelock may have been dozing, but was probably still awake. Whether Clark was asleep cannot be established from the information presently available.

The police entry into the apartment was described by the six occupants who testified before the People's Inquest and/or the Commission staff; each of the four who testified before both (Bell, Harris, Satchel, and Johnson) gave the same individual account on both occasions. Harris's testimony was also consistent, in this regard, with the statement to her lawyer and with her testimony at Hanrahan's trial, and Truelock's testimony in this regard was also consistent in his statement to Stang and at Hanrahan's trial.

From the testimony of the survivors, however, it cannot be firmly established whether police entered the front or rear of the apartment first, or whether entry at both points was simultaneous. It is evident that several of the occupants believe police entered both the front and back doors to the apartment at about the same time and were firing weapons into the dwelling as they entered, while other occupants were not in a position to make such a determination.

The occupants had difficulty establishing the exact source and timing of the first shot(s). Their vantage points were restricted, and most or all, according to testimony, were sleeping when the sounds of knocking or gunfire awakened them.

Judging from their descriptions of the shots which initiated the incident, however, it is clear that they fix the first shots as coming from the police. The statements of Harris, Bell, and Truelock further indicate that police fired either before entering or upon entering through the living room door. Johnson said that police who entered the rear also fired as they came in, but it is not clear whether that occurred before, at the same time, or after the shots were fired in the vicinity of the living room door.

Reports on Scientific Examinations of the Physical Evidence at 2337 West Monroe Street

Various reports, both official and unofficial, attempted to resolve the issue of the first shot by relying on physical evidence, especially ballistics investigation. The first such report was released by the Internal Inspections Division of the Chicago Police Department on December 19, 1969. The report, as prepared by Director Harry Ervanian, concluded:

> Physical evidence has fairly established that the occupants of the premises in question fired upon the officers who were in the process of executing the search warrant. . . .
> There is no apparent misconduct or impropriety by any of the officers involved in the incident. The evidence shows the officers were in the process of lawful execution of a search warrant issued by a judge of the Circuit Court of Cook County. Purpose of the warrant was to seize certain illegally possessed weapons which were in fact found. The officers were met with deadly force in the form of gunfire.[39]

39. Cited in *Report,* p. 60.

While the federal grand jury did not state a determination of who fired first, its *Report* strongly implies that the Panthers, and specifically Mark Clark, fired the first shot. While the *Report*'s discussion of "The Grand Jury's Assessment of the Facts," under the subheading "The Shootings: Testimony vs. Physical Facts and Evidence," does not refer to the issue of who fired first, the final pages of the *Report* quote FBI testimony that

In June of last year, the Chicago [Panther] officers told every Panther member that if you are arrested, there had better be at least one shot fired at the arresting officer or we will not bond you out.

The *Report* continues by urging that "in judging the facts of this case . . . the reader should keep the proper perspective. If officers of the law are on a legitimate and proper mission to search for illegal weapons that could endanger countless persons, *they should not be met with gun fire.*"[40] These concluding statements lead the reader to believe that the occupants fired first, while police attempted to execute a proper search. Nowhere in the *Report*'s findings, however, is it expressly stated that the occupants fired the first shot.

The issue of whether the Panthers fired first was indirectly considered by the federal grand jury when the FBI ballistics examination refuted a mistaken ballistics report of the Chicago Police Department, which indicated that two recovered shells had been fired by Harris. The *Report* discussed this error and its correction in these words:

The scientific evidence presented at the inquest consisted of the findings of the Chicago Police Department Crime Laboratory as to the crime scene search and the ballistic evidence analysis. The Sergeant who led the Crime Lab Mobile Unit stated that he arrived at the scene at approximately 5 A.M., received a briefing from Sgt. Groth, and commenced his inspection. This officer testified most emphatically that he had examined the panel in the living room door on December 4, 1969 and observed only one hole in the panel (the hole caused by the shotgun blast from within the apartment). He stated he looked for other holes in the door but could not find them, and if he did see them he would have recalled them. Before this Grand Jury, the Sergeant acknowledged that: ". . . more than one [shot] had gone through it [door]." . . .

40. Ibid., pp. 124–125; emphasis added.

Secondly, an experienced firearms examiner for the Chicago Police Department Crime Laboratory testified as to his findings relative to the ballistic aspect of the incident. The examination and findings are also discussed elsewhere in this report. Of primary significance are his findings and testimony identifying three shotgun shells as having been fired from weapons seized by the police from the premises. His findings were later proved to be in error as to two of the shells by the FBI ballistic examination. He thereafter admitted his error to the Grand Jury. [P. 69, footnotes omitted.]

As for the third shotgun shell identified by the Chicago police as having been fired from a seized weapon, the *Report* appeared to agree with Sergeant Groth's second account—that Mark Clark had fired the shot. At first he had said that Brenda Harris fired first. Subsequently he changed his mind. The *Report* stated:

At the time of this first cease fire, the only rounds that had been fired by police at the front of the apartment were two blind shots by Groth through the front doorway and three shots by Davis killing Clark and wounding Harris. There are two bullet holes in the front door of the apartment, one from the inside going towards the outside and the other from the outside coming in. Groth initially thought that the shot fired as Davis went in the door had been fired by Brenda Harris, but concluded after examining the door panel that Clark fired the first shot from behind the door. The upper hole in the door was made from the outside, with the door at approximately a 45° angle, and may be consistent with one of the shots fired by Groth. [P. 95.]

But Groth continued to insist that Brenda Harris had fired:

Groth, Davis, Jones, and Gorman all insist that a shot was fired by Brenda Harris at them as they came in the door. None of them could explain what had become of this shot, and it is not possible to draw a line from the southeast corner of the living room, where Harris was said by Davis and Groth to be on the bed holding the gun, out through the living room door. There are no holes in the west wall of the apartment. Groth believes the shot must have passed out the front door, somehow missing all of the officers in the hallway and foyer. [Pp. 95–96.]

The *Report* refers to two shots fired through the living room door —one from the inside out and the other from the outside in:

The rifled slug impact point was caused by a slug fired through the door from a point in the living room 15 inches from the door, probably by a gun at hip level. At this moment of impact, the door was open at a 45° angle. The door panel was removed from the premises by a Black Panther Party investigator on December 8, 1969. One additional hole appeared in the removed door panel, above the hole made by the rifled slug. That hole was made by a .38 caliber pistol bullet fired from the hallway into the living room, probably by Sgt. Groth. [P. 81.]

Although the *Report* tentatively identified the pistol shot as having been fired by Groth, it did not at that point speculate as to who had fired the rifled slug. After nearly thirty more pages, however, the *Report* returns to this shot:

A deer slug and its empty shell were recovered and the shell was positively identified as being fired in a shotgun which was found behind the living room door and which had on it bloodstains consistent in type with that of the deceased Mark Clark who was found lying behind the living room door. [P. 108.]

It stated no conclusion, however, as to which shot was fired first.

Herbert L. MacDonell, an independent criminologist, was approached on December 6, 1969, by attorneys for the survivors of the raid and the families of the deceased, and requested to conduct an independent examination of evidence at the premises at 2337 West Monroe Street. He agreed to conduct an impartial investigation, stipulating that he would suppress no evidence he might uncover in the course of his investigations. The attorneys for the survivors agreed in writing to this procedure, and on December 8, 1969, MacDonell examined the premises, took photographs, and collected evidence.[41]

MacDonell examined and analyzed the evidence he had collected, along with additional evidence from the premises transmitted to him on January 9, 1970, by an agent of the survivors' attorneys. He was not, however, permitted to see any of the bullets recovered from the bodies of the victims or other physical evidence in the hands of the police, including the guns collected immediately after the raid.

MacDonell reported his findings and conclusions to the attorneys for the occupants of the apartment and later testified as to his findings before the first county grand jury, the federal grand jury, and the second (special) county grand jury.

This Commission approached MacDonell in September 1970 and

41. His report is reprinted in the Appendix.

requested that he prepare for the Commission a written analytical evaluation of the ballistics evidence relating to the raid. In his report for the Commission, MacDonell stated that to determine who fired the first shot it was necessary to know whether the living room door was opening or closing when fired through. Nonphysical evidence, in his opinion, indicate that it was opening.

Although there was an inordinate quantity of firearms evidence in this case, in the final analysis only three items are necessary to reconstruct the events of greatest significance. Specifically, the question of who fired the first shot is paramount. Since only one shot was fired by the Panthers, it is only necessary to determine whether or not this was the first shot. It would be academic to prove that it were the sixth rather than the seventh, for example.

Initially, we may consider three possibilities regarding the sequence of shots. First, that the Panthers shot first; second, that the police shot first; and third, that the Panthers and the police fired the initial shots simultaneously. It is fortunate that the shotgun blast fired from within the apartment and one pistol shot fired into the living room both struck the same door panel. These events resulted in permanent physical facts that allow conclusions to be drawn as to which of the two shots was fired first. Unfortunately, however, these conclusions are based, in part, upon related events that cannot be established or proven by physical evidence alone.

1. The shotgun blast fired by the Panthers penetrated the living room door, continued across the entrance hall, struck and penetrated a partition, crossed the stairway to the upper apartment, struck an outside wall and fell to the stairs where it was recovered. I was able to look through the large hole in the living room door and sight this path to the final point of impact before the door was removed. The recovered shotgun slug was undoubtedly the projectile that was fired in the living room and ultimately penetrated the stairway walls. The presence of copper- or bronze-colored metallic paint on the slug confirms this. This is the first significant factor.

2. The slug removed from the living room east wall contained wooden fibers consistent with the living room door. It is concluded that this slug was the projectile that was fired into the apartment through the living room door. This is the second significant factor.

3. Further proof of the validity of the two previous conclusions may be established by geometry. Angles of penetration through the living room door panel have been described in detail in Section III-6. Using a scale model or diagram it will be found that projection of two lines through the door panel at their reported vertical angles will result in trajectories for each shot consistent with their respective points of impact. A tolerance of $+5$ degrees was assigned to these angles. Likewise, it is possible to view the horizontal angles

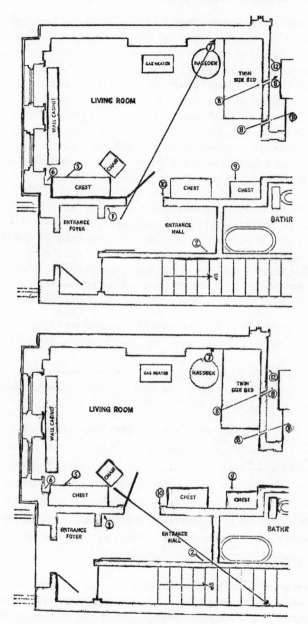

Figure 2: Diagrams showing the necessary living room door positions that satisfy trajectories of the two shots fired through this door.

of penetration from overhead and, further to incorporate them into a scale diagram of the apartment. This has been accomplished as illustrated [in Figure 2.] From these diagrams it is evident, that since the living room door has been moved 16″ to satisfy the two trajectories, then these two shots could not have been fired simultaneously. This is the third significant factor.

4. Since the two shots through the living room door could not have been fired simultaneously, the obvious question is: Which shot was fired first? The answer to this is simple, provided two additional facts are known. First, were the two shots fired at nearly the same time? Second, was the door opening or closing when the shots were fired? Physical evidence cannot establish either of these; however, there has been considerable testimony reporting that these shots occurred close together as the police were breaking in. If this is true, then there is no question regarding sequence of shots, the police fired first! A study of the diagrams clearly demonstrates why this must be so; it is elementary geometry. If, however, the living room door was being closed at the time of the shooting, it is just as conclusive that the Panther's shot was fired first. Therefore, the final proof of sequence must rest with the confidence assigned to the direction the door was traveling and the interval between shots. A liberal tolerance of ± 10 degrees would not change this conclusion.

MacDonell concluded that the door was opening at the time of the shooting and that the first shot was fired by the police:

The one shot fired out was not the first shot; the first shot was fired by the police. This conclusion is based upon previous testimony that the living room door was opening at the time of the shooting.

The only public documentation of Mr. MacDonell's examination and findings was the federal grand jury *Report*'s characterization of his testimony before the federal grand jury in a chapter entitled, "The Panther Investigation." This chapter, which is a brief critical analysis of certain aspects of the investigation and findings of the experts and attorneys retained by the survivors and the families of the deceased, summarily dismisses MacDonell's efforts as "imaginative" and "defense orient[ed]":

While some of his [MacDonell's] contributions were significant, the expert's testimony revealed his defense orientation, perhaps accentuated by the limited time he had and the briefings of counsel. For example, he proposed an imaginative theory as to who fired the first shot based upon the position of the living room door and the assumed trajectories of the incoming and outgoing rounds. He illustrated that if the door was opening at the time of the first two closely spaced shots, the incoming shot would have to be fired before the shotgun blast from within the apartment. However, if the door was closing, then the shotgun blast from within the apartment preceded the shot from outside the door. The expert stated that his opinion on who fired the first shot would be based on prior testimony establishing whether the door was opening or closing at the time. His theory excluded any other movements of the door, i.e. it could have been kicked open and bounced back. In addition, his opinion that a deer slug shotgun blast through a door at close range would not cause it to move seemed strained to the Jury and was later contradicted by FBI tests on a similar door. [P.51.]

Nowhere, however, does the *Report* set forth scientific rebuttal based upon either the fact premises set forth or the validity of the deductive reasoning employed by MacDonell in reaching his conclusion. In addition, the *Report* ignores MacDonell's assertion that his research was conducted with no external controls maintained by the Panthers:

There was never any doubt that I was receiving assistance, cooperation and courtesy from the Panthers, the attorneys, and the attorneys' assistants. Likewise, there were no questions asked nor information offered that could in any way be interpreted as showing me where to look, what to look for or where not to look. In short, I was given complete freedom to conduct the investigation as I wished without interference or direction from anyone.

Because the federal grand jury dismissed MacDonell's report so summarily, the Commission requested a police ballistics expert from a city other than Chicago to examine his report. The head of the New York City Crime Laboratory and a ballistics expert from the New York City Police Department criticized MacDonell's report for several reasons, some of which are extrinsic to the substance of the report. First, noting that MacDonell's training was principally in chemistry, they seriously questioned his qualifications as a ballistics expert. Second, they referred to technical errors in his report. For example, MacDonell referred to a .30-caliber cartridge as "probably" from "a .30 M1 carbine"; the New York City ballistic experts stated that a ballistic expert should be able to make such an identification positively. And third, they thought that MacDonell's ballistics analysis ignored ricochet possibilities and was otherwise deficient.

Primarily, however, they objected that MacDonell, a purported expert, had reached a conclusion—as to who fired the first shot—not based on physical evidence but on speculation as to the direction in which the door was swinging at the moment of the shot.

The MacDonell Report and the federal grand jury *Report* both refer to a shotgun blast fired just inside the entrance hallway into the east wall of the hallway. The blast was ignored by both the Chicago Police Department Crime Lab and the state's attorney's police; it was mentioned in both the federal grand jury *Report* and the MacDonell Report, but no particular significance was attached to it. The shot was apparently fired from Officer Jones's weapon; the wads, shot pellets, and impact points found at the scene are consistent with Jones's weapon and position.

Although Jones denies firing the shot,[42] the firing of such a shot would be consistent with the testimony of Bell and Satchel, who say they heard a shot outside the living room almost simultaneous with the pounding on the front door. The direction of the shot suggests that it may have been fired inadvertently; there is no obvious target at which it might have been aimed. In short, it seems probable that the first shot was fired by Jones as he, Davis, Groth, and Gorman broke through the outer door into the small entrance hallway.

It also seems probable that this shotgun blast precipitated Groth's shot into the living room and Davis's charge into the apartment, and, combined with Groth's shot, provoked Mark Clark's shotgun blast through the opening living room door. This initial exchange of shots —Jones's accidentally into the entrance hallway wall, Groth's into the living room, Clark's through the opening door, Davis's at Brenda Harris and Clark, and Groth's again into the room—might in turn have been the event which precipitated the entry of the police at the rear of the apartment.

Finally, it is probable that Mark Clark's shot was neither the first nor the second, but rather the third, shot fired during the raid.

42. *Report,* footnote 247.

CHAPTER 4

The Pattern of the Shooting

The opening moments of the raid, discussed in Chapter 3, were dramatic and violent. Shots were fired by Officers Jones, Groth, and Davis, and by Mark Clark. At the end of that first outbreak of firing, Mark Clark had been killed and Brenda Harris had been wounded, disarmed, and arrested. Harold Bell and Louis Truelock had fled from the living room to the rear bedroom. The living room had been secured.

Gunfire continued in the apartment for several more minutes—exactly how long is not clear—at the end of which Fred Hampton was dead and all the remaining occupants were taken into custody, four of them severely wounded. As in the case of the beginning moments of the raid, there are numerous accounts of what happened during those few minutes.

The questions of who fired at whom, and why, have been regarded as crucial by all the participants. If the Panthers engaged in the fierce gun battle described by the police, the massive return firing by police and the consequent injuries and deaths might be justified. If there was no such intensive "shoot-out" on the part of the Panthers, the actions taken by the police must be viewed in an entirely different light. In an attempt to resolve those basic questions, this chapter will present and discuss first the conflicting accounts of the police and Panthers involved in the raid, and then the physical evidence from the raid which is relevant to those questions.

An Overview

The initial public police accounts of the raid described a fierce gun battle in which police and Panthers fired at each other in an intense and extended exchange of shots. At a press conference held on the day of the raid, Assistant State's Attorney Richard Jalovec quoted Sergeant Groth as follows:

> There must have been six or seven of them firing. . . . The firing must have gone on 10 or 12 minutes. If 200 shots were exchanged, that would have been nothing.[1]

And Officer Ciszewski referred to the police "fighting" from room to room.

> The shooting must have gone on for about 5 minutes, but it seemed like 5 hours as we fought our way from room to room in the apartment. . . . With all the bullets flying around in that apartment, I don't see how we got out with only light wounds.[2]

In the initial accounts the police not only emphasized the Panthers' participation in the exchange of fire, but also attempted to lay the blame for the resulting injuries on the victims themselves. Thus State's Attorney Hanrahan, at a press conference held on the day of the raid, stated that Sergeant Groth had three times ordered a cease-fire and told the occupants of the apartment to surrender. He continued:

> The immediate, violent criminal reaction of the occupants in shooting at announced police officers emphasizes the extreme viciousness of the Black Panther Party.
> So does their refusal to cease firing at the police officers when urged to do so several times.[3]

Sergeant Groth, on the following day, was more explicit:

> We tried our best to avoid loss of life or wounding anyone. . . . I called on our men to stop shooting, and they did. I asked the other people to surrender, shouting that we had a search warrant, and they didn't obey. A man's voice shouted from one of the dark rooms in the place, "Shoot it out," and they tried it. Our men had no choice but to return their fire.[4]

1. *Chicago Today,* 5 Star final, December 4, 1969, p. 1.
2. Ibid., p. 14.
3. Chicago *Daily News,* Red Flash Edition, December 4, 1969, p. 1.
4. Chicago *Sun-Times,* Second City Edition, December 5, 1969, p. 3.

Accounts by Police and State Officials

The First Cease-Fire and Renewed Shooting

Composite Version 1: The first detailed police account of the raid appeared in the Chicago *Tribune*'s "Exclusive" on December 11, 1969, and is referred to in this report as Composite Version 1. The information for this article, including photographs, was supplied to the *Tribune* by the State's Attorney's Office.

The article reported that after Mark Clark had been shot by Officer Davis, and Davis had fallen across his body, Officers Jones and Gorman plunged into the darkened living room. As they entered, Gorman directed his flashlight into a corner of the room and saw Brenda Harris lying on a bed opposite the officers. He saw that she was wounded in her right thigh and held a shotgun in her hands. Gorman then "charged the bed and yanked" the gun from her hands, hurling it behind him toward the door. He kicked aside a round hassock near the bed, and three guns lying on it spilled onto the floor.

By this time Davis had risen to a crouch. He looked down the hallway toward the rear of the flat and saw a man carrying a shotgun duck in and out of the rear bedroom. According to Davis:

> By then, the guys had broken down the kitchen door. I saw Ciszewski in the kitchen behind the gunman and hollered for him to duck as the man fired at least one round into the kitchen. Ciszewski ducked and the shot missed.

Immediately after the alleged shot into the kitchen, Sergeant Groth ordered his men to hold their fire and "Give them a chance to come out!" The article stated that this was the first of five such cease-fire orders given by Groth during the raid. Groth was quoted as saying:

> I had men in both the front and rear of the apartment. I didn't want anyone getting hit in crossfire. But the words were barely out of my mouth before there was the whomp of a shotgun blast from the front bedroom, directly down the hall from the living room. They were firing blind because they didn't know where we were, so the charge slammed into a bathroom door almost directly across the hall.

The photographs printed with the *Tribune* "Exclusive"—which as previously noted had been provided by State's Attorney Hanrahan—

purportedly showing the inside of the apartment's bathroom door, marked by shotgun pellets that had slammed through the wood. Hanrahan was reported to have said that he would produce a ballistics expert to show in court that the Panthers had opened fire on the police.

Sergeant Groth: Sergeant Groth, at a press conference on the day of the raid, had referred to firing coming from the living room and "a second room," which Composite Version 1 apparently fixed as the front bedroom. However, he mentioned only two cease-fires, as opposed to State's Attorney Hanrahan's various reports on the same day, first that Groth had ordered three, and then "several," cease-fires. Groth said the initial cease-fire was violated by a call to "Shoot it out," followed by renewed fire.

In the filmed re-enactment of the raid, which appeared on Chicago area television on the evening of December 11 (Composite Version 2), Groth again described the first cease-fire:

I say, "All officers, stop shooting," and give 'em an opportunity for our men to get in position, and for them to come out with their hands up. And I yelled in a very loud voice, as they also do in the back room, "Come out with your hands up."
There is a shotgun blast from this first bedroom [indicates front bedroom] into that door [indicates bathroom door].

Groth testified at the coroner's inquest in January 1970 that, after the initial shooting in the front room, he stepped back into the entrance hall and ordered Officer Hughes to call for additional police assistance and to advise the officers in the rear that police were being fired upon in the front room. He then re-entered the apartment and ordered all police officers to cease firing.

They complied with my order. All at this time stopped firing. A shot rang out from one of the rooms, they resumed their firing.

Officer Gorman: Officer Gorman testified before the coroner's inquest on January 15, 1970, that he burst through the living room doorway after hearing two or three shots and a call from Officer Davis to come in. Gorman said he saw a woman sitting in one corner of the room holding a shotgun pointed toward him. He moved cautiously toward her and, when she did not move, noticed that she was wounded. He took the weapon from her and spun around, kicking over a footstool covered with handguns. He saw Officer Davis climbing off a form—Mark Clark—on the floor. He heard firing elsewhere in the apartment, and at that point Sergeant Groth called for a cease-fire.

Officer Davis: Officer Davis, testifying at the coroner's inquest on January 19, 1970, said that after he had fired at Brenda Harris and fatally shot Mark Clark in the living room, he got up off the floor and turned on a light in the room. Meanwhile, Davis said, Officer Gorman took a weapon from the hand of Brenda Harris, who had been wounded.

Looking down the hallway, he testified, he noticed a man holding a shotgun dart in and out of the back bedroom. He saw other officers entering the rear of the apartment, and warned them off, shouting, "Man behind the door." He continued:

And there was a—I saw a flash and heard noise. Sergeant Groth came in and hollered, "Cease-fire." And we tried to get all the people to come out. But no one would come out. I heard a voice somewhere state that "Shoot it out."

Federal Grand Jury Report: According to the federal grand jury *Report* (Composite Version 3), during the first cease-fire Officer Jones handed Sergeant Groth three long guns, saying, "Get them out of here." Officer Davis heard a male voice call out, "Off the pig," or "Shoot it out," or words to that effect. As Groth turned to take the guns out of the apartment, the cease-fire was broken by a shot that rang out from somewhere in the flat. After the cease-fire was violated, Davis turned on a light in the living room.

In the *Report,* various versions are recited concerning the shot that broke the cease-fire. Officer Jones said that he heard a gunshot and saw a flash as he was watching the hallway, but heard no impact of the shot and had no idea where it went. Officer Davis identified the shot as coming from the front bedroom, and said he saw a gun flash reflected on the wall of the hallway opposite the front bedroom. Sergeant Groth did not see the shot, as he had walked out of the apartment with the shotguns. Officer Gorman said only that the shot sounded "muffled" and "unusual."

Second and Third Cease-Fires and Renewed Shooting

Composite Version 1: The *Tribune* "Exclusive" reported that when the first cease-fire was terminated by a shotgun blast from the front bedroom, Officer Jones was in the living room, crouching between two wooden dressers. Jones said he saw a hand reach out from the rear bedroom, pointing a revolver or automatic pistol at the kitchen, where other detectives were crouched. "It was just about then," Sergeant Groth is reported to have said, "that I heard a voice call out from the bedroom, 'Shoot it out!' This was followed by two flashes from the [rear bedroom] I believe were from the shotgun." At this point, the police resumed firing. Minutes later, or perhaps "seconds later," Groth again ordered his men to cease firing and again called out to the occupants, "Come out with your hands up!"

Composite Version 2: In Composite Version 2, the filmed re-enactment of the raid, as the shooting resumed Officer Jones handed Groth three shotguns to be removed from the apartment. Groth walked to the front doorway and gave the weapons to Officer Hughes, who was waiting there.

Sergeant Groth: Groth testified at the coroner's inquest that he had been handed three shotguns by Jones immediately after the resumption of firing which terminated the first cease-fire and had been told to "get them out of here." Groth took the three shotguns and handed them to Officer Hughes, who was standing in the doorway. Groth then re-entered the apartment and ordered a second cease-fire, with which, he said, all officers complied.

Action at the Rear and the Machine-gunning of the Front Bedroom

The action at the front and back doors of the apartment may have proceeded more or less simultaneously; the accounts are not clear on this point. Officers at both locations reported seeing frequent flashes of gunfire. The police agreed that they returned fire, in some cases intensively, in the general direction of the fire they observed.

ACTION AT THE REAR

Composite Version 2: In the television re-enactment, Officer Carmody said he returned to the back door from the broken kitchen window, dived onto the kitchen floor on his stomach, and fired a shot into the rear bedroom. He heard a call for a cease-fire, but as he started to rise, several more shots rang out from rooms in the apartment, and Officer Broderick, who had followed him in, directed a shotgun blast toward this shooting. Carmody then heard "much more firing" and fired his second and third shots in the direction of the back bedroom. He told the officer with him in the rear that he was going to jump over a "barricade" (apparently intended as a defense against rats) blocking the way between the kitchen and dining room. At this moment, Officer Broderick heard Officer Gorman in the living room shout that he was going to start firing from the front.

Composite Version 3: According to the federal grand jury *Report* composite account, Carmody dived onto the kitchen floor and saw a gun flash from the same general area from which he had allegedly been fired upon earlier—near the doorway between the kitchen and the dining room. He fired a shot from his revolver in the direction of the flash. Ciszewski and Broderick followed Carmody through the back door into the kitchen. At this point, Carmody heard someone shout, "Hold your fire, our men are coming in the back." The grand jury *Report* apparently considers this to have been the first of several cease-fire orders issued by Groth in the course of the raid.

The *Report* states that at that time the only rounds fired by the police in the front of the apartment had been two blind shots by Groth in the living room, and three shots fired there by Davis which killed Mark Clark and wounded Brenda Harris. According to the *Report,* when Groth called for the first cease-fire, firing was going on in the back of the apartment; all the firing stopped after his order.

Officer Carmody: Officer Carmody, who had told the coroner's jury that he was fired upon while attempting to enter the apartment through the kitchen door, testified further that he re-entered the apartment by diving onto the kitchen floor, whereupon he was again fired on. He returned fire with a single shot from his revolver. As he started to rise, Officer Broderick, standing near him, fired a shotgun blast into the apartment. Carmody heard a voice in the front call out, "Hold your fire, the men are coming in the back." However, he continued, "this didn't seem like it stopped anything, seem[ed] like everything kept going." He then rose to one knee and fired two more shots into the apartment. He prepared to jump over a barricade between the kitchen and the dining room, while the officers "were yelling back and forth 'Don't jump, wait a minute.' "

Officer Broderick: Officer Broderick testified before the coroner's inquest that he followed Carmody and Ciszewski into the apartment, heard gunfire in the front of the building, and then saw what he believed to be shotgun fire coming from the front bedroom. He fired a blast from his shotgun in that direction.

Officer Ciszewski: Ciszewski testified at the coroner's inquest that he followed Carmody into the apartment and saw him "picking himself up" from the kitchen floor. Ciszewski said he saw a shotgun blast from the front bedroom, followed by "two flashes against the door of the front bedroom." He then saw Officer Broderick fire a shotgun blast from the kitchen toward the front bedroom door, and heard a call for cease-fire. Ciszewski further stated that at no time had he seen or heard Carmody fire any shots or observed any shots coming from the back bedroom area.

After Officer Broderick reportedly fired into the apartment from his position in the kitchen, Ciszewski said, Carmody announced his intention of hurdling a wooden barricade blocking the way into the dining room.

And, I told him to wait for a second. And, he waited, and I tried to—I couldn't kick it down. He said he was going to go over. We yelled to the front that Carmody was going to go over the barricade, and he went over. And, Detective Broderick went over and I covered them.

And I finally managed to kick the barricade down. At this point, we heard —I heard the Sergeant call, "Hold your fire, don't let anybody shoot."

THE MACHINE-GUNNING OF THE FRONT BEDROOM
Composite Version 1: As Carmody jumped over the barricade between the kitchen and dining room, and the Panther fire continued, Gorman, in the living room, covered Carmody with submachine gun fire, firing down the hallway and through the wall separating the living room and front bedroom. Carmody fired one round from his .38-caliber revolver as he plunged past the rear bedroom doorway

toward "shelter" against the far dining room wall.

Composite Version 2: Gorman, standing in the living room, fired a "test shot" from his submachine gun through the south wall of the living room—the wall that separated the living room from the front bedroom. After checking with Jones to ascertain that the shot had passed on through the wall into the bedroom, Gorman heard Carmody (although he may not have recognized the voice), who was then preparing to hurdle the barricade, say from the rear of the apartment: "I'm coming over."

Gorman, having been told by Jones that the "test shot" had passed through the south wall, began stitching the wall with the submachine gun. At the same time, Carmody, followed by Officer Broderick, came over the barricade and into the dining room area. Gorman described firing into the wall over Brenda Harris, who was lying wounded near it.

I put the machine gun, still on single fire, and I started, from the left side of the wall, coming across, watching where the rounds were hitting, and I went over the girl's head, down on the other side of her and I continued fire across this wall. When I gave off my last shot, I heard Sergeant Dan Groth yell "Cease-fire!" again.

Groth, after calling the cease-fire, heard a voice in the rear of the apartment call out, "Come out with your hands up." At this point, in the rear of the apartment, Broderick and Ciszewski brought Harold Bell, who had surrendered, out of the back bedroom. Both Groth and Ciszewski said they then heard a voice call out, "Shoot it out." A shotgun blast came from the front bedroom, and firing recommenced. Gorman called out to the other officers that he was going to fire, and he again proceeded to riddle the wall between the living room and the front bedroom with machine gun fire. Officer Davis began firing his carbine through the same wall. Carmody, in the dining room area, warned Gorman to move, and placed a shot into the front bedroom door. Broderick and Ciszewski also fired into the front bedroom from their positions at the rear of the apartment.

Composite Version 3: After the first cease-fire was violated, Gorman concluded that he could not safely go down the hall. He then fired one machine gun shot through the wall between the living room and the front bedroom, and asked Jones whether it had gone through. Jones said it had, and Gorman and Davis told the occupants to come out. At this time, someone shouted from the rear, "Shoot it out," and a shot was simultaneously fired in the rear bedroom.

Carmody, in the kitchen, was preparing to leap over a door blocking the entrance to the dining room. Before he could rise from his position on the floor, a shot went off behind him. Ciszewski explained to him that Broderick had fired a shot over his head, to keep the occupants of the apartment down. Broderick's shot was fired high into the front bedroom, through the east wall of the dining room. Carmody, still in the kitchen, then got up on his knees and fired two more shots toward the bedrooms.

Someone in the front called out, "Wait a minute and I will cover you," but Carmody jumped over the barricade and ran toward the north wall of the dining room, firing his fourth shot toward the rear bedroom as he ran. Broderick followed him. Gorman—without an order to fire from Sergeant Groth, who was standing behind him—then stitched the living room wall with his machine gun.

Carmody, standing against the dining room wall, heard a cease-fire called. At this time, Harold Bell came out of the rear bedroom with his hands raised. Officer Ciszewski told the grand jury that at that time, by the light of his flashlight, he saw someone lying face down on the bed in the back bedroom, his head toward the hallway, with a shotgun and an automatic pistol beside his body.

Officer Davis: Davis testified before the coroner's inquest that Officer Gorman fired a shot into the south wall of the living room— the wall separating the living room from the front bedroom—checked with Officer Jones to see whether the shot had passed through the wall, warned officers in the rear to stay back, and then fired several more shots through the wall. About this time, he said, Harold Bell surrendered out of the back bedroom.

Officer Gorman: Gorman's testimony was that, after Groth's call for a cease-fire, as he moved toward the hallway leading from the living room to the rear of the apartment, he could hear shots somewhere in the back rooms. He said that at that moment

There was a shotgun blast. It came out of this front bedroom. And, where it went, where it was aimed at, I didn't hear it hit anything, but it was out of that front bedroom.

Gorman stepped back and heard more firing in the back. He described in detail his next action:

Now, at—I thought at this time that fellows that come in the back door were running into the same thing that we just ran into, and I feared they were being killed in the back. . . . And, I know I had to do something to relieve the pressure on them. There was no way of getting down this hallway after hearing the shotgun blast come out of the first bedroom which I would have had to go past. And, seeing this doorway at the end of this hallway, I stepped back and I said to an officer who was on my right, who was George Jones, who was one of the three of us in the front room, I said to George, "Watch this shot. I am going to put one in the wall."

He said that after the single shot he warned the officers in the rear that he was going to fire through the front bedroom wall toward the back of the apartment, and with his machine gun on single fire, shot "ten or fifteen" times from left to right across the wall. Gorman said he was careful not to hit Brenda Harris, who was seated by the wall, and he took caution not to fire in a direction that would endanger his fellow officers, whom he had seen shooting out of the lighted kitchen.

Sergeant Groth then called a second cease-fire, Gorman testified. That cease-fire was broken shortly by "a loud explosion," and he heard someone shout, "Shoot it out!" Gorman fired across the wall again with his machine gun, and was joined by Officer Davis, who fired several shots from his carbine into the wall. Groth then called for the third cease-fire.

Officer Carmody: After Officer Ciszewski had kicked the barricade several times, Carmody testified at the coroner's inquest, Carmody leaped over it. As he jumped into the dining room, he fired two shots (apparently his fourth and fifth overall) in the direction of the back bedroom. A second cease-fire was announced at this point, Carmody said, and Harold Bell surrendered from the rear bedroom. Shooting resumed in the front of the apartment and Carmody heard "a loud muffled noise that sounded like it was a shotgun from the front bedroom." He fired a shot into the door of the front bedroom, and heard another call for a cease-fire.

Officer Corbett: Corbett, one of the officers who had followed Carmody into the apartment from the rear, testified that he had tried to persuade Carmody not to jump over the barricade into the dining room, fearing he would be shot. When officers in both the front and rear were apprised of Carmody's intent, however, Corbett testified that they laid down "protective fire" from both directions, and Carmody leaped into the dining room, followed by Broderick.

Surrender of Bell, Johnson, and Truelock

The police descriptions of this phase of the action include numerous references to cease-fires broken by renewed firing, and a series of surrenders from the rear bedroom where Hampton's body was found.

Composite Version 1: According to the *Tribune* "Exclusive," Sergeant Groth called out for a third cease-fire and the surrender of the Panthers. This time Harold Bell emerged from the rear bedroom with his hands in the air. Broderick and Ciszewski grabbed Bell and took him to the kitchen, where other detectives held him.

After the arrest of Bell, the third cease-fire was violated as gunfire directed at police broke out from the front bedroom. Broderick and Ciszewski fired into both bedrooms from their positions in the dining room.

Sergeant Groth called another cease-fire, the fourth, and ordered the occupants to surrender. This time a voice called from the rear bedroom, "We're coming out. Don't shoot. We've got an injured man back here." Louis Truelock and Deborah Johnson walked out and were taken into the kitchen.

Composite Version 2: According to the television re-enactment, it was during the third cease-fire that a male voice called out of the back bedroom, saying that someone in the room was injured. Deborah Johnson and Louis Truelock then surrendered from the room and were taken into the kitchen.

Composite Version 3: The federal grand jury *Report* states that, according to Davis, the second cease-fire was broken by "flashes" Davis observed coming from the rear of the apartment. Sergeant Groth believed those flashes came from the back bedroom, while Officers Jones and Gorman thought a shot had come from the front bedroom. Carmody and Broderick also stated that they saw flashes from inside the front bedroom.

After the second cease-fire was broken, Gorman again fired his submachine gun into the south wall of the living room, and Davis fired his carbine through the same wall. Neither received any order to do so from Sergeant Groth. Jones then fired two shots into the front bedroom. Broderick, who said he saw two shotgun blasts light up the door of the front bedroom, fired two shotgun blasts into the back bedroom. Ciszewski saw a flash from the back bedroom, and he fired two shotgun blasts into that room. From the dining room, Carmody called a warning to Gorman in the living room to stay back because "I am going to fire into this (front bedroom) door in case somebody is behind there." Carmody then fired a shot—his fifth or sixth— toward the front bedroom door. This was followed by gunfire from the front of the apartment. A third cease-fire was then called. During the third cease-fire, Louis Truelock and Deborah Johnson surrendered from the back bedroom.

Sergeant Groth: At the coroner's inquest, Groth testified:

At this time [during the second cease-fire] I heard one of the officers in the back say, "Come out with your hands up."
It was later determined that Harold Bell had surrendered in the back room.

During this second cease-fire, after Bell's surrender, Groth said he heard a voice (which he believed came from the front bedroom) call out, "Shoot it out." A shotgun blast was then fired out of the front bedroom, and the officers resumed firing, Groth said. He then called a third cease-fire, and the officers complied. During this third cease-fire Carmody advised Groth that two persons—later identified as Louis Truelock and Deborah Johnson—had surrendered from the back bedroom.

Officer Jones: Officer Jones, testifying before the coroner's inquest, gave a brief, rather general picture of the events which followed the police entry into the apartment. Jones described a confrontation marked by gunfire from both bedrooms directed at police. According to Jones, the shooting was interrupted three times by cease-fires called by Sergeant Groth. After the first, Harold Bell surrendered from the back bedroom, while other occupants surrendered during later pauses.

Describing gunfire from the rear bedroom, Jones recalled, "I remember specifically having heard small arms fire and a loud report from the rear bedroom."

Officer Carmody: At the coroner's inquest, Carmody stated that from the dining room he heard voices in the back bedroom shouting, "We give up," and "We have an injured man in here." Along with Officers Broderick and Ciszewski, he positioned himself outside the back bedroom, and saw a man and a woman come out to surrender.

Officer Ciszewski: Ciszewski testified at the coroner's inquest that during the cease-fire (the particular cease-fire is not specified) the officers called for the occupants to come out, and Ciszewski saw Harold Bell surrender from the back bedroom. As Bell moved forward, Ciszewski said, he saw a person lying on the bed. When Bell came out, Ciszewski turned him over to Officer Corbett in the kitchen.

Ciszewski said that while he was in the kitchen, he heard shots coming from the *front* bedroom. He stepped toward the doorway of the kitchen and saw a "flash" from the *back* bedroom, the doorway of which he had just left. He fired two shots into the back bedroom, and heard someone call, "Hold your fire." A voice in the back bedroom shouted, "Don't shoot, we have an injured man back here. We are coming out." Deborah Johnson and Louis Truelock then surrendered from that room.

Officer Davis: After Bell's surrender, according to Officer Davis's testimony at the coroner's inquest, Sergeant Groth called another cease-fire, which was followed by a call from the front bedroom to "Shoot it out." Davis thereupon joined Gorman in firing an unspecified number of shots through the south wall of the living room into the front bedroom. As Davis put it:

> We fired at a level where we figured the people [inside the front bedroom] could see the bullets . . . and realize that they should come out; and they still refused to come out of the room, and there was firing—then, Gorman went over to the door, and I heard him fire at the bedroom, at the bedroom door.

There was shouting, Davis said, and three people in the front bedroom surrendered.

When questioned, Davis placed the surrender of Johnson and Truelock somewhere in time between Bell's surrender in the rear and that of the three occupants in the front bedroom.

Davis maintained throughout his testimony that he had observed flashes and heard shots coming from both the front and rear bedrooms.

Discovery of Hampton and Wounding of Ciszewski

DISCOVERY OF HAMPTON

Composite Versions 1 and 2: After Jonnson and Truelock surrendered, according to the *Tribune* "Exclusive," Officer Ciszewski shone his flashlight into the back bedroom. In the television re-enactment, Ciszewski said:

> I see a man laying on the bed and with his feet off to this side, like in a "C," and then down on the floor I observed a shotgun by his left hand, where his hands were lying over the bed and an automatic pistol by his right hand.

Carmody, looking into the back bedroom, said in the re-enactment that he too saw the man lying on a bed, with a shotgun by one hand and a .45 automatic pistol by the other. In the re-enactment he described his actions, after entering the room, as follows:

> I didn't know if he was, uh, how bad he was injured, so I picked up—grabbed him by the wrist.

According to the *Tribune* story he dragged the man—Hampton—into the dining room "away from all those guns." In the television re-enactment he simply said he "pulled him into or onto the door which had been used as a barricade."

Officer Gorman: Gorman told the coroner's inquest that at the time of the cease-fire during which Johnson and Truelock surrendered, he replaced the partially empty clip in his machine gun with a full thirty-round clip and walked to the hallway, where he saw Officer Carmody in the rear "with somebody by the arm, up near the wrist, and he had them—well, the fellow was on the floor and he was pulling him."

Officer Broderick: Broderick testified at the coroner's inquest that he was in the dining room with Carmody and Ciszewski when Hampton's body was discovered. From that vantage point he saw Harold Bell surrender during a cease-fire—probably the second, since Broderick appears never to have heard the order for what seems to have been the first. That cease-fire was broken by a shot that Broderick heard come from the front bedroom; he began firing again and he saw and heard gunfire from both the back and the front of the apartment, most of which he thought came from the front bedroom. Another cease-fire was declared and Truelock and Johnson surrendered from the back bedroom. Broderick then saw Carmody pull out a male figure—Hampton—from the rear room into the hallway "where we could keep an eye on him." Officer Ciszewski thereupon entered the rear room and began throwing weapons out.

WOUNDING OF CISZEWSKI

Composite Version 1: As Ciszewski was throwing various weapons out of the back bedroom where Hampton had been, he was wounded in his left calf by a slug fired through the wall from the adjacent front bedroom, according to the *Tribune* story. Ciszewski then dived for safety into the kitchen.

Composite Version 2: After the discovery of Hampton by Carmody and Ciszewski, Groth was told that all occupants were out of the back bedroom but that some remained in the front bedroom. Groth said that he "pleaded," as he had earlier, with the remaining occupants to surrender.

When Carmody had pulled Hampton out of the back bedroom, Ciszewski announced that he was going into the room to remove the weapons there. As he was picking up the guns, Ciszewski "heard a shot" and felt himself "get hit." He cried out, and simultaneously he heard a second shot and a window in the back bedroom shattered next to him. Officers somewhere in the apartment shouted for him to leave the room, and Ciszewski moved out of the rear bedroom into the front portion of the dining room.

Composite Version 3: According to the federal grand jury's *Report*, it was during the third cease-fire, after the surrender of Truelock and Johnson, that Carmody went into the south bedroom and pulled Hampton out. Following Hampton's removal, Ciszewski entered the room to pick up arms, and almost immediately called out that he was shot. Simultaneously Broderick, in the dining room, saw two flashes from the front of the apartment, and returned fire by shooting his weapon into the front bedroom. Broderick then rushed from the dining room to the bathroom, broke the bathroom light, and looked into the front bedroom.

Officer Ciszewski: Ciszewski testified before the coroner's jury that Carmody had entered the back bedroom and dragged out Hampton's body, which was lying on the bed.

> At that point, it still was a long pause. And, I said I was going in the back and get some of the guns out. I went in and grabbed one that was leaning up against the wall, threw that one out.
>
> And, I reached down to pick up two other long barrel guns, and I threw those out. And, I was reaching down for the other shotgun and pistol, when a shot came—I heard a shot, and I felt the pain in my left leg and numbness, and I yelled I was hit.
>
> A second shot rang out, I heard the window to my right, I heard the glass shattering. At this point, Broderick or Carmody yelled for me to get out of the back. And, I then got out of the back of the—out of the back bedroom in back.

Asked what he did after leaving the back bedroom, Ciszewski replied, "I don't know. I stood somewhere, took some cover I think by either the kitchen—by the refrigerator or by the dining room wall." Ciszewski said that the firing continued.

> I really don't know what—exactly what happened. There were more shots. Officer Gorman went into the front bedroom. I heard a burst of fire and that was it.

Officer Broderick: Broderick testified in January at the coroner's inquest:

> I yelled to the fellows in the front to hold their fire, that Officer Ciszewski was going into the front bedroom—or in the back bedroom. He went back there and while he was still in there, I heard shots that would have to come from the front bedroom. . . .
>
> Well, at the time that Officer Ciszewski went into the back bedroom, I was in voice communication with the fellows in the front, plus I could make out their forms. I told them that John would be in the back bedroom, not to fire, and they stopped firing.
>
> So, when he went in there, there was a shot—two shots, I couldn't tell at the time. And, he came out of the back bedroom and he said that he had been hit.

Wounding and Surrender of Satchel, Brewer, and Anderson

Composite Version 1: While those in the rear bedroom were surrendering, Sergeant Groth again ordered a cease-fire—the fifth according to the *Tribune*.

I was virtually pleading with those in the front bedroom to come out. But again they fired so Broderick fired a shotgun 5 times into that room from the rear of the hallway. And I kept yelling for them to come out, but there was no response.

Gorman then approached the door of the front bedroom with his submachine gun in his hand, slammed through the doorway, and began firing.

I slammed through that doorway, firing a burst into an open closet I spotted out of the corner of my eye directly to the right inside the door. I saw two beds with the form of two people rising between them. One had what looked like a shotgun in his hands he was trying to raise clear of the bed. As he started to aim, I fired and the gun fell as he did. The second form kept rising in those few seconds and I fired again after I saw something that looked like a hand gun in a person's hand.

The first person wounded by Gorman was Blair Anderson, who, the police said, held a gun stolen from the Chicago Police Department. The second person wounded was Verlina Brewer. As Carmody plunged into the room to join Gorman, Brewer and Anderson cried out, "We give up." The police then spotted Ronald Satchel, who was also wounded, and he too surrendered.

Composite Version 2: As Broderick heard Ciszewski call out that he was wounded, he ran into the bathroom, opposite the front bedroom. From this position, he saw two people, a male and a female, between the beds in the room.

Gorman, in the living room, saw Broderick and Ciszewski as they moved into position. He saw them pump several shotgun blasts into the front bedroom—Broderick said he fired "four or five" times—and then, warning Broderick and Ciszewski to hold their fire, Gorman charged into the front bedroom doorway. In the bedroom he spied a closet to one side:

There were clothes hanging here, it was, uh, well, it wasn't clear, I couldn't see if anybody was there or not, so for my own protection, I put a short burst with the machine gun on automatic fire into that closet and swung into the doorway.

As he entered the bedroom, Gorman continued, he saw a figure holding a shotgun "coming up" between the two beds in the room.

He had a shotgun which was grayish in color, it was very vivid in my mind because of its color, and he was swinging it, and when he reached about the 45-degree angle, is where I saw him, and brought my gun across. I gave a burst to him, at the same time realizing another form was coming up. This person dropped the shotgun, grabbed groin area—this was Blair Anderson—and fell down.

The second form, still coming up, caught a blast as the gun came further across the room. Something, I don't know what the article was—I believe it to be a handgun—was in this woman's hand, because it, it just cleared the bed—that dropped to the floor, as she did.

Composite Version 3: According to the grand jury *Report,* Broderick, who had rushed to the bathroom just opposite the front bedroom when Ciszewski was wounded, saw male and female figures between two beds, but saw no weapons. He fired three to five shots into the room above the two figures. As Broderick finished firing, he saw Officer Gorman (who had reloaded his machine gun with a fresh magazine of thirty rounds) run past the door of the front bedroom firing his machine gun. Gorman placed his weapon on automatic fire and, in a low crouch, charged into the front bedroom. He fired a short burst into the closet, at the same time turning toward the center of the room. By the flickering light of his machine gun, Gorman saw one man standing up very fast between the beds with a gray shotgun in his hands. Gorman trained his machine gun on this man, firing until the man grabbed his groin and fell. As the man fell, Gorman saw another figure moving between the beds and thought he saw a handgun being raised toward him. He fired his machine gun at this figure —later identified as Verlina Brewer—until his thirty-round clip was empty and the individual shouted, "I give, I give. I am hit."

Carmody said he then rushed into the room, jumped on one of the beds and saw Anderson, Brewer, and Satchel standing in the center of the room. According to him, they were then unarmed with their hands up. There was, the *Report* stated, no firing going on in the front bedroom when Carmody went in. Carmody then escorted all three prisoners out of the room, ending the raid.

Sergeant Groth: Sergeant Groth testified at the coroner's inquest:

As they [the police] were securing the back bedroom and removing the weapons, I was pleading with the people in the first bedroom to come out. A shot rang out, apparently fired from the first bedroom. Officer Ciszewski shouted that he had been hit.

In response to the shot, Groth's testimony continued, Gorman advanced in a crouched position and fired several shots into the front bedroom. Satchel, Brewer, and Anderson then surrendered. According to Groth, all three held weapons at the time of their surrender.

Officer Gorman: Gorman testified that he heard Ciszewski yelling that he was going to enter the back bedroom to remove some weapons. The next thing Gorman heard was a gun report, "or two or three," from the front bedroom. Ciszewski, in the back bedroom, shouted that he had been hit. Gorman then saw Broderick, carrying a shotgun, move to a position inside the bathroom. About this time, Gorman said, Jones fired a shot into the front bedroom doorway, and Broderick began shooting into the same room.

I watched this fire for several seconds. And, I thought it to be ineffective fire as far as people in the front bedroom was concerned, because of the angle they had to be fired upon. And, I had some thoughts there, just how are we going to get these people out of here and after having heard shotgun fire from there, and I heard somebody—he had to be a mad man, holler, "Shoot it out." I knew that we had to do something to get them out of there, going to have to be direct confrontation.

Gorman put his weapon on full automatic fire and approached the bedroom door. "I had faith in the weapon I had," he testified. He entered the doorway and fired a short burst into an open closet to one side of the room—"I felt for my safety I had to fire in there." Gorman described the illumination from his machine gun fire as "lighting the room like candles." He saw a figure rising by one of the beds, holding "a gray colored shotgun in his hand, which was very eerie with the lighting that I had."

Gorman saw the figure point the gun directly at him.

I—quick as I could, I turned the machine gun from this closet to him, and I fired. But, as I was doing this, I felt that there was another form immediately to his right, to my left. It was a head is all I saw at the time, in the quick glance I had. But, he [the first figure] was coming down at me with this shotgun. And, I fired directly at him. And, I kept the gun pointing toward him. I was firing from the hip in this low crouch and I concentrated on him, because he was coming directly down on me with a shotgun, and I wasn't going to stop shooting until I saw that he had dropped the shotgun. And, I had it on full automatic fire, and I kept it that way until I saw this gun fall out of his hands, and he grabbed his groin area.

As this happened, he saw the second figure in the room moving again. Gorman "just continued the gun on across to this person." He heard yells from the people in the room, shouting that they were surrendering, and Gorman then stopped firing. He saw Carmody charge into the room and jump up on one of the beds, calling for the occupants to surrender. For the first time Gorman realized that there were three occupants in the room, as all came out of the room and were taken into custody by officers in the hallway. Gorman looked down at his gun and saw that he had emptied the entire thirty-round clip.

Officer Broderick: After Ciszewski was hit, Broderick testified, more gunfire followed. Broderick fired into the front bedroom "once or twice" from the dining room area, then moved into the bathroom area opposite the front bedroom. He saw "a male and female Negro between what appeared to be two single beds" in that room, and fired a blast from his shotgun in that direction. Broderick stopped firing, and Officer Gorman shot into the same bedroom with his submachine gun. Following that, Officer Carmody rushed into the room and Broderick heard people say they were "giving up."

Officer Carmody: Carmody testified that after Truelock and Johnson had surrendered from the rear bedroom, Ciszewski entered that room to collect the weapons there. Suddenly a shot rang out somewhere in the apartment, and Ciszewski cried out that he was hit. Officers shouted to Ciszewski to leave the rear bedroom, according to Carmody, and they moved to concentrate on the front bedroom.

Carmody saw Gorman firing in through the doorway of the front bedroom. He ran up alongside Gorman, and they ordered the persons in that room to come out. Three persons surrendered from the room.

Officer Corbett: After Ciszewski was wounded while collecting weapons in the back bedroom, Corbett testified, he joined other officers who were firing into the front bedroom. He fired two shots in the direction of the front bedroom.

Other General Police Accounts of the Action

Officer Kelly: Officer William Kelly testified that he had been stationed at the rear of the apartment and had not followed Carmody, Broderick, and Ciszewski when they first entered through the kitchen door. Kelly said he remained outside on the back porch for an unspecified period of time, looking into the kitchen and back bedroom windows. When he finally entered the apartment, Harold Bell had already surrendered and was on the floor of the kitchen. Kelly remained in the kitchen as the action continued, and observed firing emanating from and police firing into the bedrooms.

After a cease-fire was called, and Deborah Johnson and Louis Truelock had surrendered from the back bedroom, Kelly saw Carmody drag "an unconscious male Negro" out of that room. He thought the man was alive at the time. Ciszewski, who had entered the rear bedroom to collect weapons, was then hit by shots that "came from the front bedroom, through the wall." Kelly said he believed Ciszewski had "returned fire" at this point. Police then resumed firing at the front bedroom, but Kelly testified he fired no shots because "I would say I was real concerned of hitting another police officer, as they were all in front of me." Asked how he avoided being hit by other officers' fire, he said, "I was extremely cautious."

Officer Joseph: Officer Joseph told essentially the same story as did the other officers stationed in the rear. His only addition to their testimony consisted of his description of the events surrounding the final cease-fire. As he told it, he was in the kitchen guarding the three people who had already surrendered from the back bedroom, when Louis Truelock shouted, "Oh, my God, there is a baby in the front room." According to Joseph, Officer Carmody replied, "Why didn't you tell us?" Shortly after, a cease-fire was called and he heard "a plea for everyone to surrender." Ronald Satchel, Blair Anderson, and Verlina Brewer then surrendered from the front bedroom.

Officer Hughes: Officer Hughes said he had been stationed at the front of the building when Groth, Davis, Gorman, and Jones entered the apartment. After the initial gunfire in the front of the apartment, he testified, he had been handed three shotguns by Sergeant Groth, which he placed in the vestibule at the front. At Groth's order, he ran around to the alley in the rear of the apartment to check on the officers who had entered the house from the back.

In the alley he saw uniformed police officers, whom he warned that "those are our men inside." He ran back to the front of the apartment, collected the shotguns he had left in the outer hallway, and took them to the back alley. He then drove a truck parked in the alley around to the front of the apartment. There he saw "a lot of police cars, photographers, and so forth," and other officers bringing weapons and other materials out of the building.

Accounts of the Survivors

The use of firearms by the occupants of the apartment during the raid was a focal point of all the police and official versions of the raid, and has been a principal object of scrutiny in every official investigation of the incident. No other issue in this case has so aroused public controversy. The allegations that Panthers fired on police without provocation when the officers arrived at the apartment, shot at them as they entered, continued firing at them from three or four rooms inside the house, and ignored or violated several cease-fires are the heart of the official justification for the deaths of Fred Hampton and Mark Clark and the wounding of four of the other occupants.

The police case has been publicly disputed by the survivors, who, as quoted by Bobby Rush and the survivors' attorneys on the day of the raid, simply said that Clark and Hampton were murdered. In the accounts given in March 1970 at the People's Inquest, where six of the seven survivors testified, in October 1970 at the Commission of Inquiry hearings, where four of the six testified again, and at Hanrahan's trial in the summer of 1972, this initial charge of murder was elaborated upon by statements concerning where each of the occupants of the apartment had been and what each of them had done during the raid. The police accounts of a two-way gun battle were denied; indeed, each of the testifying survivors except Anderson (who to the Commission's knowledge was never asked) stated that he had not fired a gun at all, and Satchel, who was in the same room as Anderson, testified that there had been no weapons fired by any of the occupants of the room in which he had been; in addition, testimony was given by several that Hampton could not be wakened during the raid and was shot as he slept.

According to the survivors' public accounts of the raid, police burst into the apartment firing their weapons, ignored the pleas of the occupants to stop shooting, and continued to pour pistol, shotgun, and machine gun fire into the various rooms of the flat until all of the occupants were dead, wounded, or in custody.

In statements given to their own lawyers two weeks after the raid, by contrast, Brenda Harris admitted holding and attempting to fire a shotgun and stated that Mark Clark had also been holding a weapon; Louis Truelock, in a garbled statement that is scarcely comprehensible, stated that he had fired two rifle shots toward the rear of the apartment; Harold Bell stated that he was holding a shotgun during the raid; and Blair Anderson said that he and Ronald Satchel had each been holding a shotgun during the raid, and that he thought Satchel had fired the weapon. However, not even the most adversarial approach to the statements of the survivors would support the proposition that there was a "shoot-out."

Survivors in the Living Room

> Brenda Harris (wounded)
> Harold Bell (fled to rear bedroom)
> Louis Truelock (fled to rear bedroom)

Brenda Harris, Harold Bell, Mark Clark, and Louis Truelock were in the living room when the raid began. Mark Clark was killed immediately; his position and actions must be attested to by others. Harold Bell and Louis Truelock ran to the rear bedroom, and can account for what happened in the living room only before the major action took place there.[5]

Harris, Statement to Andrew: In the statement that Harris made in December 1969 to Francis Andrew, who was then a lawyer for the Illinois Black Panther Party, she stated that she and Mark Clark each

5. See Chapter 3.

picked up a shotgun as the police were entering the apartment. She stated that she never fired her piece; she did not say whether Clark had fired his. She said that after the initial shots, which wounded her and killed Clark, the police began shooting from the living room toward the rear of the apartment.

> They just kep shootin' in there. They was yellin', uh . . . things like . . . "There's some over in that room; and there's some over in that room. Don't shoot yourself, be careful now." One . . . you know, after they shot a little while, they said, "Is anybody hurt?" And uh, one pig said, uh, "Yeh, I got hit in the leg." He said, "You hurt bad?" He said, "No, it ain't no-thin'." Somethin', like that, you know. He said it wasn't hardly nothin' at all. And uh, they just saying, you know . . . saying, "There's some over here." You know, and uh, after they just kept shootin', uh, they went in the . . . one came in with the machine gun, and he said, "I'm going to get him with the machine gun." And uh, he stood at the door. At first he started at the door, but I don't know where he went after that. He was just shootin' back there.

She stated that she did not at any time see the officer with the machine gun fire the weapon.

The shooting stopped, she said, after the survivors in the rear said, "We give up. We comin' out."

Harris, People's Inquest Testimony: Brenda Harris testified in March 1970 before the People's Inquest that she and Clark were shot in the living room as the police entered. Immediately thereafter, she said, an officer in the living room began firing with a machine gun toward the rear of the apartment. He stopped firing for a moment and she heard voices at the rear shout, "Don't shoot any more." The officer fired again, and she heard officers calling out to one another, "There's some over there, get them." The officer with the machine gun responded by firing his weapon again. He "would start shooting and he just kept shooting until I guess—until he felt satisfied that he had killed everybody."

Harris further testified that at no time during the raid did she have a gun in her hand nor did she see Mark Clark with a gun.

Harris, Commission Testimony: In October 1970 Harris told the Commission:

> After they shot me and Mark Clark, another [officer] came in with a machine gun and he started shooting in the back with the machine gun. He

was shooting towards the back of the house, and he also sprayed the wall that I was leaning against, that the bed was against.

As the officer with the machine gun fired into the wall and toward the rear of the apartment, Harris said, she heard shouts from other police who had entered the apartment.

And the other policemen, they were saying back and forth, "There's some over here, get them." And then another said, "I think there is one over back there, get him." And he kept shooting until—until I guess he figured, you know, everybody was dead, and then he stopped, and then while he was shooting, I heard one of the occupants say back in the back, "Don't shoot anymore," but they kept on shooting.

She testified that at no time during the night of December 3 or morning of December 4 had she fired a weapon, and that to the best of her knowledge none of the other occupants had fired a weapon.

Harris, Hanrahan Trial: In August 1972, at Hanrahan's trial, Harris testified that Bell and Truelock had left the living room as the police began to enter the apartment but before any shots were fired. She sat up in bed, she said, and was shot by the entering officers, immediately following which Clark was shot. Then, she continued, the officer with the machine gun began firing from the living room (where she could see him) toward the back of the house. As the officer with the machine gun went toward the back of the apartment, and out of her line of vision, she heard the firing continue from the rear of the apartment.

She testified that at no time during the raid did she have a gun in her hands, and that she had not seen a gun in the hands of Truelock, Bell, or Clark.

Bell: Bell testified at the People's Inquest and before the Commission that he had run into the rear bedroom as soon as he heard the sound of police entry. Accordingly, his testimony sheds no light upon the events that took place in the living room. Neither his statement to Andrew nor his testimony at the Hanrahan trial has been made available to the Commission.

Truelock: Truelock's statement to Donald Stang in December 1969 and his testimony at Hanrahan's trial both indicate that he ran to the rear bedroom as the raid was beginning; like Bell's, it sheds no light upon the events that transpired in the living room.

Survivors in the Rear Bedroom

Harold Bell

Deborah Johnson

Louis Truelock

Deborah Johnson and Fred Hampton were in the rear bedroom when the raid began. Hampton was killed, and his actions can be accounted for only by others. Deborah Johnson and Harold Bell testified both before the People's Inquest and the Commission. Truelock's statement of December 22, 1969, to Donald Stang and his testimony at Hanrahan's trial have been examined by the Commission. Bell's statement to Francis Andrew and his testimony at Hanrahan's trial have not been made available to the Commission, but certain portions of his statement are quoted in the portion of the trial transcript made available to the Commission.

Bell, People's Inquest Testimony: Bell told the People's Inquest in March 1970 that he had run to the back bedroom to wake Hampton as soon as he heard the sounds of entry. As he reached the back bedroom, he said, police were entering through the kitchen door at the rear of the apartment. Upon entering the bedroom, he shook Hampton and said: "Chairman, pigs are aggressing."

Immediately thereafter, an officer with a shotgun entered the room and began shooting, while another officer was shooting in the room with a service revolver. Bell testified that he leaned against the wall for cover; then an officer armed with a shotgun stuck his weapon in through the doorway, reached around, and pulled Bell out into the hall. As Bell fell to the floor outside the bedroom, police fired more shots, some from service revolvers, into the bedroom. And after he was handcuffed and placed on the kitchen floor, he heard weapons, including automatic weapons, being fired elsewhere in the apartment. Bell testified that at no time during the morning of the raid did he have a gun in his hand.

Bell, Statement to Andrew: During the trial of Hanrahan, in connection with a motion for dismissal, one of the defense counsel read into the record the following colloquy between Bell and Francis Andrew in December 1969:

> Q [Andrew]: And did you have a shotgun in your hand at that time?
> A [Bell]: Is on tape?
> Q: Yeh.
> A: Yes.
> Q: What kind of piece did you have in your hands?
> A: I think it was automatic, I'm not sure. I don't even know whether automatic or pump.
> Q: Yeh, OK. Do you know what kind of shell it had in it?
> A: I think it was 12 gauge.

Bell, Commission Testimony: Testifying before the Commission in October 1970, Bell stated that when he heard the sound of entry, he ran through the unlighted apartment to the rear bedroom. In the back bedroom, Bell said, he saw Deborah Johnson and Fred Hampton. Hampton was lying in bed on his stomach, his head toward the open doorway, and his face turned toward the windows at the back of the apartment, with the left side of his face up. Bell said he grabbed Hampton by the shoulder and shook him vigorously, but was unable to wake him.

> I shook him twice. I called his name. I said, "Chairman, Chairman, the pigs are vamping," and I couldn't wake him.

The only response Fred Hampton made, Bell testified, was to lift his head slightly, then drop it back down.

It was then, Bell said, that he heard the police at the rear entering the apartment.

> When I could not awaken him [Hampton], I could hear the pigs coming through the back door. The noise indicated that they were entering the kitchen. I went to the side of the closet.

As Bell tried to conceal himself in the corner of the room near the doorway, he testified to the Commission, shotguns were fired into the bedroom. At the same time he heard shots that seemed to come from the front of the apartment. Bell tried to conceal himself, but was spotted by one of the officers who was firing into the bedroom.

> My movement that I had made was detected by the pigs that were firing the shotguns. He told me to come out. I was very hesitant about coming out

because of the shooting that was going on. The thought that I had in mind, if I come out, he is probably going to shoot me anyway.

Bell said he then decided to come out cautiously; crouched in a "half bent" position with his arms extended, he began to move out very slowly.

I was within arm's reach, and he reached and grabbed me behind, somewhere in the head, and he pulled me out. So I let my weight, when he pulled, I just went along with him and stumbled into the room or fell, I don't remember.

After that, he said, he could still hear shooting elsewhere in the apartment.

Bell testified that he had not seen any occupant of the apartment fire a weapon on the morning of December 4, 1969.

Johnson, People's Inquest Testimony: Deborah Johnson testified at the People's Inquest that she was awakened on the morning of the raid by somebody shaking Hampton and saying, "Chairman, wake up, pigs are here." At that time she could see shots being fired both from the back and the front of the apartment:

I kind of looked up and I could see like shots were being fired from the back and from the front. They were going both ways.

The shooting in the apartment continued, she said, until after she had been taken into custody:

I could hear the shots and so we woke up and about a few seconds after he said this, about a million pigs, they all converged at the door, you know, and so I kind of hopped on top of the Chairman a little bit and we were trying to move over like toward the wall.

So, he looked up kind of like this and all these pigs were standing at the door just shooting and he laid his head back down like that. I don't know if he was shot then or not, I assumed he was. He didn't move.

They just kept on shooting. In the meantime, the other person that came in the room, they kept saying, "Stop shooting, stop shooting, we have a pregnant woman, a pregnant sister in here."

At that time I was about nine months pregnant. They kept hollering out, they kept on shooting, kept on shooting. So, he kept on hollering out, so, finally they stopped and he said, "We are coming out with our hands up," he said, "come on out." We were coming out and it was a whole bunch of pigs. It was like two lines of them. We had to walk through them.

One of the pigs—I had on like a night shirt, like a nightgown, a robe like —and they grabbed my robe and opened it and they said, "Well, what do you know, we have a broad here." So, they pushed us into the kitchen. It was a brother laying on the floor already.

So, I heard one of the pigs say he is barely alive or he will barely make it and they started shooting again. It sounded like they were shooting all through the house.

Then I heard a sister scream and they stopped shooting. Then when she screamed, I guess they were satisfied with what they had done. They thought they had killed everybody they came to get, they stopped shooting. Another pig said, "He is good and dead now."

At no time during the morning of the raid, she testified, did she or Hampton hold a gun.

Johnson, Commission Testimony: At the hearings held by the Commission on October 26, 1970, Johnson testified about her activities just before she went to sleep as well as about the raid which occurred about three hours later. According to her testimony, she came to the apartment shortly after midnight. Upon entering the apartment she saw Hampton and Truelock talking to each other in the living room. She spoke briefly with Hampton, went to the rear bedroom, returned to the living room and spoke again with Hampton, and then returned to the rear bedroom, where she went to bed. While in bed she received a phone call and spoke briefly, hanging up before Hampton joined her in bed.

After Hampton got into bed, at about 1:00 A.M., the two of them telephoned his mother and sister and spoke with them for approximately forty minutes. During the phone call, Johnson testified to the Commission, Hampton fell asleep:

Q: But you do remember after getting off the phone awakening him, is that correct?

A: I tried to, but I couldn't.

Q: And he was asleep then, is that correct?

A: Yes.

Q: Now, it is approximately 1:30. After you were unable to awaken him what happened then?

A: I went to sleep.

Johnson further testified that the next thing she recalled was being awakened by Louis Truelock shaking Fred Hampton and saying that the police were attacking the apartment: "Chairman, wake up, the pigs are vamping." Hampton was not responding.

When Johnson awoke, she saw gunfire in the apartment:

And like I said, I looked up and I saw what appeared to be, it looked like shooting was coming from the front of the apartment to my right, and also from the back, the kitchen area, which is on my left.

Gazing at the door, she saw what "looked like about a million pigs converged at the door to that bedroom." Simultaneously, she rolled across Hampton's motionless body toward the north wall of the room, and Truelock moved onto the edge of the bed nearest the same wall. Police were firing into the room.

The mattress was vibrating real fast from bullets being shot into it. About this same time, I looked at Fred. He had raised his head up and looked at the door. He didn't make a sound. That is the only movement that he made and then he laid his head back down.

I just laid my head down because I thought I was dead and that was it.

After repeated cries by Truelock that "We have a pregnant sister in here," the police finally stopped shooting and ordered the survivors out of the room. She crossed over Hampton's body and put on a pair of house shoes that were beside the bed. Louis Truelock crossed over behind her, and both began to move toward the doorway with their hands raised. Fred Hampton lay motionless in the bed. Just as she and Truelock began to leave the room, two single shots rang out.

Johnson then saw two lines of "four to five" men each standing just outside the doorway. The men, all dressed in plainclothes, were holding drawn weapons.

There was two lines of pigs outside of the bedroom door, one on my right and one on my left. As I started walking through there, one of them grabbed the the robe I had on. They were laughing, "What do you know, we have a broad here." They pulled my robe open. One of the pigs—another one grabbed my hair and pushed me into the kitchen area.

After her capture, she said, she heard more shooting: "It sounded like they were shooting all over the house." The shooting stopped, finally, after a woman screamed to stop, and the police said, "He is good and dead now."

Johnson further testified that during the morning of December 4, 1969, neither she nor Fred Hampton touched, manipulated, or fired any kind of weapon.

Truelock, Statement to Stang: In his recorded conversation with Donald Stang on December 22, 1969, Truelock is reported to have said that as the police were entering the apartment from the front, he was heading for the rear bedroom. At the time he left the living room, he said, he did not have a gun in his hands, although there were many weapons around the apartment. Before he reached the rear bedroom, he heard shots from the front of the apartment, although he could not identify the type of weapon from which the shots had been fired.

By the time he got to the dining room, the police were entering the rear of the apartment.

Soon as I entered the dining room the back door here of the kitchen flew open and there was an officer standing there with a machine gun. And he began to fire soon as the door came open, it came open with him firing. And there were two officers on their knees right beside him, standing there at the door.

He then crawled into the rear bedroom.

Truelock said that upon reaching the rear bedroom, he then tried to wake Hampton, who seemed to be drugged. Hampton's only comment, Truelock continued, was to tell him to get into the bed and keep Deborah Johnson between the two of them. Hampton then once again lapsed into unconsciousness. Hampton was, Truelock said, lying on his back.

As Hampton, Johnson, and he lay in the bed, Truelock said, Officer Davis and then another officer shot Hampton in the head with their service revolvers.

During all this time, according to Truelock, Bell was standing in the room, near the window, and surrounded by three shotguns.

Truelock stated that he tried to give up once, but that before he and Deborah Johnson were allowed to surrender the police fired more shots into the bedroom. After he and Johnson were out of the room, Truelock said, more police continued to shoot into Hampton's bedroom.

Later in the conference, Stang purportedly asked Truelock, "Did anyone have a gun in his hands?" Truelock initially answered "No," and then changed his story to say that Bell might have had a gun and that he, Truelock, had fired two shots:

Q: Did anyone have a gun in their hands?

A: No, there wasn't. Bell was standing in between the three guns, now, it was rather dark and I couldn't see whether he had his hand on the guns or not, and I know he was standing there between three guns, and I only could see this one, when the officers began to fire. Up until that moment, I didn't even know that Bell was in the room.

Q: As far as you know, did anybody in the house get off any shots at all, including yourself?

A: Oh, there were two shots fired, and uh, at this point here [where the hallway enters the dining room] there were two shots fired [toward the kitchen].

Q: . . . Who fired them?

A: I fired those two.

Q: With what?

A: With a rifle.

Q: What kind of rifle?

A: It was an automatic pump, I'm trying to think what caliber it was, somewhat of a . . . I don't recall what caliber it was, it was someone's rifle that was at the crib [the apartment], and I, first thing that I could see when I entered in and saw them shooting, you understand. We had a rifle that we kept right along here in this room here, a rifle we kept . . .

Q: In the dining room?

A: In the dining room, yeah. We had a chair right along here. And we kept the rifle right alongside, I can't recall if this . . .

Q: When did you do it?

A: When I left the washroom, and passed the washroom, I automatically picked the rifle up, and when I got to this stage right here [at the entrance to the dining room] and saw the door fly open, and uh, firing from the machine gun, in order to try to clear my way through to the Chairman's room, I fired the rifle which made everybody kind of get to the side, and then I went right into the room.

Q: As far as you know, you didn't hit anybody?

A: No, didn't no one get hit. There wasn't no one there but Gloves [Davis], and these other three officers, and I didn't want anybody hit. The officer that got hit he was hit during the firing up in the front, when the bullets were coming through the walls.

Later in the conversation, Truelock returned to the subject of how Hampton had been killed.

The sergeant from the State's Attorney's office and Gloves [both took out their revolvers], and Gloves laid his revolver out on his elbow like this, aimed right at the Chairman's head, at the Chairman's body, and shot.

He stated that, in addition to the first two shots that hit Hampton, the police continued to fire at him after everyone else was out of the bedroom.

Truelock, Hanrahan's Trial: At Hanrahan's trial, in August 1972, Truelock stated that he at no time saw Harold Bell holding a gun, that at no time during the raid had he fired any shots, and that Hampton had not told him to keep Deborah Johnson between the two of them —that, in fact, Hampton had been unable to utter a sound. The remainder of his testimony, which fills approximately three hundred pages of trial transcript, adds little to an understanding of the events of the raid.

Survivors in the Front Bedroom

> Ronald Satchel (wounded)
> Verlina Brewer (wounded)
> Blair Anderson (wounded)

All three persons who were sleeping in the front bedroom were wounded in the raid. All three said that police fired at them many times, a fact that police testimony corroborates, though the police stated that each of the three was armed and that the police fired, in effect, in self-defense. Satchel and Brewer publicly denied that they had either fired or even held any weapon, and Satchel also stated that Anderson (who was never asked) similarly had not touched any weapon. At Hanrahan's trial, however, defense counsel read from a statement in which Anderson said that both he and Satchel had shotguns in their hands during the raid.

The police gunfire from the living room into the front bedroom was described by four of the survivors: by Brenda Harris, who observed it from the living room, and by Ronald Satchel, Verlina Brewer, and Blair Anderson, who were in the front bedroom.

The surrender of the three occupants of the front bedroom ended the raid.

Satchel, People's Inquest Testimony: Satchel testified at the People's Inquest that he had been awakened by a knock on the door, followed shortly thereafter by shots. As he awoke, he said, bullets were going through the front bedroom. The three occupants of the room fell to the floor for protection.

While they were on the floor, a voice had called to them to "come out," but they had hesitated to move because the firing outside the room was continuing. Satchel then heard one of the officers say "he was going to put something in the room that would get us out." It occurred to Satchel that tear gas might be thrown into the room, but instead another barrage of bullets tore into the room. All three occupants were hit by the gunfire. The three moaned, and Satchel heard a voice outside say that they had been shot. Satchel heard an officer order them to come out or be killed. Satchel's testimony continued:

I couldn't get up because I was shot in the stomach twice and in the leg and each hand and the other people were shot, I didn't know where they were shot at.

I tried to get up, they told us to turn the light on in the room. Somehow I managed to prop myself over the bed and I turned the bedroom light on.

Satchel then saw several armed men standing at the doorway of the bedroom, pointing weapons at him and the other two occupants. The three were ordered out of the room.

Asked whether occupants of the apartment had fired at the police at any time, Satchel replied:

I can only answer for the people in the particular room I was in and no one in that room fired, no one in that room even had a weapon.

Satchel, Commission Testimony: Satchel testified at the Commission hearings that he, Verlina Brewer, and Blair Anderson were sleeping in the front bedroom when the raid began. Satchel was awakened by the sound of knocking at the front door, followed by several gunshots. Upon hearing the gunfire, he began putting on his pants and at the same time awakened Anderson and Brewer and told them to get on the floor. The three dropped to the floor between the beds.

At first, he testified, it had seemed to him that the shots were being fired from the front portion of the apartment, but after dropping to the floor he noticed firing that seemed to be coming from the rear.

Voices called for the occupants to come out of the bedroom, but when the gunfire outside continued, the three of them remained in the bedroom. He continued:

Next time, the voice said, "If you don't come out, we will put something in the room that will make you come out." And then after that, then it was a rapid succession of gunfire. I remember being hit by—you know—what was evidently a bullet. I was hit about five times altogether, and the other people in the room were also hit and we—let's see, it was one young lady there and she hollered and myself and another young man, we moaned.

Satchel testified that he then heard a voice order the occupants to come out of the bedroom and turn on the lights in the room.

I remember saying that I couldn't move, but you know, fearing being shot again, I managed to turn the light on and I seen—I am not sure of the number, but it was at least two figures at the doorway, and they told me to get up and come out of the room, you know, and I was hurt.

The men at the doorway were white males, dressed in plainclothes, and were holding weapons.

Satchel testified that he could not identify any of the persons he saw in the apartment the morning of the raid other than the occupants of the apartment. Asked whether the unidentified persons were members of the police department, he responded: "Well, I didn't know, I wouldn't have known at the time. They didn't have uniforms and they didn't have badges. They didn't present badges to me." He further testified that the intruders did not announce to him or in his presence to other occupants of the apartment that they were police officers.

Satchel testified that during the raid he did not see any occupant of the apartment with a weapon.

Anderson, Statement to Andrew: During the trial of Hanrahan in the summer of 1972, one of the defense counsel quoted from a statement made by Anderson to the Black Panthers' lawyer in December 1969, in which Anderson admitted that he and Satchel had both handled shotguns during the raid:

And [Satchel] said "The pigs are . . ." and I grabbed Verlina, and I grabbed a shotgun. Then he [Satchel] grabbed a shotgun. We got down on the floor.

It seemed like someone kicked the door open or something, right before I heard, when I think I heard Doc shooting.

Anderson, People's Inquest Testimony: Anderson testified at the People's Inquest that he, Brewer, and Satchel were asleep in the front bedroom when the raid began. He was awakened, he said, by Satchel telling him, "The pigs are here." He heard "a lot of noise," and dropped to the floor with Brewer and Satchel.

Anderson testified that he heard pistol, shotgun, and machine gun fire, which continued uninterrupted through calls to halt firing, and that bullets were coming through the walls of the bedroom.

First it was pistols, you know, just coming from the walls and then shotguns and then the dude hollers, he said, "Halt fire," and then he said, "Come on out," or something and before they even finished talking they started shooting again, and they kept on shooting and it sounded like they were starting with shotguns.

The shots sounded like they were coming from all directions and then they hollered "Halt fire" again and then all of a sudden I heard a dude holler, "Halt fire" and then all of a sudden machine guns came through the wall, we were on the floor, I tried to push myself under the bed and machine guns went through again.

The machine gun firing halted temporarily, Anderson said, and then resumed:

It came from down, it was down lower this time. They busted paint buckets by my foot down by the foot of the bed where we were laying the paint buckets were busted. The mattress was jumping, plaster was jumping all over the place.

Anderson heard shouting outside the room. Then more shots came into the bedroom and suddenly the wall was struck by a blast which carved out a "moon-shaped hole." The three occupants yelled that they had been hit; Anderson was bleeding freely from wounds in the groin area. The police stopped firing and ordered them to come out.

Brewer, People's Inquest Testimony: Verlina Brewer testified at the People's Inquest that she was awakened by the sounds of "a whole lot of gunfighting" and by Satchel saying, "Get on the floor, the pigs are here." She said she and Satchel lay on the floor between the beds while the police "kept on shooting for a long time." She continued:

Then they just kept on shooting and finally I don't know how long they shot in, but it was for a pretty long time and finally, you know, we were all hurt pretty bad, and I don't remember what we said, but anyway the pigs started shooting and they kicked the door open, you know, and then they started going out to the dining room and then out to the kitchen and I can't remember exactly who went first, you know, but I saw they were kicking people and everything and then first I didn't even know I was shot in the leg and I started walking and I fell and this pig put this gun to my head talking about "Get up, mother fucker," you know, and I got up and went in the kitchen and people were laying on the floor and some people were standing up and I was standing up against the refrigerator and then they—they snatched me, they snatched me from the kitchen to the dining room.

She testified that at no time during the raid did she have a gun in her hand.

The Commission's Analysis of the Testimony

One basic theme is presented in the numerous police versions of the raid—that despite heavy firing from the Panthers who were occupying the apartment, the police were nonetheless able to subdue and capture them; that although the police tried valiantly to effect the arrests without violence or bloodshed, they were repeatedly forced to resort to more violence when every effort on their part to achieve a cease-fire was frustrated by the Panthers' resuming fire.

The survivors tell a very different story. Although no survivor saw more than a limited part of the action, each of those who testified, except Truelock, denied having fired a gun during the raid, and Truelock's testimony is not credible. None of the survivors, except Anderson, testified to hearing an order to cease firing, and his testimony is that the cease-fire orders were ignored or promptly violated by the police. On the other hand, in the statements that certain of the survivors made to their own lawyers shortly after the incident, they contradict in material aspects their public statements.

One conclusion is obvious: the testimony will not—cannot—be determinative. The basic questions remain: Were shots fired by the occupants at the police? Were the occupants even preparing to fire at the police? In short, was the massive firepower of the police justified?

Or was the essence of the police action simply murder in the guise of the service of a search warrant?

The physical evidence, although it cannot resolve all the above questions, does answer the first, and has significant implications for the resolution of the remainder.

The Physical Evidence

The Physical Evidence as Presented by the Grand Jury

In January 1970 a federal grand jury was established to make an "exhaustive inquiry into all the facts surrounding the incident." In the course of this inquiry, the grand jury attempted to develop and analyze the physical evidence. The jury's *Report* describes the procedure it followed:

The best methodology available to the Grand Jury, and the one adopted, was first to attempt to collect every possible item of physical evidence recoverable; second, to submit all of such evidence together with all weapons known to have been on the premises to the FBI Laboratory in Washington for definitive ballistics analyses; third, to have a scale model of the apartment constructed by the FBI exhibit section, showing as nearly as possible, the location of all bullet holes and furniture; fourth, while this was being done, to try to resolve all issues not related to the scene, e.g., the conflicting autopsy reports and the Hampton drug question, and to hear any relevant testimony from neighborhood residents, collect and analyze all news accounts and copies of the television reenactment; fifth, after being fully briefed on what the physical evidence showed and what it did not show, to hear testimony from each of the participants.

The Grand Jury recognized that because of the pending state prosecutions and their suspicion of any "establishment" proceeding, the survivors might be reluctant to testify. It was hoped, however, that they could be persuaded to reconsider since the principal focus of the proceeding was to determine if their civil rights had been violated.

This was the course taken. After appropriate court orders were entered, all of the weapons seized at the apartment, all of the police weapons carried that morning and all of the physical evidence in the possession of the Chicago Police Crime Laboratory was obtained and forwarded to Washington. After appropriate orders had been obtained from Chief Justice Power of Cook County Circuit Court, attorneys for the surviving occupants produced all of the materials removed by them from the apartment. Several FBI agents spent approximately twenty-four days sifting through the considerable debris at the apartment and recovering other items of evidence. All of this material was turned over to the FBI for careful expert appraisal and report. [Pp. 25–26.]

The physical evidence relevant to the events that took place during the raid consisted of the following:

1. The apartment at 2337 West Monroe.
2. Parts of the apartment which were severed shortly after the raid.
3. The weapons which were present in the premises that night, either in the possession of the occupants ("seized weapons") or in the possession of the police, transported and used by them as part of the police armament for the raid ("police weapons").
4. Cartridges or components of cartridges recovered at the scene of the raid or from the bodies of the occupants of the apartment.

Of that physical evidence, the ballistics evidence is by far the most significant.

Although the FBI's analysis of ballistics evidence relating to the raid has never been made public, a room-by-room summary of the analysis, showing bullet-impact points and the location of bullets and shell casings, is included in the grand jury *Report* on pages 79 to 89. The grand jury's summary indicates that between eighty-three and one hundred shots were fired during the raid. Only one of those shots was fired from a seized weapon. That single shot was fired through the living room door from a shotgun which the evidence indicates was held by Mark Clark.[6]

The eighty-two to ninety-nine shots fired by the police included seven fired from revolvers, twelve to twenty-five fired from shotguns, nineteen fired from the single carbine and forty-four to forty-eight fired from the one machine gun. Many of these shots were fired "blind"—for example, forty-two shots were fired through the living room wall into the front bedroom, and eighteen of those went through the front bedroom into the rear bedroom.

The mere number of bullets fired by the police presents only a partial picture of the overwhelming firepower employed by them. A perhaps more telling picture is portrayed by the *Report*'s description of the south (rear) bedroom (for diagram, see pp. 52–53):

6. See Chapter 3.

Examination of the south bedroom reflected nineteen entry bullet holes (8) on the north wall, of bullets fired from the living room, as well as eight entry holes of bullets fired from the north bedroom doorway or through the closet of the north bedroom. At the time of the FBI examination of the south bedroom, there were two apparent 12 gauge double ought buck shotgun blast impact points (16) on the east wall, fired into the room from the bedroom doorway, and several apparent impact points on the shutters, south wall window frames and south wall (8) made by bullets fired south from the living room or southeast into the north bedroom from its doorway. (17) The mattress of the bed from which Hampton was dragged contained many bullet fragments; the foot of the bed had been struck by a shotgun blast from the doorway; this shotgun blast was reflected in the lower east wall of the bedroom in line with the foot of the bed in films taken at the scene on December 4, 1969. This portion of the wall had been torn out at the time of the FBI examination. The west window on the south wall was shot out by a police officer firing from the dining room (18). This shotgun blast impacted on a neighboring shed outside and to the east rear of the apartment (18).

The Chicago Police Department and the Black Panther Party investigators each retrieved eleven items of physical evidence from this room, and the FBI recovered four more at the time of its examination of the premises. There were no impact points or other physical evidence of any firing originating in this room. [Pp. 84–85.]

Before the FBI conducted its ballistics investigation, the Chicago Police Department conducted its own. The police investigation was criticized by the federal grand jury on several grounds:

1. Except for a few items of physical evidence collected by crime lab officers, the materials were unclassified as to locus of recovery.
2. No fingerprints were preserved.
3. The police weapons were not submitted for examination, although it is standard practice that they be so submitted.
4. The crime lab's report, although inadequately prepared, was presented to the state grand jury as evidence to consider for indictment of the surviving occupants.
5. Two shells fired by Officer Ciszewski's shotgun were improperly identified as having been fired from a seized weapon, and the crime lab report contained additional ballistics errors as well.
6. The crime lab examiner testified that pressure from the State's Attorney's Office prevented him from conducting adequate tests. [Pp. 88–89.]

Testimony vs. Physical Facts and Evidence

The grand jury *Report* states that its "major concern . . . has been the irreconcilable disparity between the detailed accounts given by the officers and the physical facts and evidence examined and reported by the FBI."[7] The *Report* goes on at length to describe how the disparities were pointed out to the police prior to their testifying before the federal grand jury—and how the police adhered to the testimony they had given at the coroner's inquest. It then continues by noting major disparities and trying to explain them.[8]

The *Report* cites several theories suggested by the police or others to explain the discrepancies, but rejects each of the theories:

Several officers suggested that during the period when the Panthers had control of the apartment, some of the evidence could have been removed either intentionally or by some of the thousands of spectators who toured the scene. One of the officers provided the name of a news reporter who had allegedly witnessed one of the Panther guides remove one .45 cal. shell casing from the dining room area. The reporter was located and confirmed this story, but the individual who allegedly removed this shell has not yet been located.

While it is conceivable that some items could have been removed from the premises in the manner suggested, the theory falls far short of explaining the total discrepancy. First, the theory does not explain the absence of bullet holes or marks from the alleged firing. Secondly, the possibility of intentional concealment by Panther agents seems implausible. Pursuant to Court order attorney Andrew turned over some two hundred items of potential evidence including numerous bullets, lead fragments and shell casings, on his oath that this was everything removed from the apartment under his direction. Moreover, since neither he nor his ballistics examiner had access to any of the Panther weapons, it would have been impossible for them to determine which items to turn over and which to conceal. Finally, the statistical probability that sight-seers removed almost all of the evidence of Panther shots and almost none of the evidence of police shots is astronomical.

Another theory suggested was that changes had been made to significant items and structures after the police left the apartment. The Grand Jury was concerned enough over this possibility to request the FBI to run spectographic analyses of the bathroom door to see if it had been replaced. The paint samples from the door, its hinges, the door jamb and the adjacent walls

7. *Report,* p.108.
8. Ibid., pp. 108–113.

matched. The door had not been replaced.

Similarly, the FBI did all that could be done to determine if bullets passed out either the front or the rear of the apartment. Although one can never negative this possibility entirely, the investigation covered all of the surfaces of the doors, the porches, and the surrounding buildings and no evidence of bullet impacts were found. Also, a marked brick was removed from a building across Monroe Street and tested without positive results.

Another suggestion was that some of the bullets and expended shells could have landed in the storage boxes, clothing, debris and rubbish in the apartment, from which it was never recovered. Again, while this could be a possible explanation for a few items, it seems rather unlikely that all of the missing evidence was lost. Moreover, FBI agents did sift through all of the debris in the apartment, finding in the process pieces of lead as small as 1.25 grains, and none of the identifiable items recovered were attributable to Panther weapons. [Pp. 111–112.]

The *Report* then suggests that the officers may have been lying. Yet, although it rejects the various theories offered by the police to explain the disparity between their testimony and the physical evidence, and although the police reject what the *Report* terms the most "plausible" explanation for the disparity, the *Report* concludes that it "is not persuaded from the evidence available to it that the officers are intentionally falsifying their stories. Accordingly, the Grand Jury is unable to determine that there is probable cause to believe that there has been a violation of the testimonial oaths taken by" the police.[9]

Among the evidence available to the grand jury were ballistics and other laboratory findings prepared by Herbert L. MacDonell, a consulting criminalist. Subsequent to his testifying before the grand jury, MacDonell prepared a written report, which is reprinted in the Appendix. Although different physical evidence was available to MacDonell from that available to the FBI, his tests confirm that only one shot was fired by the apartment's occupants.

The evidence available to MacDonell did not permit him to determine the total number of shots fired. But his examination did show that the police had fired their assorted weapons sufficiently often for forty-six shots to have been fired into the living room walls, forty-two rounds to have entered the front bedroom from the living room, thirty rounds to have entered the back bedroom, and a few shots to have hit

9. Ibid., p. 113.

miscellaneous other locations. Some of those shots are included in more than one category.

In short, although certain details in the FBI ballistic analysis cannot be verified by MacDonell's report, the crucial finding that only one round was fired from a weapon held by an occupant, while the police fired their weapons time and again, is corroborated.

The Commission's Analysis of the Physical Evidence

Some of the questions raised by the testimony cannot be answered by the physical evidence. For example, the physical evidence does not resolve the number of cease-fires, if any, called by the police; it does not resolve questions concerning the sequence of events during the raid; and it does not resolve questions of what the occupants of the apartment were doing during the raid.

The scientific evidence does resolve that there was no "shoot-out" —that except for the one shot probably fired by Mark Clark, all the shooting was by the police; that each cease-fire, if any were called, was violated by the police; and that the police testimony concerning the raid was clearly not an accurate account of the events of the raid.

Whether the police lied is not certain. Their motive for doing so, given the gravity of their action, would have been obvious. But another explanation, the suggestion which the federal grand jury described as the "most plausible," although denied by the police, is available: that police mistook the firing of other officers as gunfire of the occupants. Given the mutual fear, distrust, and hostility between the police and the Panthers such a reaction to any gunfire in the context of the raid would be plausible. It would not, however, justify the initial firing by the police after each cease-fire. Moreover, even a conclusion that the police did not lie would not end the inquiry. Two deaths were still caused by the police and four other individuals were wounded.

The federal grand jury *Report* concluded that although the raid was not professionally planned or properly executed, and although the result of the raid was two deaths, four injured occupants, and seven improper criminal charges, there was insufficient evidence to establish probable cause that the police had willfully violated the occupants' civil rights.

The fact that neither the state's attorney nor the police have been indicted for their roles in the planning and execution of the raid[10] on 2337 West Monroe Street raises disturbing questions about the degree to which improper police or prosecutorial conduct is presently subject to any orderly system of correction and control and about the license which condonation of these individuals' actions may give or seem to give to other officials in other circumstances to act capriciously without fear of any real restraint by "the authorities." These questions are particularly troubling in the present context of prevalent police-community tension and alienation; on a larger scale they are of grave importance to any individual who espouses views or engages in political activities which may be abhorrent to some in positions of power or authority.

10. State's Attorney Hanrahan, Assistant State's Attorney Jalovec, and twelve members of the Chicago Police Department, including eight officers who participated in the raid, ultimately were indicted, but for their actions after the raid. Their trial ended in an acquittal at the conclusion of the prosecution's case. See Chapter 7.

CHAPTER 5

The Shooting of Fred Hampton

Fred Hampton was shot four times during the raid, twice in the head. The circumstances of his death have been a major source of controversy. Was he murdered—deliberately shot by an officer who could see him lying helplessly on the bed? Was he hit by bullets fired blindly through the north wall of the south (rear) bedroom? Did shots fired wildly in the dark from the kitchen or dining room to the west cause his death? Was he lying on the bed when he was hit? Do the position of his body and the nature of his wounds indicate the trajectory of the bullets, the rooms from which they came and the guns from which they were fired?

It is very difficult legally to justify the vast amount of shooting throughout the apartment by the police when only one shot can be ascribed with confidence to any occupant, even if other occupants did have weapons and were attempting to fire them. Beyond that issue, however, it remains critically important to determine whether Fred Hampton was hit by bullets fired blindly or by shots deliberately fired into his head as he lay on the bed.

The possibility that Hampton might have been killed by gunfire of other occupants of the room can be readily dismissed. There is no physical evidence that any gun was fired by Fred Hampton or any of the three other occupants of the bedroom in which he died. No marks within or without the room indicate that any bullet was fired from within the room. None of the guns alleged to have been found within the room is reported to have been examined to determine if it was fired during the raid, and no cartridge case or shell was discovered that was identifiable with any such gun. It would have been exceedingly diffi-

128

cult for any survivor from the room to have disposed of cartridge cases or shells, and it is improbable that subsequent searches of the room would have failed to discover them. Though four officers who entered the rear of the apartment testified that occupants of the south bedroom fired at them, the federal grand jury found that "There were no impact points or other physical evidence of any firing originating in this room."

The federal grand jury's summary of the FBI ballistics report specifically identified thirty-one police gunshots entering the south bedroom: twenty-seven fired through the north wall of the bedroom, from either the living room or the front bedroom, and four shotgun blasts fired through the south bedroom door. No specific findings were made with respect to the pistol shots which Carmody testified to having fired directly into the rear bedroom, although the grand jury *Report* stated that the mattress in the rear bedroom was found to contain many bullet fragments. Since no marks caused by pistol fire from the doorway were found on the walls, floor, or ceiling, pistol shots into the room must have hit the mattress, Fred Hampton, or both.

No officer testified that he had fired at Hampton, or that he believed he had hit him, in contrast to police statements that they had fired at Mark Clark, Brenda Harris, and the occupants of the north (front) bedroom.

The south bedroom was small, more than half of its floor space covered by a queen-size bed. Of the four people in the room, only Hampton was hit, though two others, Bell and Truelock, were apparently standing and moving at times during the shooting. Two, Johnson and Truelock, were alleged to have been on the bed during much of the shooting, between Hampton and the front rooms of the apartment, from which many of the bullets which entered the south bedroom were fired.

The police closest to the rear bedroom speculated that Hampton was hit by bullets fired from the living room. However, the probability of one man being hit four times by gunfire through the north wall and three persons escaping unscathed in these circumstances seems very slim, particularly where two of the three persons are between the person hit and the alleged source of the firing.

No report was made of any effort by any official investigation to analyze the trajectory of the bullets that struck Hampton, though a wound in his left shoulder was identified by the federal grand jury as "probably" caused by a police .30-caliber carbine fired from the living room. No report explains the authorities' failure to find and examine the bullets that struck Hampton's head.

A careful examination and analysis of police and Panther statements, of ballistics tests, of autopsy reports, and of official investigations are necessary to make a judgment as to the manner in which Hampton died.

The Statements and Testimony of the Police

In order to place the death of Hampton in context, it is useful to recapitulate some of the events that took place in the apartment during the raid, as described by the police.

Events at the Rear of the Apartment

Throughout the police versions of the raid, as detailed in Chapters 3 and 4, there is reference, albeit unsupported by the physical evidence, to gunfire from the occupants directed at the police. Much of that gunfire is attributed to the occupants in the rear of the apartment. Immediately after the raid, for example, Assistant State's Attorney Richard Jalovec, quoting Sergeant Groth (who was said by Jalovec to have been at the rear of the apartment), stated that as the police broke through the kitchen door, they "were met by a blast of shotgun fire as they smashed inside."[1]

Officer Ciszewski, who with Officer Carmody entered the apartment through the kitchen, told newsmen at a conference held on the day of the raid that the police had been met with a burst of shotgun fire at the back door, followed by further intensive firing from the rear of the apartment after they entered.

Other statements attributed to Ciszewski and to Carmody, describing the same moments, appeared the same day in the Chicago *Daily News*, Red Flash Edition. For example, Ciszewski stated: "My partner [Carmody] tried to get through the window and was cut with

1. *Chicago Today*, December 4, 1969.

flying glass. We finally got into the rear room. . . . I saw flashes coming from the middle and back bedroom to my right." Similarly, Carmody was reported to have said: "I kicked in the back door and went to the rear window. Two other policemen were covering the door with me. Shots were fired through the back window. Flying glass hit my right hand. . . . We went inside after the shooting stopped and there were two dead men."

In the composite version that appeared on December 11, 1969, in the Chicago *Tribune,* Carmody is said to have reported three shots fired toward him from the back bedroom as he tried to get into the kitchen. He backed away, smashed a window in the kitchen, and then returned to the back door. As he dove onto the kitchen floor, he fired a pistol shot into the back bedroom. At that point he heard a call for a cease-fire, but as he started to rise, several more shots rang out from rooms in the apartment, and Officer Broderick, who had followed Carmody into the kitchen, directed a shotgun blast toward the shooting. Carmody then fired two more pistol shots toward the back bedroom.

Testifying before the coroner's inquest, Carmody reported seeing three shots fired in his direction from a handgun, and a hand holding a handgun pointing directly at him from the area where the dining room, rear bedroom entrance, and kitchen entrance adjoined. The kitchen was reportedly lighted at the time. When he finally dove onto the kitchen floor, he said, he saw another shot fired from the same direction as the previous three, and he returned fire with several shots.

Officer Joseph, who was stationed at the rear of the apartment, testified that before Carmody broke through the kitchen door he heard "a loud shot, followed by sporadic fire," which "sounded like small arms." When Carmody kicked open the door, he said, Joseph saw two flashes indicative of small arms fire and the tip of a gun in the area of the rear bedroom. At that point, Carmody retreated from the doorway and broke the kitchen window.

Officer Ciszewski testified at the coroner's inquest that he had heard "three rapid pops" from the rear of the apartment as Carmody kicked at the door, immediately following which Carmody backed away. He further stated, however, that although he had seen shots from the front bedroom, he had seen no shots at any time coming from the back bedroom area. Ciszewski also testified that at no time had he seen or heard Carmody fire any shots, and that he saw Broderick fire his shotgun from the kitchen toward the front bedroom door.

Broderick also testified that he had fired his shotgun toward the front, rather than the back, bedroom, in response to shooting that he heard from the front of the building and shotgun fire that he saw coming from the front bedroom.

According to the summary in the federal grand jury *Report,* Carmody, leading the raid in the rear of the apartment, went into action as the front door was smashed open. Upon hearing a loud bang inside the apartment, which he believed to be a shotgun blast, he kicked in the kitchen door. As he began to enter the apartment, he saw three gun flashes and a hand holding a gun protruding around the corner of the doorway between the kitchen and dining room, and he quickly backed out of the door. Ciszewski, waiting outside the back door, heard three "poplike" shots. Carmody went over to the kitchen window and smashed it with his gun, cutting his hand in the process. Seeing that the burners were lit on a stove just below the window, Carmody decided not to enter that way and returned to the kitchen door.

Carmody then dived through the kitchen doorway onto his stomach. As he did so, he saw a flash from the same general area from which he said he had been fired on earlier—near the entrance between the kitchen and the dining room—and fired a shot from his revolver in the direction of the flash. Ciszewski and Broderick followed Carmody through the back door into the kitchen. At this point, Carmody heard someone shout, "Hold your fire, our men are coming in the back."

According to the *Tribune* "Exclusive" on December 11, 1969, Carmody, after Broderick's shotgun blast, jumped over the barricade between the kitchen and dining room. Officer Gorman, in the living room, covered Carmody by firing his machine gun down the hallway and through the wall separating the living room from the front bedroom. Carmody fired one round from his .38-caliber revolver as he plunged past the rear bedroom doorway toward cover against the far wall of the dining room. At that point Sergeant Groth called out for a cease-fire and Harold Bell surrendered from the rear bedroom. The cease-fire was then broken as gunfire directed at the police reportedly broke out from the front bedroom, whereupon Broderick and Ciszewski began firing their shotguns from the dining room into both bedrooms. Another cease-fire was called by Groth, and Deborah Johnson and Louis Truelock surrendered from the back bedroom. Carmody looked into the room and found Hampton lying face down on the bed. According to Carmody, Hampton's head lay toward the bedroom door.

He was lying with his arms hanging over the foot of the bed. On the floor at his right hand was a .45 caliber automatic and at his left a shotgun. I could see he'd been hit, but I didn't know if he was alive or dead. All I knew was that that room was full of shotguns and rifles and ammo. So I grabbed him by the wrists and dragged him into the dining room away from all those guns.

A moment later Ciszewski, who was throwing weapons out of the rear bedroom, was wounded by a shot fired from the front of the apartment.

According to the television re-enactment of the raid on the day of the *Tribune* "Exclusive," Carmody heard gunfire as he was lying on the kitchen floor, and Broderick fired a shotgun blast from the kitchen toward the area of this shooting. Carmody heard more firing, and fired two revolver shots toward the rear bedroom. As Carmody told the other police in the kitchen that he was planning to hurdle the barricade, Broderick heard Gorman shout from the living room that he was about to start machine-gunning from the front. Gorman began shooting, and Carmody, followed by Broderick, went over the barricade and into the dining room. A cease-fire was called by Groth, during which Bell surrendered from the back bedroom to Broderick and Ciszewski. Both Groth and Ciszewski said they then heard a voice say, "Shoot it out," followed by a shotgun blast from the front bedroom. Gorman once again began firing into the wall between the living room and the front bedroom, and Davis commenced firing his carbine through the same wall. Carmody shot his pistol from the dining room into the front bedroom door, and Broderick and Ciszewski also fired into the front bedroom. Sergeant Groth then called another cease-fire, during which Deborah Johnson and Louis Truelock surrendered from the rear bedroom. After their surrender, Officer Ciszewski said, he shone his flashlight into the rear bedroom.

I see a man laying on the bed and with his feet off to this side, like in a "C," and then down on the floor I observed a shotgun by his left hand, where his hands were lying over the bed and an automatic pistol by his right hand.

Carmody also said he saw a man lying on a bed in the back bedroom, with a shotgun by one hand and a .45 automatic pistol by the other.

I didn't know if he was, uh, how bad he was injured, so I picked up—grabbed him by the wrist and I pulled him into or onto the door which had been used as a barricade.

Sergeant Groth was then told that all the apartment's occupants were out of the back bedroom, but that some remained in the front bedroom. Groth said he "pleaded" with the remaining occupants to surrender.

Ciszewski announced that he was going into the back bedroom to remove the captured weapons. As he was picking up guns in the room, Ciszewski heard a shot and felt himself hit. As he cried out, he heard a second shot, and a window in the back bedroom shattered next to him. An officer somewhere in the apartment shouted for him to leave the room, and Ciszewski moved out into the front portion of the dining room.

During the cease-fire in which Johnson and Truelock surrendered, Officer Gorman, who had been firing the machine gun through the living room wall, reloaded the gun with a thirty-round clip. Looking down the hallway he saw Carmody "with somebody by the arm, up near the wrist, and he had them—well, the fellow was on the floor and he was pulling him." Gorman then heard Ciszewski yell that he was going to enter the rear bedroom to remove some weapons, whereupon one to three gun reports came from the front bedroom, and Gorman heard Ciszewski cry out from the back bedroom that he had been hit.

At the coroner's inquest Carmody testified that as Deborah Johnson and Louis Truelock were surrendering, he noticed a body lying on its stomach on the bed, with the head toward the doorway, feet dangling off the side of the bed toward the back of the apartment, arms dangling over the end of the bed toward the doorway, and the face turned toward the wall (i.e., the front of the apartment).

He entered the rear bedroom, and "noticed the man had blood on him." He grabbed the body by the left wrist and pulled it out into the dining room. As he did so, he saw two shotguns and a .45 pistol near the bed where the body lay.

I pulled him out not knowing how bad he was injured, and for fear that if I left him in there, one of us would have to stay and watch him, and if there was more shooting, one of our people would be in the back bedroom and we didn't know what would happen to him. Or if he wasn't injured too bad, he could grab one of these guns.

Carmody identified the man as Fred Hampton, and testified that he had not known at that time whether Hampton was dead or alive.

Carmody said that Officer Ciszewski then entered the rear bedroom to collect the weapons there. Suddenly a shot rang out somewhere in the apartment, and Ciszewski cried out that he was hit. Officers shouted to Ciszewski to leave the rear bedroom, and they moved to concentrate on the front bedroom.

Carmody saw Gorman, toward the front of the apartment, firing his machine gun through the doorway of the front bedroom. He ran up alongside Gorman, and they ordered the occupants of that room to come out. Three persons surrendered from the room.

Officer Ciszewski testified at the coroner's inquest that after Johnson and Truelock had surrendered from the back bedroom, Carmody entered the room and "dragged out" the body lying on the bed. He continued:

At that point, it still was a long pause. And, I said I was going in the back and get some of the guns out. I went in and grabbed one that was leaning up against the wall, threw that one out.

And, I reached down to pick up two other long barrel guns, and I threw those out. And, I was reaching down for the other shotgun and pistol, when a shot came—I heard a shot, and I felt the pain in my left leg and numbness, and I yelled I was hit.

A second shot rang out, I heard the window to my right, I heard the glass shattering. At this point, Broderick or Carmody yelled for me to get out of the back. And, I then got out of the back of the—out of the back bedroom in back.

Asked what he did after leaving the back bedroom, Ciszewski replied, "I don't know. I stood somewhere, took some cover I think by either the kitchen—by the refrigerator or by the dining room wall." After he was wounded, Ciszewski said, the firing continued.

I really don't know what—exactly what happened. There were more shots. Officer Gorman went into the front bedroom. I heard a burst of fire and that was it.

Ciszewski also gave detailed testimony with respect to the position of Fred Hampton's body at the time he first saw it, during Harold Bell's surrender. He said the body was lying on the bed, head toward the doorway with arms dangling over the end of the bed toward the door. His hands reached to the floor, Ciszewski said, and a pistol lay about three to four feet away from his right hand, on the floor. The head faced the north wall, toward the front of the apartment. As Bell was surrendering, Hampton's body was the only other figure Ciszewski saw in the back bedroom.

Under questioning, Officer Ciszewski testified that he had at one point fired two shots "high into" the back bedroom, from a position in the dining room "directly in line of the doorway." He did not say when in the course of the raid these shots were fired. He did, however, testify that he did not believe any of his shots had hit Fred Hampton. On the question of who shot Hampton, he engaged in the following exchange with Special Deputy Coroner Martin Gerber:

DEPUTY GERBER: Officer Ciszewski, do you now have an opinion from your observation in that apartment, as to whose shots may have hit Fred Hampton?
A: No, maybe some of the bullets that came through the wall.
DEPUTY GERBER: Through the wall from where and fired by whom?
A: Probably in the living room, fired by Detective Gorman.
DEPUTY GERBER: From the submachine gun, sir?
A: Yes, sir.
DEPUTY GERBER: Is that your best opinion from your observations as to who must have hit him?
A: Yes, sir.

Broderick testified at the coroner's inquest:

I yelled to the fellows in the front to hold their fire, that Officer Ciszewski was going into the front bedroom—or in the back bedroom. He went back there and while he was still in there, I heard shots that would have to come from the front bedroom. . . .

Well, at the time that Officer Ciszewski went into the back bedroom, I was in voice communication with the fellows in the front, plus I could make out their forms. I told them that John would be in the back bedroom, not to fire, and they stopped firing.

So, when he went in there, there was a shot—two shots, I couldn't tell at the time. And, he came out of the back bedroom and he said that he had been hit.

After Ciszewski was hit, Broderick testified, more gunfire followed. Broderick fired into the front bedroom "once or twice" from the dining room area, and then moved into the bathroom area opposite the front bedroom. Broderick stopped firing, and Officer Gorman shot into the same bedroom with his submachine gun. Altogether, Broderick said, he had fired ten shots into the bedrooms, but did not know whether any had struck Hampton. Officer Corbett, who had followed Carmody, Ciszewski, and Broderick into the kitchen, added only one element to their testimony. He said that when Carmody plunged past the barricade, officers from both the front and rear laid down protective fire.

Officer Kelly, who was also stationed at the rear of the apartment but who did not immediately enter the kitchen, testified that, when he finally entered, Harold Bell had already surrendered and was on the floor of the kitchen. From the kitchen, Kelly saw gunfire coming from both bedrooms. He remained in the kitchen as action continued, and observed further firing emanating out of the bedrooms; he also saw police firing into those rooms. After a cease-fire was called and Deborah Johnson and Louis Truelock surrendered from the back bedroom, Kelly saw Carmody drag "an unconscious male Negro" out of that room. He thought the man was alive at the time.

Gunfire by Police Entering the Front of the Apartment

While accounts of police gunfire from the front of the apartment vary in the police statements made between December 4 and the coroner's inquest, the physical evidence of that gunfire was marked on the walls of the apartment.

Most of the firing from the front of the apartment came from Officer Gorman's machine gun, to which the FBI attributed forty-four of the seventy-six cartridge cases of shells recovered, and thirty-two of the fifty-six bullets recovered. The most detailed descriptions of the firing of the machine gun are in statements made by the police at the coroner's inquest. There Sergeant Groth testified that, after the living room had been secured, he had called for a cease-fire. Officer Gorman in turn testified that, after Groth's call for a cease-fire, he could hear shots somewhere in the back rooms. Then, he said:

There was a shotgun blast. It came out of this front bedroom. And, where it went, where it was aimed at, I didn't hear it hit anything, but it was out of that front bedroom.

Gorman stepped back, and heard more firing in the rear of the apartment. He described his next actions in detail:

Now, at—I thought at this time that fellows that come in the back door were running into the same thing that we just ran into, and I feared they were being killed in the back. . . . And, I know I had to do something to relieve the pressure on them. There was no way of getting down this hallway after hearing the shotgun blast come out of the first bedroom which I would have had to go past. And, seeing this doorway at the end of this hallway, I stepped back and I said to an officer who was on my right, who was George Jones, who was one of the three of us in the front room, I said to George, "Watch this shot. I am going to put one in the wall."

After firing the single shot, Gorman testified he warned the officers in the rear that he was going to fire through the front bedroom wall toward the back of the apartment, and, with his machine gun on single fire, shot "10 or 15" times from left to right across the wall. Gorman said he had been careful not to hit Brenda Harris, who was sitting by the wall, nor to fire in a direction that would have endangered his fellow officers, whom he had seen shooting out of the lighted kitchen.

Sergeant Groth then called a second cease-fire, Gorman testified, which was broken shortly by "a loud explosion," and a shout to "Shoot it out!" Gorman again fired his machine gun across the south wall of the living room, this time joined by Officer Davis, who fired several shots from his carbine into the wall. Davis testified:

We fired at a level where we figured the people [inside the front bedroom] could see the bullets . . . and realize that they should come out; and they still refused to come out of the room, and there was firing—then, Gorman went over to the door, and I heard him fire at the bedroom, at the bedroom door.

Gorman further testified that after his second machine-gunning of the south wall of the living room, during a third cease-fire called by Groth, he replaced the partially empty clip in his machine gun with a full thirty-round clip and walked to the hallway, where he saw Officer Carmody in the rear "with somebody by the arm, up near the wrist, and had them—well, the fellow was on the floor and he was pulling him." He then saw Officers Jones and Broderick fire shots into the north bedroom.

I watched this fire for several seconds. And, I thought it to be ineffective fire as far as people in the front bedroom was concerned, because of the angle they had to be fired upon. And I had some thoughts there, just how are we going to get these people out of here and after having heard shotgun fire from there, and I heard somebody—he had to be a mad man, holler, "Shoot it out." I knew that we had to do something to get them out of there, going to have to be direct confrontation.

Gorman then put his weapon on full automatic fire and approached the north bedroom door. "I had faith in the weapon I had," he testified. He "slammed through that doorway" and fired into an open closet on the south side of the room:

There were clothes hanging here, it was, uh, well, it wasn't clear, I couldn't see if anybody was there or not, so for my own protection, I put a short burst with the machine gun on automatic fire into that closet and swung into the doorway.

While firing at the closet, Gorman noticed a man elsewhere in the room.

I—quick as I could, I turned the machine gun from this closet to him, and I fired. But, as I was doing this, I felt that there was another form immediately to his right, to my left. It was a head is all I saw at the time, in the quick glance I had. But, he [the first figure] was coming down at me with this shotgun. And, I fired directly at him. And, I kept the gun pointing toward him. I was firing from the hip in this low crouch and I concentrated on him, because he was coming directly down on me with a shotgun, and I wasn't going to stop shooting until I saw that he had dropped the shotgun. And, I had it on full automatic fire, and I kept it that way until I saw this gun fall out of his hands, and he grabbed his groin area.

Officer Gorman then saw Carmody enter the room and jump on one of the beds, calling for the occupants to surrender. He looked down and saw he had emptied the entire thirty-round clip in his machine gun. The shooting had ended.

The Statements Made by the Survivors

Deborah Johnson: Deborah Johnson testified in March and October 1970, before the People's Inquest and the Commission, that she had awakened in the rear bedroom to find Louis Truelock shaking Hampton and calling to him to wake up. Miss Johnson was lying on the south side of the bed, her head to the west toward the bedroom door, her feet toward the east wall of the house. She lay partially on her left side, turned toward Hampton, who was between her and the north wall between the front and rear bedrooms. Hampton's body, she said, lay in the same position it was in when he fell asleep hours earlier, lying on his stomach, arms partially extended and interlocked, hands palms down on the bed. Johnson said the right side of Hampton's face lay against the mattress, so that his face was turned toward her and the south wall of the bedroom. The back of his head was toward the bedroom's north wall, which separated it from the front bedroom. Hampton's head was pointed toward the west wall and the open doorway of the bedroom, his feet toward the east wall.

Johnson stated that, despite the noise of the shooting, she and Truelock were unable to wake Hampton. As gunshots began to be fired into the rear bedroom from the doorway, she said, she rolled across Hampton's motionless body toward the north wall. At the same time Truelock moved onto the edge of the bed nearest the same wall. The mattress was vibrating rapidly as shots hit it. She saw Hampton's head rise for an instant, then fall back onto the bed as the figures at the doorway continued firing into the bedroom.

So, he looked up kind of like this and all these pigs were standing at the door just shooting and he laid his head back down like that. I don't know if he was shot then or not. I assumed he was. He didn't move.

She did not see him move again.

After continued further firing by the police, and repeated calls by Truelock to stop shooting, the gunfire finally ceased. Johnson and Truelock crossed over Hampton's body and emerged from the bedroom with their hands up, and were taken into the kitchen. As she was leaving the bedroom, Johnson testified, she heard two single shots.

Johnson said that in the kitchen, where she saw Harold Bell lying on the floor, she and Truelock were handcuffed and placed facing against the kitchen wall. At that point, she heard a voice say, "He is barely alive and he will barely make it." More shooting followed, and a voice said, "He is good and dead now."

Harold Bell: Harold Bell also testified before the People's Inquest and the Commission. He stated that he had been sleeping in the living room when he was awakened by thuds on the front door and two shots. He said he immediately ran to the back bedroom to awaken Hampton. While he was attempting to wake Hampton up he heard shots in the front of the apartment and "a window broke or the door being forced open or bursted open." Bell described Hampton's position at this point in much the same manner as did Deborah Johnson —lying stomach down on the bed, facing the south wall of the bedroom, with his head toward the west side of the bed and his feet toward the east. Bell said he grabbed Hampton by the shoulder and shook him twice, calling his name, but could not wake him. The only response Hampton made was to raise his head once and drop it back down. According to Bell, Hampton's head at that point still lay facing the south bedroom wall.

"When I could not awaken him," Bell continued, "I could hear the pigs coming through the back door. The noise indicated that they were entering the kitchen. I went to the side of the closet." According to Bell's testimony, about three or four shotgun blasts were fired directly into the bedroom from the doorway, and another officer was firing a revolver into the room. At the same time he heard shots that seemed to come from the front of the apartment. He said that he tried to conceal himself, but was detected and told to come out. He moved cautiously in a "half bent" position toward the door and was grabbed and pulled out. As he fell to the floor outside the bedroom, police fired more shots into the bedroom, including shots from a service revolver. Bell said he was taken into the kitchen, handcuffed, and placed on the floor. One of the men placed his foot on Bell's neck and pointed a shotgun in Bell's ear, Bell testified, while other men entered the apart-

ment from outside through the kitchen door. As this was taking place, more shots were fired into the back bedroom, and Bell said he heard police saying, "That's Fred Hampton, that's Fred Hampton." He did not know for sure, but believed that at this time Hampton had already been shot to death. As the firing in the apartment continued, Bell heard people screaming, "I am shot." At another point he heard one of the armed men who had entered the apartment say, "I seen his toe move, he is not dead." Bell also told of hearing one of the men say, "We should kill all of the dirty motherfuckers." When the shooting finally ended, Bell was taken out of the apartment through the front door.

On the way out I saw the body, I saw Fred's body. I saw where he had been shot or that he had been shot in the head, and I was told to keep moving, look straight ahead, and taken out and put into the wagon.

Louis Truelock: In the statement given by Louis Truelock to Donald Stang on December 22, 1969, he stated that when he got to the rear bedroom, he tried to wake Hampton to tell him about the raid that was, by then, already in progress. Truelock said that Hampton, although he appeared to be drugged, told Truelock to get into bed with Deborah Johnson and himself and to keep her between them.

Truelock stated that he got into bed with Hampton and Johnson, following which Officer Davis reached the door of the rear bedroom holding the machine gun. Davis is reported by Truelock to have handed the machine gun to another officer and then to have fired his service revolver at Hampton's head. Another officer, whom Truelock did not name, then reportedly also began to fire at Hampton's head with his service revolver. Davis and the other officer continued firing, Truelock said, until they had emptied their revolvers; then, under cover of the machine gun, they reloaded their revolvers and once again fired them until they were emptied.

Truelock's statement placed Hampton on the south portion of the bed, in a position from which one could see out of, and thus could also be seen from, the door of the rear bedroom; Johnson was in the middle of the bed and Truelock on the north side, next to the wall separating the front and the rear bedrooms. Hampton was lying on his back, Truelock said, with his head to the side.

After Hampton had been shot, and Johnson and Truelock had been removed from the rear bedroom, Truelock said, Sergeant Groth asked one of the officers if he knew who they had just shot, to which the officer responded that it was Fred Hampton. In response to the queston "Is he dead?" the officer answered, "I don't know, I saw him wiggle his toe." Truelock said that the officer with the machine gun then began firing at the bed, in which Hampton still lay, and about six other officers emptied their revolvers in the direction of the bed; Hampton was then dragged out of the bedroom by his hair.

Truelock testified in August 1972 at Hanrahan's trial. At that time he reaffirmed the statement he had made to Stang that Hampton was on his back on the south portion of the bed, Johnson was in the middle and he was on the north edge. He also testified, however, that Hampton had not *told* him to get into the bed and keep Johnson between them; rather, he said, it appeared that Hampton was trying to say that. "Just looked like [Hampton] was trying to say something and his eyes were more or less slowly moving in his head." In addition, Truelock stated that at no time had he seen any wounds on Hampton, but thought that Hampton had been wounded before Truelock and Johnson surrendered because his reactions were not normal—he never fully awakened during the raid. Truelock also stated that Officer Davis was not the officer he had seen with the machine gun during the raid.

The Pathological Evidence and the Reports of Autopsies

The pathological evidence relating to the death of Fred Hampton is found in three principal sources: (a) the autopsy performed by the Cook County coroner; (b) the autopsy performed by Dr. Victor Levine; and (c) the autopsy performed by Dr. Charles S. Petty. The third autopsy was commissioned by the federal grand jury in an attempt to resolve the controversy which had arisen from the conflicting findings of the first two autopsies.

The Autopsy by the Cook County Coroner

On December 4, 1969, Hampton's body was removed from 2337 West Monroe Street to Cook County Hospital, where he was pronounced dead at 5:40 A.M. At 6:05 A.M., the body was delivered to the morgue, and later that day an autopsy was performed on it.

The only existing documentation of this autopsy is contained in a "Pathological Report and Protocol." According to the federal grand jury *Report*, the autopsy was performed by a junior or assistant pathologist who later dictated some notes into a dictating machine. A few days later, at the request of the acting director of pathology, the assistant prepared a handwritten draft report on the autopsy. The acting director personally revised and edited this report through several drafts, and signed the final version of the "Protocol" on December 12, 1969. The assistant's original notes were lost or destroyed.

The following findings regarding Hampton's body are derived from the "Protocol":

1. Hampton was shot twice in the head. One shot entered in front of the left ear and exited at the right forehead, leaving a large wound. The other shot entered the right side of the neck, below the right ear, and exited at the left side of the throat. Both head wounds were through and through; no bullet was recovered from either.
2. Hampton was shot in the left shoulder. A .30-caliber carbine bullet was recovered in the left pectoral muscle from this wound.
3. Hampton's right forearm exhibited a graze wound; no bullet identifiable with that wound was recovered.
4. Hampton's stomach was opened by the pathologist, but finding the contents to be fluid he made no analysis of the contents.
5. Cause of death: through-and-through bullet wound of head lacerating brain.

The Autopsy by Dr. Victor Levine

On December 5, 1969, at the request of Hampton's family, Dr. Victor Levine, former chief pathologist for the Cook County Coroner's Office, performed an autopsy on Hampton's body. The autopsy was performed at the Rayner Funeral Home, 3654 West Roosevelt Avenue, Chicago, Illinois, where the body had been taken from the morgue. Dr. Levine was assisted and observed in his autopsy by Dr. Earl M. Caldwell, Dr. William Thomas, Dr. Quentin Young, a senior medical student, and an attorney for the Hampton family.

A summary of Dr. Levine's findings, derived from the autopsy report he prepared, is as follows:

1. Hampton was shot twice in the head, both shots traveling from right to left. One shot entered at the right forehead and passed through the brain; the track of this shot was probed to a point behind the left eye; no exit wound was found. The other shot entered in front of the right ear and exited at the left side of the throat. No bullet was recovered by Dr. Levine from either wound.
2. Hampton suffered a bullet wound on the left shoulder, suggesting a graze wound passing from front to back of the top of the shoulder. No bullet was recovered by Dr. Levine from that wound.
3. Hampton suffered a bullet wound of the right forearm, suggesting a graze wound passing from the radial to the ulnar side of the forearm. No bullet was recovered by Dr. Levine from that wound.

At one of several press conferences held by Dr. Levine after his autopsy he suggested that the coroner must have found and removed a bullet from behind Hampton's left eye. He also indicated that the wounds were consistent with Hampton's having been shot from above and behind while in a reclining position.

The Autopsy Commissioned by the Federal Grand Jury

In an effort to resolve the questions raised by the different findings of the first two autopsies, the grand jury obtained an order for exhumation of the body, and commissioned Dr. Charles S. Petty, chief medical examiner for the county of Dallas, Texas, to perform a third autopsy. The autopsy was conducted at the Veterans Administration Hospital, Shreveport, Louisiana, from 6:00 P.M., February 16, 1970, until 12:30 A.M. the following day.

Observing the autopsy were: for the Cook County State's Attorney's Office, Assistant State's Attorneys Thomas Hett and Hick Motherway, Dr. Jerry Kearns of the Cook County Coroner's Office, and Dr. William P. Mavrelis, pathologist; for the Hampton family, Francis E. Andrew, an attorney, and Dr. David Spain, a pathologist. For the United States Government, in addition to Dr. Petty, were present Assistant Attorney General Jerris Leonard, Deputy Assistant Attorney General James Turner, four Deputy United States marshals and two special agents of the FBI.

The significant findings of the third autopsy, summarized from Dr. Petty's report, are as follows:

1. Hampton was shot twice in the head, both shots passing right to left. One shot entered the right forehead and exited from a wound in front of the left ear which was clearly visible when the sideburn covering it had been shaved away. The other shot entered in front of the right ear, and exited from a wound on the left side of the throat. Both wounds were through and through, and no bullet was recovered by Dr. Petty from either wound.

2. Hampton suffered a gunshot wound of the left shoulder. The track of this wound extended to the underlying muscle, but no specific track could be established through the muscle itself. No bullet was recovered by Dr. Petty from this wound.

3. Hampton suffered a graze wound from a gunshot, on the posterior aspect of the right forearm. This may have been caused by the bullet striking Hampton's shoulder or by one of the bullets which struck his head, or it may have been caused by a fourth bullet. The bullet was not recovered by Dr. Petty.

4. The Coroner's Office had not, contrary to the statement in its report, opened the stomach of the body; the stomach was found attached and unopened.

The Federal Grand Jury Report on the Autopsies

The federal grand jury accepted as determinative the results of the "extraordinarily thorough" third autopsy. The results of that autopsy differed materially from the results of the first two, which also differed materially from one another. Accordingly, the grand jury's *Report* turned to a discussion of the autopsy procedures used and the resultant controversy. Its conclusion was, basically, that the errors made by the Cook County coroner—misidentifying an entry wound on the right forehead as an exit wound (and the related misclassification of the exit wound in front of the left ear as an entrance wound), erroneously placing the location of the other head wound on the right side of the neck instead of the right cheek, and misrepresenting the procedures followed in stating that the stomach had been opened—were caused by understaffing.

The major problems in the coroner's findings appear to be based on the understaffing which required the examination to be conducted by a pathologist of restricted licensure without the direct supervision of a certified pathologist. Fortunately, the misdescription of the right head wound and the erroneous classification of the left[2] forehead entrance wound as a wound of exit, does not seem to have had a substantive effect in this case. [P. 57.]

The grand jury was considerably less lenient in its criticism of the second autopsy, however, and considerably harsher in its evaluation of the effect of that autopsy on the controversy surrounding the case.

The errors in the second autopsy are harder to understand. The principal pathologist was assisted and observed by two pathologists, a physician and a medical student. It seems incredible that all of them could have missed the exit wound near the left ear. This mistake combined with the mistaken drug analysis,[3] the erroneous classification of the shoulder wound as a graze, the confusion over the recovery of a bullet by the coroner and the defense counsels' predeliction for accusatory press conferences, contributed significantly to exacerbating community tensions. Plainly, a careful and objective approach to the second autopsy could have prevented this unnecessary conflict over the cause of death. [P. 57–58.]

The Commission's Analysis

Aside from presenting and briefly discussing the results of the various autopsies, the federal grand jury's *Report* scarcely deals with the precise manner of Hampton's death except to state that "presumably, one of these bullets [fired through the wall between the living room and the front bedroom] (a .30 caliber carbine bullet) was the one recovered from Hampton's body."[4] The bullet "recovered from Hampton's body" was from the wound in his left shoulder. The bullets from the fatal head wounds were never reported to have been recovered. The *Report* does not discuss the position of his body as described at the People's Inquest by the survivors or before the grand jury by the police, or as suggested by bullet fragments and blood in the bed on which Hampton died.

The relevance of these issues to the question whether Hampton was

2. None of the three autopsies referred to any "left forehead entrance wound." All three found a wound in the *right* forehead, which the coroner mistakenly identified as an exit wound. Apparently the federal grand jury *Report* intended to say "right" rather than "left" in the quoted passage.
3. The issue of drug analysis is discussed in Chapter 6.
4. *Report*, p. 83.

murdered is clear. The Commission, although obviously hampered by the absence of evidence which could have been obtained only by official investigative bodies, has nonetheless attempted to answer the question. In this connection, the Commission asked Dr. David Spain, who was present as an observer of the Hampton family at the third autopsy, but whose observations had not been documented, to prepare a written analysis of his interpretation of the pathological findings.

Dr. Spain's Report

Dr. Spain submitted his report to the Commission on December 29, 1970, two months after the Commission had made its request. It restates the findings of the third autopsy that Hampton was shot twice in the head, with both wounds passing along a trajectory from right to left at a downward angle, and that he suffered two additional wounds, a graze wound of the right forearm and a wound of the left shoulder.

Dr. Spain's report adds, however, a statement of his conclusions as to *how* Hampton was shot:

According to the location of the bed in the south bedroom, the door leading into this bedroom and the bullet holes through the walls, the most likely logical position of Fred Hampton's body at the time of the shooting was that he was lying on his right side with his head turned towards the right, his right arm under his head, and his face turned towards the south wall. This position can account for all of the entry wounds and their trajectory as coming from the direction of the open door. No other position can logically account for the trajectory and direction of all the bullet wounds. This would indicate that the body of Fred Hampton, was in full view of the individual who shot him, and that that individual was able to see that he was lying in a defenseless position. Paraffin tests performed on Fred Hampton's body at the time of the third autopsy were completely negative [indicating that he had not fired a weapon immediately before his death].

Because of his conclusion with respect to Hampton's position at the time he was shot, Spain disagreed with the federal grand jury's conclusion concerning the impact of the autopsy errors made by the Cook County coroner:

I must disagree with the conclusions of the Federal Grand Jury report to the effect that "fortunately, the misdescription of the right head wound and the erroneous classification of the left forehead entrance wound as a wound of exit does not seem to have had a substantive effect in this case." The final and correct placement of these wounds had a substantive effect on this case in that it indicated that Fred Hampton was shot in full view of the killer while in a defenseless position, and not in a blind shoot-out.

The Commission does not agree with Dr. Spain that the only position of Fred Hampton's body which can logically account for the trajectory and direction of all the bullet wounds is the position he has described. If Hampton's body was in the position he describes, the bullets which struck Hampton could indeed have been fired from the direction of the open doorway, but only if the weapon or weapons firing the shots were close to the level of the floor, which seems improbable. His report does render a valuable service, however, in raising the questions of whether the wounds indicate the direction or directions in the apartment from which the bullets inflicting them were fired; whether Hampton was lying on the bed when struck; if so, in what position; and whether he moved. Dr. Spain's report also demonstrates the significance of the Cook County coroner's erroneous findings that one bullet entered on the left side of Hampton's head and exited on the right, while the other traveled in the opposite direction. The coroner's autopsy would suggest either that the fatal bullets were fired from different directions or that Hampton was moving in the room, while the other autopsies would indicate that he was shot by gunfire from a single direction while still on the bed.

The physical evidence from the second and third autopsies clearly establishes that the two head wounds were caused by bullets which struck Hampton's head at approximately the same angle from above and slightly behind, entering on the right side of the head and exiting on the left. The .30-caliber carbine wound in the left shoulder and chest struck the body in the shoulder and moved downward to the chest. Thus all three shots struck the body at a similar angle. The downward angle of the shots makes it very unlikely that Hampton was erect when hit. It is also improbable that he moved after one shot and was later hit at generally the same angle. Therefore, all three shots probably came from the same direction. If Hampton was lying on the bed in the position described by Officers Ciszewski and Carmody, on his stomach, head toward the doorway on the west wall, feet toward the east wall and face toward the north wall, then all three wounds would line up with trajectories of bullets fired from the doorway.

The Cook County Coroner's Report

The medicolegal examination of Mark Clark and Fred Hampton by the medical examiner of the Cook County Coroner's Office was under the authority of, and pursuant to, an Illinois statute.[5] This statute requires the examiner's conclusions to the extent possible from the evidence available to him, as to the cause of death. The purpose and justification for such medicolegal "examinations"—examinations for the purposes of the state, as distinguished from the private medical examination of deceased persons—is to obtain the conclusion of the medical examiner as to cause of death.[6] The common understanding of those experienced in this area is that "cause of death" means the primary and secondary or other related factors which contribute to the ultimate determination of whether a death has been occasioned by natural or unnatural causes, and if the causes are found to be unnatural, then whether they were by accidental or by criminal act. If there is evidence of criminal conduct, the examiners are to seek to collect and develop, by the employment of their scientific methodology, evidence of the crime.

The determination of the cause of death, therefore, may be the result of a complex value judgment—upon the conclusion of the autopsy.[7]

The report form used by the Cook County Coroner's Office provides for a determination and description of the "Conditions, if any which give rise to the above Immediate Cause (A)." This information, the development of which is an essential element of the coroner's role, was not stated in the report, nor has it been otherwise furnished by the coroner. There was no apparent effort to use the expertise of the coroner to reconstruct, to the extent the available physical and scientific information made possible, what actually happened to Fred

5. Ill. Rev. Stat. 1967, Ch. 31, para. 10.2.
6. See U.S., Armed Forces Institute of Pathology, *The Medico-Legal Autopsy Laws of the Fifty States and the District of Columbia* (Washington, D.C.: Government Printing Office).
7. *People* v. *Fiddler*, 45 Ill. 2d 181, 258 N.E. (2d 359), 361 (Ill. 1970).

Hampton, or to determine who inflicted the fatal wounds, or to explain the cirumstances and conditions of his death insofar as they might relate to the issue of culpability. What is demonstrated by the coroner's conduct, as generally by the governmental investigations of the incident of December 4, 1969, is the outright failure of officials to do their duty in a professional manner. The public was not presented with an irreconcilable conflict between conclusions reached by experts as a result of thorough investigations, examinations, and appraisals of physical and scientific evidence, but merely with the confused and inconclusive consequences of a failure to seek, analyze, or report the facts.

The coroner's examinations of the deaths of Mark Clark and Fred Hampton not only ignored the purposes of the cited Illinois law, as evidenced by the lack of thoroughness of the investigation of the cause of death, but also ignored the procedures established by law to assure such a thorough and complete investigation. Those procedures include requirements that neither the deceased nor any property of the deceased be handled or moved except with the coroner's permission.

§10.5 REMOVAL OF BODIES—PERMIT—EXCEPTION—VIOLATION
No dead body which may be subject to the terms of this Act, or the personal property of such a deceased person, shall be handled, moved, disturbed, embalmed or removed from the place of death by any person, except with the permission of the coroner, unless the same shall be necessary to protect such body or property from damage or destruction, or unless necessary to protect life, safety, or health. Any person knowingly violating the provisions of this Section is guilty of a misdemeanor.

§10.6 CORONER TO BE NOTIFIED—VIOLATION
Every law enforcement official, funeral director, ambulance attendant, hospital director or administrator or person having custody of the body of a deceased person, where the death is one subject to investigation under Section 10 of this Act, and any physician in attendance upon such a decedent at the time of his death, shall notify the coroner promptly. Any such person failing to so notify the coroner promptly shall be guilty of a misdemeanor, unless such person has reasonable cause to believe that the coroner had already been so notified.

The purpose of the Illinois law was to bring the medical examiner into the scene as soon after the time of death as possible and with as little change in the surroundings as possible, so as to facilitate his ability to make the judgments required of him by his office. In the case of deaths in which the police are involved, it is of the greatest importance that the statute be complied with, since any challenge to the police account of the facts may make an independent evaluation of crucial relevance.

The police in the December 4 raid received their directions from the State's Attorney's Office. The presumption that they knew the law is great, as is the presumption that they were sensitive to compelling legal and social needs for strict compliance with that law. Under the circumstances, the failure of the police to perform their duty raises the question whether officials wanted an on-the-scene investigation by the Coroner's Office contemporaneously with the event. Of course, the police faced the particular difficulty of being in a neighborhood that would presumably be hostile to their conduct of the raid. The illegal removal of the bodies of Hampton and Clark and the failure to seal the apartment for some days could be attributable to police apprehension about the community's response. But whatever the precipitating motivation—fear, inefficiency, or deliberate intent to conceal evidence—the law has been circumvented, and the truth rendered more difficult to determine.

The Federal Grand Jury Report

It is doubtful that there was legal authority for a federal grand jury to issue a report in May 1970. Neither the Constitution, federal statute, nor established practice provided such power. Regardless of legal authority,[8] however, the federal grand jury *Report* of the raid was inadequate—inadequate not only as a substitute for indictments but also as an exposition of what happened during the police action. The *Report* has every quality of a whitewash. Two people were dead and four seriously injured. Police had fired scores of rounds of ammunition; Panthers had fired one shot, at most. Assistant Attorney General Jerris Leonard, who headed the federal investigation, had led members of the Commission of Inquiry with whom he met in Justice Arthur Goldberg's office in early 1970, to believe that indictments

8. The *Report* generally, including questions concerning its legality, is discussed in Chapter 8.

would be forthcoming. Instead, there was an insufficient report and no legal action.

No aspect of the federal grand jury *Report* more clearly exposes its inadequacy than does its treatment of the death of Fred Hampton. The grand jury did not try to determine when Hampton was killed, who fired the shots that struck him, and under what circumstances, whether he was awake and moving during the incident, the direction from which the bullets that killed him came, the angle at which they struck, the location and position of his body, whether others were still in the room when he was fatally wounded, whether it remained possible to test firearms allegedly seized in the room to determine if they had been discharged or whether any bullets or fragments found in the room could be matched with specific weapons or identified as having caused Hampton's head wounds. Since the grand jury's legal function was to determine whether the police had unlawfully killed, wounded, or assaulted persons—even if only in an attempt to determine whether the police had deprived the occupants of federally protected rights, contrary to law—it is incredible that it made no effort fully to analyze the circumstances under which Hampton was shot.

The grand jury did cause a new autopsy to be performed, from which it confirmed that Hampton's head wounds were caused by shots entering on the right side of his head and exiting at lower points on the left side, but it made no effort to fix the precise angles, as could readily have been done. Nor did it discuss Dr. Levine's assertion in the second autopsy that the fatal bullets were fired from above and slightly behind Hampton's head. The grand jury saw no significance in the error in the coroner's report which described the bullets as entering the head from opposite directions, yet this issue would seem critical in determining the directions from which the bullets came and the probable circumstances under which they were fired. The grand jury's silence about the manner in which the bullet wounds were inflicted on Fred Hampton left the nature and agent of his death unresolved; indeed, it left nothing but the unchallenged speculation of the police that Hampton was slain in a blind "shoot-out."

Only one other comment concerning the shooting that caused Hampton's wounds is made in the grand jury's *Report*. In the section entitled "Scientific Analysis of the Physical Evidence Found in the Apartment," the *Report* notes that:

Examination of the north bedroom walls and furniture revealed that all forty-two shots fired into the south wall of the living room passed into the north bedroom and that eighteen of the forty-two shots passed through the south wall of the north bedroom into the south bedroom; presumably, one of these bullets (a .30 caliber carbine bullet) was the one recovered from Hampton's body. [P. 83; reference note omitted.]

It was not necessary simply to speculate about the source of the .30-caliber carbine bullet. The bullet was found in Fred Hampton's body. Tests could have been made to determine whether it was fired from Officer Davis's carbine, whether it could have inflicted such a wound after having passed through two walls, whether it was mis-shapen by impact with walls, whether particles of paint or building materials traceable to the walls were found on it. If such tests were not made, officials were derelict; if they were, the results should have been made known.

The Commission's Analysis

Facts are rarely easy to find after a traumatic event. Here the difficulties are compounded by changes, ambiguities, and omissions in official accounts. Nevertheless, some conclusions can be reached with reasonable certainty.

No shots were fired by the four occupants of the south bedroom. Despite early statements by police that they were fired upon from this bedroom, and despite Louis Truelock's statement that before reaching the south bedroom he had fired two shots toward the back of the apartment, no physical evidence exists to support these statements. No cartridges, bullets, or bullet holes were found attributable to gunfire from within the room. The alleged shotgun blasts from the occupants in the south bedroom into the adjacent rooms could not have been fired as stated by police. Despite all the police facilities for investigation there is no test showing that any gun allegedly found in the south bedroom was fired. Such tests should have been made in the course of ordinary investigative procedures. They could have been made after controversy arose.

Fred Hampton was never fully conscious during the police presence on the premises, although it appears likely that he moved his head once. If he moved from the bed, there is no explanation of how he got back on the bed. The similar angles at which the bullets struck him make it highly unlikely that he moved after first being hit. Deborah Johnson and Harold Bell both described him as being unconscious on the bed throughout; Louis Truelock described him as having been barely conscious for one brief moment. The accounts of several officers describe a body on the bed. The angle at which the bullets struck his body makes it more likely that he was in a horizontal than in a vertical position.

If Fred Hampton was unconscious throughout the raid, there must be some explanation of why the noise of the shooting and Truelock's efforts did not awaken him. The question whether he was drugged is treated in a later chapter. There would seem to be no possibility that any of the first shots of the raid hit him. Bell and Truelock were able to move from the front of the apartment to the south bedroom before police entered the house. The testimony of the police is that Officer Davis did not fire his carbine toward the south of the house until after Officer Gorman had strafed the south wall of the living room once, and the wound caused by the carbine bullet would not have been likely to cause an immediate loss of consciousness.

Police gunfire from the front of the house probably did not hit Hampton. In the small bedroom it is improbable that random, blind gunfire would have hit Hampton four times and left the other three occupants untouched. Shots fired from the north would have had to penetrate walls which stopped most of the bullets before one could have hit Hampton's head. Moreover, Hampton's two head wounds were only inches apart and the shoulder wound little more than a foot away. The pattern of firing from the front room makes it unlikely that three bullets would be so close together, particularly after traveling through two walls and the front bedroom. Deborah Johnson and Louis Truelock stated that they were on the north side of the bed, between Hampton and the line of fire from the north, during much of the firing from the front of the apartment. It seems even less likely that Hampton could have been hit by fire from that direction while they escaped unscathed. If any bullet from the north had entered and exited from Hampton's head, it would not have been likely to hit the mattress because of the near horizontal path it would have followed. With its force largely expended, such a bullet should have been found in the south wall of the bedroom—certainly, it should have been found somewhere in the room.

If the later police accounts of the firing are credible, Fred Hampton was dragged from the south bedroom before Officer Gorman fired his machine gun from the hallway into the closet of the north bedroom and the bedroom itself. Gorman himself described seeing Carmody drag someone from the rear bedroom before he fired into the north bedroom closet. Ciszewski had been wounded in the rear bedroom after Hampton was removed and before Gorman fired into the closet. Carmody, after having removed Hampton from the south bedroom, entered the north bedroom as Gorman was firing, thus ending the raid. It was therefore not machine gun fire into the north bedroom closet that penetrated the wall and hit Fred Hampton.

The shots which struck Fred Hampton almost certainly were fired from or through the doorway into the room. The trajectory from that position and the angle of the wounds in Hampton's head and shoulder are consistent with the testimony of all the witnesses as to Hampton's position on the south side of the bed and with the statements of Officers Carmody and Ciszewski that he lay with his head toward the door. The latters' statements that Hampton was facing the north wall of the bedroom are not supported by the testimony of the survivors. Johnson and Bell both testified that while they were attempting to awaken Hampton he lay with his face toward the south bedroom wall; Truelock stated that Hampton was on his back. Johnson's testimony that Hampton raised and then dropped his head as she moved over him to the north side of the bed does not indicate whether his head dropped to the same position; Bell, however, specifically stated that after Hampton's head dropped back onto the mattress it was still facing the south wall.

Although no definite answer can be reached from this apparently contradictory testimony, it does not seem implausible that Hampton's face could have been turned from the south to the north wall between the time that Johnson and Bell saw him and the time he was killed. Such a change in position might have been caused, for example, by

Johnson and Truelock climbing over Hampton's body to surrender from the room, by the impact of the shot which wounded his shoulder, or by a spontaneous movement by Hampton.

It is difficult to determine whether Hampton was shot while Bell, Johnson, and Truelock were in the room or after Bell, or all three, had been removed. The probability is that Hampton was alone on the bed when shot. Neither Johnson, Truelock, nor Bell remembers seeing blood on Hampton. Bell, Johnson, and Truelock were not hit. They were in the room when early shotgun blasts and pistol shots, which probably hit no one, were fired into the room. The direction of the shotgun blasts indicates they were not directed at occupants, and Hampton's wounds do not seem to have been caused by shotgun blasts. Pistol shots apparently fired into the room before anyone left it may have hit the mattress. In so small a room—the doorway was only a few feet from the bed—all occupants could have been hit by gunfire directed at any one of them. But it is unlikely that Hampton could have been hit four times and Johnson and Truelock, behind him on the bed, not hit at all.

The shots in Hampton's head, their closeness to each other, and their proximity to the shoulder wound indicate that they were fired by persons who could see their target. If Hampton could be seen and was then shot, it is likely that Johnson and Truelock, if on the same bed, could also have been seen and shot. It is therefore probable either that Fred Hampton was shot after the other occupants were removed from the room by an officer or officers who could see his prostrate body on the bed, or that Hampton was deliberately selected as the sole target.

CHAPTER 6

Was Hampton Drugged
at the Time of His Death?

During the entire course of the raid Fred Hampton alone among the occupants of the apartment did not awake. One explanation which has been suggested for his failure to be aroused by the shooting, the commotion, or the specific attempts by other occupants to awaken him is that he had been drugged.

Such a conclusion might help to explain how Hampton happened to be shot three or four times and killed while the other three people in the same room were not even wounded. More importantly, it would raise the further questions of how and why Hampton was drugged. Speculation on the latter points in turn raises again the unanswered question about the planning of the raid: why fourteen heavily armed police officers attempted to execute a search warrant in the predawn hours rather than at a time when there was reason to believe that the premises to be searched would be empty. For if the evidence were to indicate that the police or the state's attorney knew not only that Hampton would be at the apartment, but also that he would be drugged, it might lead to a very serious inference that the entire raid was merely a camouflage for Hampton's murder.

Unfortunately, of the many issues considered in this report the questions of whether, how, and why Hampton was drugged are among the most difficult to resolve. Although a substantial amount of information is available on the issue of whether he was drugged, the evidence on the questions, "If so, how and why?" is so sparse that answers to those questions can only be highly speculative and inferential.

The evidence relating to whether Hampton was drugged falls into two categories: testimony and other data concerning toxicological evidence, and testimony about Hampton's behavior immediately prior to and during the raid.

The testimony relating to Hampton's behavior immediately prior to and during the raid has been discussed in Chapters 4 and 5. It is sufficient to restate here that Hampton fell asleep in the middle of a telephone conversation at about 1:30 A.M. on December 4, approximately three hours before the raid; that specific attempts by Deborah Johnson to wake him at that time failed; and that further attempts by the survivors to wake him while the raid was in progress also failed. Hampton's only observed movement during the raid was to raise and then drop his head.

This chapter will discuss the toxicological evidence and the various questions raised by that evidence.

The Toxicological Evidence

Following Hampton's death a number of tests, some official and some private, were reportedly conducted on Hampton's blood. Although the tests may have had more than one purpose, one of their objects was to determine whether any barbiturates were present in Hampton's bloodstream when he died.

The Cook County Coroner's Office: December 5, 1969

Shortly after Hampton was determined to be dead, his body was transported to the Cook County Coroner's Office, where an official autopsy was performed. According to the coroner's chemist, a sample of Hampton's blood, labeled 69–2170, was taken during the course of the autopsy. The coroner's chemist and his assistants then performed an ultraviolet test on a blood sample, labeled 69–2171,[1] which was also identified as Hampton's blood. This test "failed to show the presence of barbiturates."

Dr. Victor Levine and Dr. Eleanor Berman: December 12, 1969

On December 5, 1969, Hampton's body was removed to a private funeral home and, at the request of the Hampton family, a second autopsy was performed by Dr. Victor Levine, the former chief pa-

1. The FBI later identified sample 69–2171 as Hampton's blood, and sample 69–2170 as coming from the deceased Mark Clark.

thologist for the Cook County Coroner's Office. Dr. Levine removed two samples of blood: the first, loose blood from a body cavity, and the second from a vein. On December 9, 1969, Dr. Levine delivered both samples, marked C–69#1 and C–69#2, to Dr. Eleanor Berman, a toxicologist and acting director of the Department of Biochemistry, Cook County Hospital, with instructions to see what she could find in the blood. At the time, Dr. Berman did not know that the blood was Fred Hampton's. She refrigerated the blood from December 9, 1969, until December 12, 1969, when she performed ultraviolet spectrophotometry (U.V.) and thin layer chromatography (T.L.C.) tests on both samples. The method of storage of this blood between December 5 and December 9, 1969, is unknown.

Dr. Berman testified before the federal grand jury that her U.V. results had shown the presence of unknown foreign substances in the blood. Accordingly, she ran a routine drug screen for acid and neutral substances and the alkaloid family of drugs. Her T.L.C. results for both blood samples were positive for barbiturates (secobarbital), but negative for all other drugs. Based on further tests, she estimated the secobarbital concentration to be in the range of 4.1 to 4.5 milligrams percent. Dr. Berman identified an additional foreign substance in the blood as salicylate.[2]

Dr. Berman stated:

Analyses were performed on Samples 1 and 2 simultaneously. No. 1 contained secobarbital 4.1 mg per cent and alcohol 40 mg per cent. No. 2, secobarbital 4.5 mg per cent and alcohol 50 per cent. The alcohol content was determined by the modified Widmark reaction. I did not perform a Gas Chromatography test because my equipment was in disrepair. At the time I conducted the above tests, I noticed that the blood had already begun to deteriorate.

After Dr. Berman's tests on December 12, 1969, the Berman-Levine samples of Hampton's blood were refrigerated until January 22, 1970.

The Cook County Coroner's Office: December 22, 1969

On December 22, 1969, by special order of the coroner, a second analysis was performed by the Coroner's Office upon the samples of

2. A substance apparently unrelated to whether Hampton was drugged.

Hampton's blood taken by that office on December 4. This analysis also "failed to show the presence of barbiturates."

By January 7, 1970, there had been public disclosure of the findings of the second autopsy, including the finding as to the presence of drugs in Hampton's body at the time of his death.

The federal grand jury *Report* referred to press conferences at which Dr. Levine appeared and said that he had given "his opinion that the level of the seconal present in the body would have placed the subject in a deep stupor." The *Report* continued:

These reports, especially the alleged presence of drugs, were widely published in the media together with comments from Panther leader Rush and others that this fact proved the assassination theory.

Shortly thereafter, the coroner's office announced that an analysis of samples of Hampton's blood retained from its autopsy showed that no seconal was present. [P. 54.]

Dr. Victor Levine and Dr. Berman: January 22, 1970

On January 22, 1970, Dr. Berman, in the presence of Dr. Levine, again tested blood sample C–69#1 for barbiturates. She testified before the federal grand jury that her Beckman Chart (U.V.) curve disclosed the continued presence of foreign substances in the blood and that her T.L.C. plate again established the presence of secobarbital and salicylate. Above the spot which Dr. Berman had identified as secobarbital, a larger spot also appeared which she identified as protein. A photograph of this T.L.C. plate was taken by Dr. Levine.[3] By running concurrent standards Dr. Berman estimated a secobarbital concentration of 3 milligrams percent.

FBI Analysis: February 3, 1970

The federal grand jury, recognizing the conflict in the results reached by Dr. Berman and the coroner's chemist, undertook to resolve the inconsistency.

First, it subpoenaed all of the pathologists, chemists and supporting personnel who had participated in the autopsies together with their photographs,

---

3. The U.V. Beckman Charts from Dr. Berman's original analysis were not retained, nor were photographs made of the first T.L.C. plates. At the time of her initial tests, as previously noted, Dr. Berman did not know the source of the blood she was testing or the potential significance of the results.

X-rays and reports and heard the analysis of each. Second, it ordered that the retained blood samples from both autopsies should be submitted to the FBI Laboratory for a complete serological study. Finally, when it became apparent that the conflicting findings were irreconcilable from available evidence, it obtained an order of exhumation and commissioned Dr. Charles Petty, Chief Medical Examiner for the County of Dallas, to perform a third autopsy in the presence of physicians and attorneys representing the Coroner and the Hampton family. [P. 54.]

The FBI Crime Laboratory collected four blood samples under grand jury subpoena—two from the Coroner's Office (Clark and Hampton) and two from Drs. Levine and Berman (Hampton). It is not known under what conditions the blood was stored or transported between the date on which the samples were subpoenaed and the date of the FBI tests, which were performed, according to the federal grand jury *Report,* on February 3, 1970.

The federal grand jury *Report* asserts that: "The expert from the FBI Laboratory testified that he had conducted the most specific and sophisticated test known for secobarbital—gas chromatography[4]—on all of the blood samples submitted." He concluded that no secobarbital was present in the blood samples that he analyzed.

The Federal Grand Jury's Autopsy: February 16, 1970

By order of the federal grand jury, a third autopsy was performed upon Hampton's exhumed body. The findings are contained in the "Report and Protocol" of Dr. Charles S. Petty, chief medical examiner for the County of Dallas. Dr. M. F. Mason, toxicologist, had received from Dr. Petty the following specimens from the embalmed body of Fred Hampton: (1) muscle tissue, (2) vitreous humor, (3) liver, (4) brain, (5) kidney, (6) bloody fluid from spinal canal, (7) bone marrow, and (8) stomach and contents (the latter diluted). The examination requested was "tests on appropriate specimens for the presence of the barbiturate derivative, secobarbital."

Dr. Mason performed his tests on March 9, 1970, more than three months after Hampton's death on December 4, 1969, and reported as follows:

---

4. This was the test Dr. Berman could not employ due to malfunctioning equipment.

Result of Examination:
(8) Stomach content fluid: no barbiturate was detected.
(2) Vitreous humor: no barbiturate was detected.
(3) Liver: no barbiturate was detected.
(6) Bloody fluid (from spinal canal): no barbiturate was detected.

The presence of secobarbital (and other barbiturates) in quantities sufficient to have had any significant pharmacological action at the time of death of the subject has been excluded.

Dr. Mason reasoned that his failure to find secobarbital in the March 9 examination necessarily excluded the presence of sufficient secobarbital "to have had any significant pharmacological action" at the time of death. This conclusion settled the drug question for the federal grand jury. It concluded in its *Report* that Fred Hampton was not drugged at the time of his death:

The autopsy conducted by Dr. Petty at the Shreveport, Louisiana Veterans Hospital, with Grand Jury attorneys present, was extraordinarily thorough. An X-ray study of the entire body was made, and color and black and white photographs were taken at every stage of the examination. This autopsy conclusively confirmed the findings of the FBI and the coroner's chemist that there was no trace of drugs in the body through extensive cultural analyses of the stomach, kidneys, liver, brain and other organs; samples of these organs were contemporaneously obtained by the Hampton family pathologist and the coroner's pathologists. [P. 55.]

The Commission's Investigation

Because the procedures followed pursuant to the federal grand jury's order for an investigation into the drugging issue seemed to leave a number of questions unanswered, the Commission pursued its own investigation. In addition to eliciting reports and comments from Dr. Berman herself, it sought professional analysis of the available reports and documents from a number of experts. These were Walter Booker, professor and head of the Department of Pharmacology, Howard University College of Medicine; Walter G. Levine, associate professor of Pharmacology, Albert Einstein College of Medicine; Bernard Davidow, chief, Food and Drug Laboratory, New York City Department of Health; and Dr. Leo Goldbaum of the Armed Forces Institute of Pathology. The Commission also asked Ivan Rayner, Fred

Hampton's mortician, to disclose the quantities of embalming fluids he used in preparing Hampton's body for burial; the Commission was the only group investigating Hampton's death which contacted Mr. Rayner.

The issues to which these experts addressed themselves were the validity of Dr. Berman's tests and the probative value with respect to the issue of the presence of barbiturates in Hampton's blood at the time of his death of both the FBI tests performed on two-and-one-half-month-old blood samples and the third autopsy tests performed on a strongly embalmed body three months after its preparation for burial.

Mr. Rayner stated that Hampton's body had been heavily embalmed, since he had not known how long the body would remain unburied:

The following substances were used in the preparation of the body. Two bottles of Lithol (Index 32), an arterial fluid, were injected in the veins. Each bottle contained sixteen (16) ounces and was diluted with two and a half (2–1/2) gallons of water. Lithol (Index 32) is manufactured by the Embalmers' Supply Company of Westport, Connecticut 06880.

The organs, which were found in a plastic bag supplied by the Coroner, were embalmed with two (2) sixteen (16) ounce bottles of Cavrex (Index 28), a cavity fluid used on the viscera. The Cavrex (Index 28) was used in a full strength non-dilute state. Cavrex (Index 28) is manufactured by the Embalmers' Supply Company of Westport, Connecticut.

I decided to use two (2) bottles of Lithol (Index 32) and two bottles of Cavrex (Index 28) because it is a strong dosage, since I did not know how long the body would remain before burial and I took the precaution of using enough to guarantee against deterioration of the body.

Professor Booker was apprised of the embalming procedure followed by Mr. Rayner before his opinion to the Commission was delivered. He stated that the FBI tests, if they were to be reliable, would have to have compensated for the strong dosage of embalming fluid; Mr. Rayner has stated, however, that except for the Commission letter no inquiry was made of him as to how Hampton's body had been prepared for burial. Professor Booker found as follows:

In my professional opinion, Extraction, Saponification, and/or T.L. Chromatography, Elution and U.V. Photometry analysis of organ tissue would conclusively establish the presence or absence of Secobarbital in the organs or body of a person three months after death only if done by a person who is familiar with the likelihood of interfering substances such as Cavrex-Esco and Lithol; and further that necessary steps must have been taken to compensate for their presence in the body or organs when the organs have been placed in a plastic bag and bathed in 32 ounces of the concentrated fluid Cavrex-Esco for three months or in a body embalmed for three months with two quarts Lithol (28 index) to two gallons of water.

It is my further professional opinion that the presence of Cavrex-Esco in or around the organs or Lithol (28 index) in the body for a period of three months would significantly interfere with or make difficult the Extraction process which is essential for the identification and estimation of barbiturates.

It is my further professional opinion that the problem of Extraction is so complicated when Cavrex-Esco or Lithol (28 index) are present in or around an organ or the body that the fact that no secobarbital was found in a test three months after death and embalming is not satisfactory proof of the absence of secobarbital from the body at the time of death.

Professor Levine similarly stated emphatically that the failure to detect secobarbital in the tissues of a body embalmed for three months prior to the analysis does not constitute irrefutable proof that a substantial amount of the drug was not present at the time of death. He also noted that the dual factors of the presence of embalming fluid and deterioration of the body made ordinary testing unreliable.

After careful consultation with my colleagues and after reviewing the pertinent medical and scientific literature, I can say unhesitatingly that a negative finding for secobarbital analysis in the postmortem tissues of a human body that had been embalmed approximately three months prior to this analysis does *not* constitute irrefutable proof that a substantial amount of the drug was not present at the time of death. [Emphasis in original.] The technical problems of extracting and identifying barbiturates are difficult enough using blood or urine specimens obtained from a living individual. Identification of the drug from other tissues is even more difficult and the recoveries tend to be somewhat lower than from body fluids. *The effect of embalming fluid plus deterioration which occurs despite embalming are factors whose influence on the analytical procedure cannot be readily determined. In my opinion, it is indeed possible that these factors may have prevented the recovery of the barbiturate from the tissues by accepted methods of extraction.* [Emphasis added.]

Dr. Davidow stated that neither a thin layer chromatography nor a gas chromatography test conducted one and a half months after death would be reliable unless the blood sample had been frozen, or at the very least refrigerated, for the entire period. In addition, he said, the presence of the embalming fluids would have made it extremely difficult to detect any secobarbital in bodily organs three months after death.

Before responding to your specific questions regarding the determination of secobarbital in blood, I would like to make an important preliminary observation. Secobarbital is an unsaturated barbiturate which means that it is relatively unstable and will decompose much more rapidly than most other commonly employed barbiturates. Thus, the answers stated below depend, to a large extent, on the initial concentration of secobarbital, the length of time involved and the skill of the person testing for its presence.

It is my professional opinion that 4.1 to 4.5 mg of secobarbital per 100 ml. of blood is a potentially lethal dosage which will definitely result in coma unless the individual is a barbiturate addict.

It is my further professional opinion that a qualified person using proper techniques would be able to detect significant levels of secobarbital in a blood sample by using either a Thin Layer Chromatography test or a Gas Chromatography test.

In any case, it would be difficult to determine if either of these two tests would show the presence of secobarbital one and a half months after the sample was taken, without knowing the conditions of storage. Blood or serum samples containing secobarbital should be frozen or refrigerated to preserve the presence of the barbiturate. Any other method of storage would result in deterioration of the secobarbital. As the temperature of the storage area increases, the rate of deterioration of the secobarbital will also increase.

In my professional position, unless the sample is frozen I do have serious doubts about the validity of a test performed one and a half months after the sample was taken because, as noted above, secobarbital is relatively unstable in aqueous solutions, and is more unsaturated than most other commonly employed barbiturates. Therefore, secobarbital will deteriorate and break down into other products, which may not be detected in an analysis for secobarbital.

Even if secobarbital were in the organs of a body at the time of death or thereafter, it would be extremely difficult for any test to be positive three months after death, when two quarts Lithol (28 index) and two gallons of water were injected into the body and the organs were bathed in 32 ounces of Cavrex-Esco. The reasons for this are twofold. First, the extraction process would be complicated by the presence of these materials. Second, the effect of these interfering substances would serve to dilute the amount of secobarbital in the blood and organs to the point where its presence may no longer be detected.

As part of its investigation, the Commission contacted Dr. Berman and received from her two letters describing the analyses of Hampton's blood conducted by her and commenting on the FBI analysis. Several of the points raised in her letters warrant emphasis. With respect to her analyses she noted first that before the blood samples were delivered to her on December 9, 1969, they had been stored under conditions not known to her but they had not been frozen, and that the samples were not frozen by her either before her first analysis on December 12, 1969, or her second test on January 22, 1970; second, she said, she conducted in each analysis two separate tests, an ultraviolet spectrophotometric scan (U.V.), which showed the presence of foreign substances in the blood, and a thin layer chromatography (T.L.C.) test, the result of which was her determination that one of the foreign substances was secobarbital.

Dr. Berman took sharp exception to the FBI's conclusion, based on tests conducted by Joseph Gormley, that no secobarbital was present in Hampton's blood. First, she stresses the absence of testimony by Gormley concerning how the blood was stored. Second, she disagrees with Gormley's testimony that secobarbital in solution does not deteriorate. Third, she disagrees with Gormley's analysis of her tests. He had testified that Dr. Berman relied on U.V. tests to identify the secobarbital; Dr. Berman reiterated that her U.V. tests had been used only to show the existence of a foreign substance, not to identify it, and that the identification had been based upon the T.L.C. test. Finally, she rebutted several of Gormley's statements about the procedures which she had followed:

After having read the Grand Jury testimony of FBI special agent, Joseph Leo Gormley, I would like to make several comments. First, Mr. Gormley did not state how the blood was stored for the ten days following my test of January 22, 1970, or the size of the blood sample used in his tests. Second, contrary to what Mr. Gormley stated, secobarbital in solution is rather unstable and does deteriorate. Deterioration is more rapid in alkaline solutions. The blood samples discussed were alkaline. Rate of deterioration is dependent upon temperature also. For example, solutions are less stable at room temperature than in refrigerator. Therefore, Mr. Gormley's negative findings of secobarbital are not by any means conclusive.

Before proceeding I want to make a critical point. My U.V. test was only for the purpose of determining if the blood was pure or contained a foreign substance. It was not done for the purpose of specifically identifying the nature of any impurities as Mr. Gormley suggests. The results of my Beckman Chart showed only that the blood contained foreign substances. My TLC test then disclosed that the foreign substance was secobarbital plus salicylate. The salicylate was not mentioned in my report because its presence was not considered significant at the time.

There is also a question in my mind about the methodology used by Mr. Gormley in his Gas Chromatography. He does not indicate the conditions of the procedure. What type columns were used? What type detector? What were the temperatures of the column, detector, and injector part, etc. Also, how did the extraction and re-extraction procedures described affect recovery of secobarbital?

Mr. Gormley's Beckman Chart clearly shows that the blood he tested was not pure but did indeed contain a foreign drug substance. In my professional opinion that substance is salicylic acid. My TLC preparation also showed the presence of salicylate. Indeed the curve on my Beckman Chart is exactly the kind of curve you would expect to find if a salicylate and secobarbital were both in the same blood sample. Instead of clean peaks at 237–40 and 295 (as you would expect to find with barbiturates) you would have one upward line moving from peak to peak between 290, 255 and 240. While Mr. Gormley's Beckman Chart shows the characteristics of a salicylate, my tracing was not specific. This change could indicate that the secobarbital had already deteriorated by the time of his analyses. However, salicylates being much more stable continued to be present. Thus, with the deterioration of the secobarbital, the U.V. tracing of Gormley showed definite peaks at 237 and 295 for the salicylate present.

Mr. Gormley spent some time discussing the significance of adding strong or weak alkali or acid solutions to a weak alkali extract of a chloroform extract of a blood sample. However, this procedure is only valid or useful if only one single drug substance is recovered. As I noted above, my U.V. test showed that more than one foreign substance could be in the blood sample. Therefore, I did not follow the procedure suggested by Mr. Gormley because in this case it would not have contributed to the clarification of the problem.

I also wish to take strong exception to Mr. Gormley's statement that the tracing of an extract of 2 ml. of blood containing 4.5 mg% of secobarbital would have gone off the chart. The tracings on our standard solutions treated as are the blood specimens stay on the chart at concentrations below 6 mg%. Known standards and blank solutions are run concurrently with unknowns and compared to measure concentration.

2 ml. of blood were acidified to about pH 6 with 0.1 normal hydrochloric acid and extracted with 40 ml. of washed chloroform. Thirty-five ml. of the chloroform extract were in turn extracted with 5 ml. of 0.5 normal sodium hydroxide.

If I have further comments I will send them along. I invite the Commission to submit my Grand Jury testimony and Mr. Gormley's Grand Jury testimony to impartial toxicologists for analysis and comment. I am confident that they will be in substantial agreement with my observations.

In an effort to resolve the conflicting toxicological evidence, the Commission once again contacted Professor Booker. He reviewed the federal grand jury testimony of Dr. Berman and Mr. Gormley, as well as Dr. Berman's letters to the Commission. In addition, he spoke with Dr. Berman about the testing procedures she had followed. Professor Booker, in a series of letters, the last of which was written jointly with Dr. Goldbaum, concluded on the basis of both Dr. Berman's and Agent Gormley's tests that Hampton's blood was not normal; on the basis of Dr. Berman's analysis he concluded that the foreign substance in Hampton's blood was a barbiturate. The full text of those letters is as follows:

Herbert O. Reid
Executive Director
Commission Inquiry
880—3rd Avenue
New York, New York

DEAR DR. REID:
At your request, I have reviewed the Grand Jury Testimony and exhibits of Dr. Eleanor Berman and Joseph Gormley, as well as Dr. Berman's letters to you dated February 24, 1971. I have also personally talked to Dr. Berman to ascertain the methodology she employed in performing the tests on the samples of Fred Hampton's blood.

Both Dr. Berman and Joseph Gormley appear to possess more than the minimum qualifications to satisfactorily and accurately perform the necessary tests to determine if secobarbital was present in a blood sample. I have been informed that since 1948 Dr. Berman has personally conducted or supervised approximately 50,000 similar tests. This is far in excess of the number necessary to qualify her as being proficient with the testing methods she and Mr. Gormley used. Unless shown otherwise, I would be inclined to accept either persons's professional judgment. Therefore, I disagree with Mr. Gormley's suggestion that Dr. Berman is not sufficiently experienced or qualified as being unsupported by the facts.

I have reviewed the methodology used by Dr. Berman and Mr. Gormley on the Hampton blood samples and have concluded that the procedures employed were proper and should have resulted in accurate findings. Yet, the findings of Berman and Gormley are in clear conflict. It is difficult for me to resolve or pinpoint the discrepancy between these two analyses if the tests were performed under standard and well accepted conditions and procedures of laboratory discipline.

I cannot agree with Mr. Gormley's assertion that Dr. Berman's curve would have gone off the chart before it had peaked, as it would be impossible for anyone to come to such a conclusion unless the sensitivity of Dr. Berman's equipment and its settings were known to the observer. What Mr. Gormley has done is to raise a quantitative issue but he has applied it to a qualitative situation; that is, difference of opinion regarding the possible level of barbiturate should not be taken to mean no barbiturate is present.

I have examined the Beckman chart of Dr. Berman and concluded that her curves show the presence of several foreign substances in the blood. However, it is impossible to ascertain from her charts the exact nature of those foreign substances.

In her Grand Jury Testimony, Dr. Berman stated that she performed an ultraviolet test for the limited purpose of determining if the blood sample was normal. She testified that she did not rely upon her ultraviolet test to identify the specific substance found in the sample. For this she said she used a T.L.C. test.

Mr. Gormley, in his testimony, does not refer to Dr. Berman's T.L.C. test, but, nonetheless, concludes that Dr. Berman was in error. To sustain his position, Mr. Gormley would have to explain away Dr. Berman's T.L.C. results which he has not done. All that Mr. Gormley has established is the point that Dr. Berman concedes—that her ultraviolet test (as opposed to her T.L.C.) does not establish that secobarbital was the foreign susbstance in the blood sample.

I have also examined Mr. Gormley's Beckman chart. My conclusion is that his curves, like Dr. Berman's show that the blood sample was not normal and that several foreign substances were present. Although it is impossible to determine what the foreign substances might be without examining Mr. Gormley's standards, it is clear that more than one substance is present since his chart shows more than one peak at the same optical density.

If you have any further inquiries, I shall be happy to respond.

Sincerely,
(signed) WALTER M. BOOKER, Ph.D.

WMB:pj

\#

Herbert O. Reid
Executive Director
Commission Inquiry
880—3rd Avenue
New York, New York

DEAR DR. REID:
At your further request, I have examined a photograph of Dr. Berman's T.L.C. plate which shows the result of her tests done on January 22, 1970.

Dr. Berman's T.L.C. results, as depicted in the photograph, corroborates the initial findings of her ultraviolet test that a foreign substance was in the blood. In my professional opinion, that picture taken, together with the peaks on her Beckman Chart curves, establishes that the foreign substance in the blood sample C169 #1 was a barbiturate.

Unfortunately, the picture of Dr. Berman's T.L.C. plate is not of the highest quality, thus making it difficult to conclusively establish the precise identity of the barbiturate. However, the height and shape of the second spot on the blood sample C169 #1 compares favorably with the secobarbital standard and in all probability is secobarbital.

The tail which is clearly present in the blood sample C169 #1 means that another foreign substance was in the blood sample. The fact that this substance shows as a tail instead of a spot establishes that Dr. Berman's standards were pure.

After having examined all of the available material in this matter, I feel confident in stating that the evidence does establish that Fred Hampton's blood was not normal; that a barbiturate and other foreign substances were present; and that the barbiturate was, in all likelihood, secobarbital. I have seen nothing, including the testimony of Mr. Gormley, which would alter these opinions.

Sincerely,

(*signed*) WALTER M. BOOKER, Ph.D.

WMB:pj

#

Herbert O. Reid
Executive Director
Commission Inquiry
880—3rd Avenue
New York, New York

DEAR DR. REID:

At your further request, Dr. Leo Goldbaum, of the Armed Forces Institute of Pathology and the Howard University College of Medicine, and I have examined the following material:

1. Grand Jury testimony of Dr. Eleanor Berman.
2. Grand Jury testimony of Mr. Leo Gormley.
3. Grand Jury testimony of George Christopoulos.
4. Photograph of Dr. Berman's T.L.C.of January 22, 1970.
5. Letter to H.O. Reid from Dr. Booker, dated February 17, 1971.
6. Letter to H.O. Reid from Dr. Davidow, dated February 18, 1971.
7. Letter to H.O. Reid from Ivan E. Rayner, II, dated February 23, 1971.
8. Letter to H.O. Reid from Dr. Berman, dated February 24, 1971.

9. Letter to H.O. Reid from Dr. Berman, dated February 24, 1971.
10. Letter to H.O. Reid from Dr. Booker, dated March 2, 1971.
11. Letter to H.O. Reid from Dr. Booker, dated March 4, 1971.
12. Pathological Report of Dr. Toman, December 4, 1969.
13. Autopsy Report of Dr. Levine, December 5, 1969.
14. Autopsy Report of Dr. Petty, March 9, 1970.

We consulted on this matter for a period of several hours and arrived at the following conclusions:

1. Dr. Berman's T.L.C. results, as depicted in the photograph, corroborate the initial findings of her ultraviolet test that a foreign substance was in the blood. In our professional opinion, that picture, taken together with the peaks on her Beckman Chart curves, indicates that the foreign substance, an acid compound, in the blood sample C–69 #1 was a barbiturate.

2. Unfortunately, the picture of Dr. Berman's T.L.C. plate is not of the highest quality, thus making it difficult to conclusively establish the precise identity of the barbiturate. However, the height and shape of the second spot on the blood sample C–69 #1 compares favorably with the secobarbital standard and in all probability is secobarbital.

3. The tail which is clearly present in the blood sample C–69 #1 means that another foreign substance was in the blood sample. The fact that this substance shows as a tail instead of a spot establishes that Dr. Berman's standards were pure.

4. After having examined all of the available material in this matter, we feel confident in stating that the evidence does establish that Fred Hampton's blood was not normal. Based on Dr. Berman's T.L.C. picture, coupled with her experience of performing such tests, it is likely that a barbiturate was present; and the strong suggestion is that the barbiturate was secobarbital, although specific staining could have clinched the point.

Sincerely,
(*signed*) WALTER M. BOOKER, Ph.D.

WMB:pj

The Commission's Analysis of the Toxicological Evidence

On December 12, 1969, Dr. Berman tested samples of Fred Hampton's blood taken before the embalming of his body on December 5, 1969, and found that significant amounts of secobarbital were present. Her subsequent tests performed on January 22, 1970, resulted in the same finding.

The federal grand jury, on the basis of the findings of the FBI expert, Joseph Gormley, of Gormley's criticisms of Dr. Berman's work, and of the results of the third autopsy, concluded that Dr. Berman's results were wrong and that the findings of the Cook County coroner's chemist were right.

On the basis of the review conducted by the experts contacted by the Commission, the Commission has concluded that the probative value of the results of Mr. Gormley's tests is questionable. The experts contacted by the Commission specifically noted that the validity of the tests performed by Dr. Berman and by Mr. Gormley would depend, in large measure, on the manner in which the blood was stored between the time it was taken and the time it was tested. Dr. Berman noted that as early as December 12, 1969, the blood samples taken on December 5 had begun to deteriorate. Although she testified that the samples had been refrigerated during the four days between their delivery to her and her initial tests, she could not say how they had been stored prior to delivery, nor did she know how they were stored between December 13, 1969, and January 22, 1970, when she performed a second series of tests. Further deterioration of the blood may account for the decreased amount of secobarbital (3 mg. percent) found in her second, as compared to her first, test.

Mr. Gormley's tests on those same samples were not performed until February 3, 1970. Although Gormley's testimony and the federal grand jury *Report* suggest no lack of certitude about his results, the record is silent as to the conditions under which the samples had been stored—a major factor bearing on the probative value of his test.

The conclusion in the federal grand jury *Report* also rests in large measure on the results of the third autopsy. Those results are based on the testing of samples taken from Hampton's body three months after it was embalmed. It was reported that no trace of barbiturates was found. There is no mention in the autopsy report, as far as the Commission can determine, of any knowledge on the part of those performing the autopsy about the procedures followed by the mortician in preparing Hampton's body for burial. Indeed, the mortician, Ivan Rayner, indicates that the Commission was the only investigative body which asked him how he had prepared the body. Moreover, Mr. Rayner stated that he used large amounts of embalming fluids on

Hampton's remains because of his uncertainty about the length of delay before burial.

Knowledge by the persons conducting the autopsy of the types and amounts of embalming fluid used in the preparation of the body was crucial, in the view of Drs. Booker and Davidow, to the ability to make effective tests and to evaluate those tests appropriately. In the opinion of Drs. Booker and Davidow and of Professor Levine, the dilution and deterioration of the samples caused by the embalming fluids during the three months before the third autopsy might have made impossible a determination of whether barbiturates had been in the body at the time of death. Booker and Davidow noted that the quantities of fluids used in the embalming process would have made the conduct of the tests extremely difficult because the fluids would have seriously complicated the process of extraction by which the presence of barbiturates was determined. In the absence of any reference to these points in the federal grand jury *Report,* and in view of Mr. Rayner's statement that no one other than the Commission had sought any information from him about the embalming, the Commission can assign little or no probative value to the toxicological results of the third autopsy on which the federal grand jury relied so heavily.

At this point, the inquiry turns again to Dr. Berman's tests and criticisms of them made by Mr. Gormley and the federal grand jury. Dr. Berman performed her first tests a week after Hampton's death on blood samples taken prior to embalming and less than twenty-four hours after he died. Dr. Booker indicates that the T.L.C. tests which Dr. Berman used and her methodology "were proper and should have resulted in accurate findings." The results of her second set of tests on the same blood sample were confirmed upon examination of her Beckman Chart and the photograph of her T.L.C. results by Drs. Booker and Goldbaum, as stated in Dr. Booker's letter of March 12, 1971.

Yet the federal grand jury chose to accept the FBI's contrary findings and its criticisms of Dr. Berman's techniques as conclusive. The defects in the FBI's analysis of its own test results are discussed above. Its criticism of Dr. Berman's work is also defective. Mr. Gormley and the federal grand jury chose to center on Dr. Berman's U.V. tests and to ignore the T.L.C. tests, although the results of her T.L.C.

tests were before the grand jury. Mr. Gormley argued that Dr. Berman's U.V. test could not detect the presence of secobarbital. Dr. Berman agrees and stated that the U.V. test was performed only for the purpose of determining whether foreign substances were present in Hampton's blood. The T.L.C. tests performed on December 12, 1969, and January 22, 1970, while deemed appropriate and conclusive by Drs. Booker and Goldbaum, were ignored by Mr. Gormley and the federal grand jury. The latters' silence on that point negates their attempted refutation of Dr. Berman's findings. The federal grand jury's *Report* also contains a confirmation of the findings of the Cook County coroner's chemist's test result on Hampton's blood:

The chemical analysis of Hampton's blood was also done in the coroner's office. It appeared to be a professional and competent job and reached a correct result. [P. 57.]

But the only test said to have been performed by the coroner's chemist was the U.V. test, precisely the test which both Mr. Gormley and Dr. Berman agreed could not detect the presence of secobarbital. There is no indication anywhere in the record that the coroner's chemist went on to conduct the much more specific T.L.C. test which Dr. Berman performed. And according to Dr. Booker both Mr. Gormley's and Dr. Berman's U.V. tests showed the presence in the blood of foreign substances.

Moreover, the Cook County Coroner's Office records contain a document which throws even more doubt on the thoroughness of the procedures employed by that office. On a printed Cook County form entitled "Analysis Sheet," the only analysis requested on Fred Hampton on December 4, 1969, is "alcohol." Not "alcohol and drugs" nor "alcohol and barbiturates"; just "alcohol." Under the blank space left for "conclusions" there are two notations. The first, in bold open script, reads as follows: "Analysis of blood failed to show the presence of alcohol, R.S. 12/8/69." The second, in tight neat print and apparently with a heavier pen, reads: "Analysis of blood failed to show the presence of barbiturate, E.P. 12/8/69." The facts that the request on the analysis sheet sought only an analysis for alcohol, that the first notation dealt only with alcohol, and that the second notation dealing with barbiturates is written in a distinctly different hand raise the question of whether, in fact, any analysis was done to test for barbiturates.

In summary, the Commission is presented with analyses by the FBI and the federal grand jury which failed to deal with issues which were crucial to the conclusions they reached. We also have before us the conclusions reached by Dr. Booker in consultation with Dr. Goldbaum, after examination of the recordation, photographs, charts, and other documentation of Dr. Berman's tests which she maintained had demonstrated the presence of secobarbital in Fred Hampton's blood. After examination of that evidence, Drs. Booker and Goldbaum reached the professional judgment that:

1. Fred Hampton's blood was not normal.
2. The acid compound found in the blood was a barbiturate.
3. The barbiturate in Fred Hampton's blood in all likelihood was secobarbital.

The Commission is hard pressed to make any conclusive finding, based on the scientific evidence available, that Hampton was drugged, although it seems highly probable. The Commission is convinced, however, that the FBI and the federal grand jury rejected Dr. Berman's findings and conclusions on insufficient grounds.

Administration of the Drug: Possibilities

The possibility that Hampton was drugged presents some of the most difficult questions of the entire raid. How did he come to be drugged? Did the police know in advance that he would be drugged? Did they, in fact, arrange the drugging?

There has not been disclosed to the Commission any clue to the manner in which a drug might have been administered to Hampton. This much, however, is clear from interviews with those who knew him: Hampton was not a barbiturate addict, he did not take drugs, and he was known to oppose drug use by others. Thus self-administration of a drug, particularly in as strong a dosage as Dr. Berman reported she found, is highly unlikely. There is no record that barbiturates, prescription slips, or other evidence of drugs were recovered from anywhere in the apartment by the survivors, their attorneys, or investigators employed by them. No such evidence is known to have been recovered by any of the official investigators.

There is uncontroverted evidence—by the admission of police and the State's Attorney's Office—that an FBI informant, and possibly one other informant, had been present in the apartment in the days preceding the raid. Whether this infiltrator might have been instrumental in administering a drug to Hampton on the evening of December 3, or early in the morning of December 4, cannot be determined from the evidence now available to the public and this Commission. The government has resisted all attempts to disclose the identity of the informant or the extent of the informant's activities, and the Commission has no power to compel any such disclosures.

Whether Hampton was drugged, and, if so, how he came to be drugged, may never be known with any degree of certainty. The only investigative authorities that had the power to obtain information that might have answered these questions have declined to do so. The implications compelled by the facts demand an official investigation, yet none is forthcoming. Clearly culpability for this failure to determine the truth lies with the very parties which might be most seriously implicated by the truth, the parties to which our society has entrusted the fair and impartial enforcement of the law.

CHAPTER 7

Conduct of City, County, and State Officials in the Aftermath of the Raid

One of the many controversies arising out of the raid has related to the conduct following the raid of city, county, and state officials charged with the investigation and prevention of crime and the administration of justice. The performance of certain of those individuals has been discussed in a number of contexts throughout this report in connection with specific issues. This chapter will bring together a discussion of certain of those issues along with other matters dealing with the postraid performance of local governmental officials.

The examination centers on the proceedings and actions of (1) the Chicago Police Department, and in particular its Crime Laboratory and Internal Inspections Division,[1] (2) the Cook County Coroner's Office, (3) the Cook County State's Attorney's Office, and (4) the two Cook County grand jury investigations of the raid. In order to keep the several official proceedings in chronological perspective, the following discussion is presented as much as possible in order of actual occurrence.

The Initial Police Action after the Raid

Removal of the Survivors and the Bodies of the Deceased

When the gunfire inside the apartment at 2337 West Monroe Street ended, the seven survivors were taken into police custody: three of them were removed to jail and the remaining four, all seriously wounded, were transported to Cook County Hospital under heavy

1. The Internal Inspections Division (IID) has since been renamed the Internal Affairs Division.

guard. Police also removed the dead bodies of Fred Hampton and Mark Clark. Guards were placed at the apartment to seal the premises.

According to the police testimony before the federal grand jury, their "first priority" after the shooting stopped "was to remove the dead, wounded and those under arrest."[2] Pursuant to Illinois law, however, that priority was misplaced. As discussed in Chapter 5 of this report, Illinois statutory law requires prompt notification of the coroner by any law enforcement official having custody of the body of any person whose death is suspected of having been sudden or violent, and prohibits the moving or removal without the coroner's permission of any such body or the personal property of any such deceased person, "unless the same shall be necessary to protect such body or property from damage or destruction, or unless necessary to protect life, safety, or health."[3] There is no evidence that the failure of the police to comply with the statute was required to protect the body of Hampton or Clark or was otherwise necessary "to protect life, safety, or health."

One obvious purpose of the Illinois law is to assure that the medical examiner arrives at the scene of death as soon after the death as possible, so that he can adequately perform the functions of his office. The police who removed the bodies received their instructions from the State's Attorney's Office, which must be presumed to be familiar with the law. By moving the bodies in the apartment from the locations in which they died, and then removing them from the premises entirely, the police on the scene severely hampered the coroner's ability to perform his duty of determining the immediate and underlying cause of death. The inference is compelling that the State's Attorney's Office simply did not want a contemporaneous on-the-scene investigation by the Coroner's Office.

Search by the State's Attorney's Police

The police who participated in the raid also testified before the federal grand jury that their second priority, after the removal of the survivors and of Clark's and Hampton's bodies, was to "recover all

2. *Report,* p. 36.
3. 31 Ill. Stat. Ann. §§ 10.5–.6; see p. 225, *supra.*

the physical evidence."[4] In fact, the state's attorney's police began their search of the apartment while the occupants of the apartments were being removed by other officers of the Chicago Police Department (who had responded to the radio call for assistance transmitted by the state's attorney's police).[5] The state's attorney's police testified that after beginning their search, they decided that the job of gathering evidence could best be performed by a mobile unit of the police Crime Laboratory (MCLU). However, that testimony was directly contradicted by Police Superintendent James Conlisk, who stated that all evidence collection was performed by the state's attorney's police, who refused to allow the MCLU to participate.[6] In either event, the state's attorney's police collected a number of spent cartridges and other items,[7] including weapons, and transported them, unmarked as to location of recovery,[8] to the State's Attorney's Office.

Search by the Crime Laboratory

Deputy Superintendent of Police Merle Nygren testified that he arrived at the apartment within six or seven minutes after the call of the state's attorney's police for assistance was transmitted over the police radio. Nygren ordered the MCLU to the apartment and instructed a field lieutenant of the Chicago Police Department to post two uniformed police guards each at the front and rear doors of the apartment.[9]

Before the MCLU arrived, a police evidence technician responded to the police radio transmission and reached the apartment, where he was told by an unidentified plainclothes officer that "They shot through the back door and we want a picture of the hole in the back door."[10] He was conducted to the kitchen, where, at the officer's request, he photographed a sheet with a hole in it draped over the back door. He made no further examination of the sheet or of the door

4. *Report,* p. 36.
5. Ibid., p. 42.
6. Ibid., footnote 12.
7. Ibid., p. 48. The total number of items of ballistics evidence collected by the state's attorney's police, exclusive of weapons, was 62.
8. Ibid., pp. 42–43.
9. Ibid., p. 37.
10. Ibid., p. 43.

behind it. Before leaving, but without instructions to do so, he photographed the body of Fred Hampton, which had been dragged out of the rear bedroom into the area between the bedroom and the dining room, and may have photographed the body of Mark Clark, which lay near and slightly behind the living room door at the front of the apartment.[11]

The MCLU arrived at the apartment at about 5:15 A.M. and examined the premises for about ninety to ninety-five minutes. The MCLU supervising sergeant testified later that he had concentrated on finding evidence that shots had been fired at the raiding officers; as evidence of such gunfire, he said, he found one shot through the living room door and two questionable shots in the north bedroom. At the coroner's inquest the sergeant emphatically testified that he saw only one hole in the living room door; later, before the federal grand jury, he stated that "more than one [shot] had gone through it."[12] Neither the evidence technician nor the officers from the MCLU removed the damaged panel in the living room door which contained the gunshot holes. Neither tagged the seized weapons or attempted to preserve fingerprints on them.[13] The MCLU recovered only seven items of ballistics evidence (cartridges, slugs, etc.) on the morning of the raid, although investigators and attorneys representing the survivors subsequently recovered a total of forty-three items of such evidence.[14] Twelve days after the raid, the MCLU recovered an additional eight items of ballistics evidence.

With regard to the initial police search of the premises, the *Report* of the federal grand jury observed:

The joint crime scene search by the three branches of local law enforcement —the State's Attorney's Police, the duty evidence technician from the Task Force and the Mobile Unit from the Crime Lab, was conducted in a crowded

11. The photographer denied photographing the body of Mark Clark, because, he said, it had been removed before he had the opportunity to take such pictures. Sergeant Groth, however, asserted that the photographer *did* photograph the body of Mark Clark, and said he was later informed that the photographs "did not turn out" *(Report,* p. 44).

12. *Report,* p. 69. The two shots in the bedroom were later conceded to be from police fire.

13. Ibid., p. 44.

14. Ibid., p. 48.

situation in a high crime area under considerable pressure to get the job done. However, any crime scene investigation which uncovers barely half of the relevant evidence must be seriously questioned. The explanation for the limited work done by the Crime Lab team is clear. The sergeant in charge agreed that the crime scene investigation was conducted, not to obtain all the available evidence, but, to try to establish the authenticity of the account given by the raiding officers. [P. 48.]

Security of the Apartment

At 7:30 A.M. the police guards who had replaced the officers assigned by Deputy Superintendent Nygren to secure the premises left the scene, allegedly because they were told a radio order had been issued to relieve them. No such order was found on the tapes routinely made by monitoring all police radio communications. The apartment was then left unguarded and unsealed until December 17, 1969, when the coroner said he realized from reading newspaper reports of Panther "tours" through the premises that the apartment was not sealed.

Summary

The initial examination of the premises by the state's attorney's police and MCLU seems to have been conducted primarily to gather evidence that would support the raiding officers' accounts. The police had, contrary to law, removed the bodies of Clark and Hampton from the apartment. They had not tagged the seized weapons as to location where found, nor had they sought to preserve fingerprints. They failed to seal or secure the premises to preserve vital evidence, and they left behind important items of evidence such as the living room door panel. Whether the singularly inadequate efforts of the police to obtain, identify, and preserve evidence was due to gross incompetence or was a deliberate attempt to obscure the truth, they have contributed largely to the confusion and conflict which surround the raid.

Pretrial Publicity and the State's Attorney's Office

Beginning with the many versions of the raid given to the press by participating officers on December 4 and succeeding days, continuing through the dramatic press conferences of State's Attorney Edward Hanrahan in which alleged "seized Panther weapons" were displayed and accounts were given of police bravery under fire, and culminating in the "exclusive" Chicago *Tribune* story and the filmed television re-enactment of the raid, a stream of conflicting accounts emphasizing the courage of the raiding officers and the dangerousness of the Black Panther Party issued from the State's Attorney's Office.

The first stories were brief, dramatic, personal accounts of the incident which, as demonstrated elsewhere in this report, were frequently erroneous. The early statements by the state's attorney were vague accolades of police conduct; on December 8, 1969, State's Attorney Hanrahan stated that "a more detailed statement would be improper in view of criminal charges pending against survivors."[15] Within three days, however, his position had changed dramatically.

On December 11, 1969, Hanrahan unleashed a two-pronged campaign to publicize the "official" version of the incident. A front-page "authorized" exclusive, drawn from the principal police participants, was published in the morning by the Chicago *Tribune*. That same night the local CBS-TV outlet broadcast an "official re-enactment" of the raid, in which the raiding officers depicted their own roles. Both accounts reached large audiences in the Chicago area.

With regard to these productions, the federal grand jury *Report* observed:

Thus, the smoke had hardly cleared before Panther spokesmen claimed murder, and their claims were published. Similarly, the injured policemen made immediate statements to the press at the hospital which were either grossly inaccurate or grossly distorted. The ensuing escalations have been described in the first part of this report and culminated in a television spectacular being acted out by the policemen who did the shooting. While we can understand the State's Attorney's position—that he felt obligated to respond to widely published charges made by Panther spokesmen—the jurors cannot accept this as justifying the extraordinary television show or the exclusive (and in part erroneous) *Chicago Tribune* account. The Grand Jury does not understand how the right to a fair trial can ever be guaranteed when the major prosecution witnesses all give a detailed testimonial re-enactment. [P. 118.]

Thus, while "rejecting" the state's attorney's justification for the publicity, the *Report* states that the grand jurors "understood" his position—a posture of the grand jury which negates its rejection.

15. Ibid., p. 14.

This Commission also rejects the state's attorney's justification, but it expressly declines to dilute that rejection. The Commission finds that the stream of detailed, often erroneous, and always widely publicized, pretrial statements and "official accounts" emanating from the State's Attorney's Office created a hostile public atmosphere, severely damaged the course of subsequent official investigations, stimulated prejudicial speculation in the press and public arena, and very likely precluded the possibility of a fair trial for *any* participants in the incident who might be accused of wrongdoing.

The Internal Inspections Division Investigation

On December 11, 1969, Superintendent of Police James Conlisk announced that the Internal Inspections Division of the Police Department had commenced an investigation of the raid. This investigation was immediately suspended, however, when the jurisdiction of the IID over the state's attorney's police was questioned. Thereafter, at State's Attorney Hanrahan's request, the investigation was reinstated, and Superintendent Conlisk directed a "complete, comprehensive investigation of the facts."[16]

The IID was a division of the Chicago Police Department responsible for investigating allegations of police misconduct. In interviews with citizens of Chicago, including members of the bar, the working press, and prominent businessmen, the Commission found a widespread belief that the IID was so biased in favor of police officers that it offered little or no promise that citizens' complaints against policemen would be impartially investigated and resolved. The Commission found long-standing complaints in the black community that the IID was not responsive or objective in dealing with alleged police misconduct against black citizens. These doubts about the lack of professionalism and impartiality of the IID were hardly allayed when the results of the IID investigation, which exonerated the police, were published on December 19, 1969.

The grand jury *Report* quotes Captain Harry Ervanian, the director of the IID, as having promised that all background information relat-

16. Ibid.; pp. 59–60.

ing to the raid would be reviewed, including "arrest records from the raid, all physical evidence, statements from witnesses, and photographs of the apartment."[17] However, the federal grand jury's inquiry into the IID's handling of the investigation revealed a picture quite contrary to that painted by the IID and the superintendent of police.

Because the IID investigation and proceeding were not open to the public, the Commission, in its discussion of the IID, has of necessity relied on the facts relating to the IID presented in the federal grand jury's *Report*. The *Report* states that, although Captain Ervanian had promised that all background material would be reviewed, the grand jury's examination of IID files, which had been obtained by a subpoena, disclosed

no records of contact with neighborhood residents, no indication of a visit to the premises, no ballistic analysis of the officers' weapons compared to the recovered bullets and empty shells, and no detailed or substantive accounts of the incident by the fourteen individual officers. [P. 60.]

When State's Attorney Hanrahan expressly requested that the IID investigation be conducted, Superintendent Conlisk ordered Deputy Superintendent John Mulchrone to supervise the investigation, as a replacement for Lieutenant Robert Kukowinski, then head of the excessive force unit of IID and the officer who would normally have been in command. Mulchrone selected Chicago Police Sergeant John Meade (a former assistant state's attorney) to "advise him" on the conduct of the investigation. Sergeant Meade prepared a list of questions to be asked of, and answers to be given by, the fourteen policemen who had participated in the raid. These questions were based primarily on Meade's review of the officers' version as presented in the filmed television re-enactment.[18] Sergeant Meade himself testified that he "took the version of the officers as being a truth," and "assumed that everything they said was true." There were no questions that "tended to test the truth and veracity of these officers," and the questions and answers were "designed to spell out the result of the inquiry."[19]

17. Ibid., p. 15.
18. Ibid., p. 62.
19. Ibid., pp. 63–64.

The questions and proposed answers prepared by Sergeant Meade were discussed on December 16 by him and Deputy Superintendent Mulchrone with Assistant State's Attorneys Jalovec, Meltreger, and Sorosky, and with Sergeant Daniel Groth. Groth "examined and altered the questions and answers."[20]

The thirteen state's attorney's police under Groth's command on the night of the raid then conferred privately with the three assistant state's attorneys before the questioning began, and were briefed as to the nature of the questions they would be asked.[21] The procedure of questioning employed by Sergeant Meade was to obtain Sergeant Groth's "agreement" on the proposed questions, and then "to obtain agreement from the other thirteen officers with Sergeant Groth."[22]

The three assistant state's attorneys later represented their role at the questioning as "observers," but the Chicago police officials conducting the investigation believed that the three had been present as attorneys for the fourteen police officers to be questioned. Under questioning before the grand jury, Captain Ervanian, director of the IID, admitted that "this was not a normal nor a complete investigation." He conceded further that the circumstances of the incident had not been developed "with any great degree of accuracy," and that he had failed to carry out his duty as director. The *Report* cites the following exchanges between a grand juror and Captain Ervanian:

Q: Captain, let's be candid—now, with the State's Attorney's office represented at this meeting, and the man who led this raid, or the service of this warrant, and the way the questions were drafted, and the ultimate questions which were actually asked of these officers, Captain, do you think it would be any way unfair for a reasonable person to come to the conclusion that this was nothing but a whitewash?

A: The way you describe it, no, sir. . . .

Q: Again, Captain, do you think it would be unfair or unreasonable for a person to come to the conclusion, even adding the facts of the crime lab report, that this was a whitewash?

A: I would agree, sir, that this was a very bad investigation, yes, sir. . . .

Q: Well, it was extremely bad, wasn't it?

20. Ibid., pp. 62–63.
21. Ibid., p. 63.
22. Ibid., pp. 62–63.

A: Yes, sir.

Q: As a matter of fact, have you seen one as bad as this one?

A. No, sir. [Pp. 65–66.]

Implicated in what Captain Ervanian conceded was a "whitewash" were himself, Superintendent Conlisk, Deputy Superintendent Mulchrone, and Sergeant John Meade of the Chicago Police Department, State's Attorney Hanrahan, and Assistant State's Attorneys Jalovec, Sorosky, and Meltreger, and Sergeant Daniel Groth and the thirteen state's attorney's police under Groth's command on the raid —in short, the hierarchy of the two principal law enforcement agencies in Chicago and Cook County and the actual participants in the raid. Superintendent Conlisk, informed by the grand jury of the unusual mode of questioning employed by Sergeant Meade, said he was "aware that the questions to be asked the officers might have been discussed with the Assistant State's Attorneys." But when told that the proposed answers had also been prepared and discussed with the assistant state's attorney, Conlisk said, "I am flabbergasted to think that such a thing could exist."[23]

The *Report*'s assessment of the investigation conducted by the IID concluded:

The performance of this branch of the Chicago Police Department—the branch dedicated to impartial and objective investigations of police conduct —was so seriously deficient that it suggests purposeful malfeasance. The regular channels of the IID were bypassed. Instead of a complete investigation of any of the factual controversies raging in the press, the investigation consisted only of gathering all police reports, soliciting cooperation from counsel for persons accused of crimes (knowing that no defense counsel would permit pre-trial statements by an accused) and asking the officers involved a few simple conclusory questions in which they denied wrongdoing. No officer was given the opportunity to explain what happened in detail and all the subordinate officers were asked only to ratify their sergeant's account—which itself was based not only on prepared questions, but suggested answers composed by a police department lawyer and shown to the sergeant in advance.

Nor did the IID investigate any potential violations of police department regulations by the officers. For example, the General Order 67–14 relating to the use of deadly force in making an arrest, specifically prohibits the following practices:

23. Ibid., p. 65.

1. Firing into crowds
2. Firing over the heads of crowds except on specific order of a member of the Department above the rank of Captain
3. Firing at a fleeing car except one in which a person who has attempted or committed a forcible felony is riding
4. Firing warning shots in the case of individuals where the use of deadly force is not permitted *(even when deadly force is permitted, warning shots will not be fired when they are likely to injure persons other than those against whom deadly force is authorized)*
5. *Firing into buildings or through doors when the person fired at is not clearly visible.* [Emphasis the grand jury's.]

Even the media accounts available to the IID clearly frame an issue as to whether the police department's own regulations were violated.

Moreover, the publication of the results of this "investigation," in the view of the Grand Jury, was misleading to the general public by inferring that a legitimate investigation was held. The Grand Jury found a more detailed account of the raid in the *Chicago Tribune* than it did in the IID files. . . .

An organization charged with the responsibility of evaluating the conduct of police officers must have public credibility to succeed. The facts in this case show that the IID's performance does not deserve such confidence. [Pp. 122–123.]

The federal grand jury's finding that the IID "whitewash" suggested "purposeful malfeasance" was limited to a criticism of the structure and method of Internal Inspections Division investigations. The *Report* chastised the IID for failing to conduct a complete investigation of the "factual controversies raging in the press," and yet itself ignored one of the most stridently argued of those controversies: whether the police officers had intentionally falsified their accounts of the incident, and whether the State's Attorney's Office and other law enforcement agencies had been accomplices in that falsification. The allegation of such deliberate falsehood should have been at the core of any evaluation of the IID investigation.

The Cook County Coroner's Office

The performance by the Cook County Coroner's Office has been discussed in some detail in Chapters 5 and 6 of this report, and will be reviewed only briefly here. The conclusion of the Coroner's Office based on its examination of Fred Hampton's body can be summarized as follows:

1. Hampton was shot twice in the head. One shot entered in front of the left ear and exited at the right forehead, leaving a large wound; brain tissue was tremendously lacerated. The other shot entered the right side of the neck, below the right ear, and exited at the left side of the throat. No bullet was recovered from either wound.
2. Hampton was shot in the left shoulder. A .30-caliber carbine bullet was recovered in the left pectoral muscle from this wound.
3. The right forearm exhibited a graze wound, no bullet recovered.
4. The stomach was opened by the pathologist, but finding the contents to be fluid he made no analysis of the contents.
5. Cause of death: through-and-through bullet wound of head lacerating brain.
6. Ultraviolet tests on blood samples failed to reveal the presence of barbiturates.

Finding (1) was contradicted and rejected by the private autopsy performed at the request of the Hampton family on December 5, 1969; by the autopsy performed at the request of the federal grand jury on February 16, 1970; and by the report of Dr. David M. Spain, who analyzed the evidence for this Commission. Both the second and third autopsies and Dr. Spain concurred that *both* shots into Hampton's head passed along a trajectory from right to left at a downward angle.

Finding (4) was contradicted and rejected by the third autopsy, which found that the stomach had *not* been opened.

Finding (6) implies without expressly stating that there were no drugs in Hampton's body at the time of his death and during the raid. The Commission's experts and their analyses of the evidence contradict that implication, concluding that Hampton probably was drugged with a barbiturate.

Beyond these contradicted and possibly erroneous findings, other questions have been raised about the conduct of the Cook County Coroner's Office. The autopsy results were initially dictated into a machine. The report ultimately issued had gone through several drafts after it was first written up. The critical original dictabelt, which could have been compared to the final report, was reported to the federal grand jury to have been "lost."[24] The Coroner's Office's toxicological

24. Ibid., p. 120.

analysis appeared in the form of rebuttal to the findings of a private toxicologist, rather than as an objective and rigorous scientific inquiry. The failure to place a coroner's seal on the apartment at 2337 West Monroe Street until twelve days after the raid complicated the investigation and preservation of evidence. And the use of an unlicensed pathologist and pathology assistants to perform highly technical procedures seems likely to have increased substantially the risk of error.

Perhaps the most critical failing of the Coroner's Office was the failure to fulfill the responsibilities delegated to that office to determine "cause of death." The statute under which the medicolegal examination of Mark Clark and Fred Hampton was made[25] requires the examiner to determine, to the extent possible from the available evidence, the cause of death; indeed, the report form used by the Coroner's Office in the present case calls for a description of the "Conditions, if any, which give rise to the above Immediate Cause [of death]." This information was not furnished in the coroner's report, nor has it been furnished since the completion of that report. None of the facilities of the Coroner's Office was employed to examine the available physical and scientific evidence and information to determine who inflicted the fatal wounds, and under what circumstances and conditions, or to consider how these factors might relate to the issue of culpability.

The Coroner's Inquest

After considerable public agitation and pressure, Andrew J. Toman, the Cook County coroner, announced that a special "blue-ribbon" coroner's jury composed of six prominent citizens, black and white, would be constituted to conduct an inquiry into the deaths of Fred Hampton and Mark Clark. On December 30, 1969, the coroner appointed attorney Martin S. Gerber as a special deputy coroner to preside over the inquest. Toman also announced that, because of the existence of contradictory versions of the events of the raid, cross-

25. 31 Ill. Rev. Stat. Ann. § 10.2.

examination would be permitted.[26]

The coroner's inquest was convened by Special Deputy Coroner Gerber on January 6, 1970. On that date, and although the survivors had already announced their refusal to participate, Gerber was quoted as having said: "If there is not a full hearing, only those who refuse to testify will be responsible."[27]

Throughout the course of the public inquiry, Gerber made statements to the press indicating his evaluation of the proceedings and even his speculation as to the ultimate verdict. This latter action led to public criticism of Gerber by the jurors.

On January 18, 1970, Gerber was interviewed on television (WLS-Ch. 7) and suggested what verdict the "blue ribbon" jury would reach. The following day the jurors publicly admonished Gerber for making such statements specifically asking the Special Coroner ". . . not to allow [himself] to be interviewed by television people or other media." Gerber retorted that he was the coroner and the jury should not criticize him. A juror replied that if Gerber allowed himself to be interviewed again, the jury would criticize him again. Gerber, seeking to have the last word, said he would not allow such criticism; a juror replied that Gerber would not stop such criticism. [Pp. 69–70.]

As fifty deputy sheriffs stood guard in the courtroom through twelve days of testimony, the special deputy coroner—as was his privilege—controlled the questioning of witnesses and, when he himself deemed further inquiry unnecessary, simply instructed counsel to stop questioning the witness.[28] Exchanges, often acrimonious, between Gerber and attorneys representing the survivors of the raid were common, and ranged from arguments over procedure—such as refusal to consider the validity of the search warrant—to attacks on the presentation of evidence. All fourteen of the officers who participated in the raid testified. Their testimony, analyzed elsewhere in this Commission's report, was marked by notable internal inconsistency and contradictions of prior accounts they had given.

Testimony was also given by a firearms examiner from the Chicago police Crime Laboratory. The testimony of this ballistics expert, who stated that two shotgun shells recovered from the apartment had been

26. Chicago *Tribune,* December 31, 1969.
27. *Chicago Sun-Times,* January 6, 1970.
28. *Report,* pp. 68, 70.

fired from a weapon identified as belonging to Brenda Harris, was contradicted by the report of the FBI Crime Laboratory. The expert subsequently admitted that the shells had been fired from a police weapon in the possession of Officer Ciszewski.[29] Neither the ballistics expert hired by attorneys for the survivors nor the pathologist or toxicologist retained by the Hampton family was asked to testify.

On January 22, 1970, the coroner's jury returned a verdict of justifiable homicide, "based solely and exclusively on the evidence presented."[30]

The federal grand jury found that "it is questionable whether the continuation of the [coroner's] inquest system is in the best interests of justice":

The office of the Coroner, in Illinois as in other states, is a combination of archaic and statutory functions. The office is presently required by law. This investigation established reasonable grounds to question whether the continuation of that office is desirable.

The inquest function is archaic in origin and of doubtful relevancy. The findings of a Coroner's jury as to cause of death are immaterial; they neither prevent nor require prosecutions. [P. 120.]

The Commission concurs with that finding of the federal grand jury. The Commission also finds, however, that the proceedings in this inquest raise serious questions about the inquest's objectivity and impartiality. The presentation of evidence was limited almost entirely to police officers and technicians who later proved to have given substantial erroneous testimony. The control of the proceedings vested in the special deputy coroner was exercised to curtail examination of police witnesses. The inquest based its verdict on incomplete and one-sided evidence[31] although evidence adverse to the police was readily available even without the participation of the survivors. In short, despite weaknesses in the system, an inquest that might have

29. This finding by the FBI Crime Laboratory will be discussed more fully in the following section.

30. *Chicago Today,* January 22, 1970.

31. The federal grand jury later rationalized that this result was inevitable in light of the survivors' refusal to testify, and appropriated this same excuse after failing to bring in any federal indictments.

helped determine the facts was misused, and instead contributed to confusing the issues.

The Police Crime Laboratory

As has been noted above, ballistics evidence relating to the raid was collected for the police both by the state's attorney's police and the mobile unit of the Crime Laboratory. All of that evidence, irrespective of who retrieved it, was ultimately submitted to the Crime Laboratory for examination. Of all the evidence analyzed by the crime lab, only the relatively few items actually recovered by the MCLU officers were marked as to location of recovery; no attempt had been made to preserve fingerprints on any items, and none was observable;[32] and the seized weapons were displayed at the state's attorney's press conference before submission to the crime lab. In addition, the police weapons carried on the raid were not submitted to the crime lab for examination or testing.

In view of the defects in the evidence examined by the crime lab, it is not surprising that the analysis submitted by the lab's ballistics expert, John Sadunas, was contradicted by later investigations. Most seriously, the crime lab expert misclassified two shells fired from Officer Ciszewski's weapon as having been fired in a gun allegedly held by Brenda Harris. The federal grand jury *Report* detailed several other types of errors in the crime lab report.[33]

In explaining why he had filed such an error-filled report, on the basis of which he had testified before both the coroner's inquest and the county grand jury which indicted the survivors, Sadunas explained that to have refused would have cost him his job.[34] He indicated that if such insufficient and poorly handled evidence had come from the Chicago Police Department, he would have refused to make even an examination, much less a report; as a result of daily pressure from the State's Attorney's Office, however, and of fear of being discharged if he failed to cooperate, Sadunas performed a concededly

32. *Report,* p. 88.
33. Ibid., p. 89.
34. Ibid.

inadequate analysis of the evidence made available to him (which did not include all of the police weapons), and signed reports which he himself admitted were unsatisfactory and "preliminary in nature," although not so indicated.[35] As the *Report* of the federal grand jury observed:

> While any firearms examiner can be excused a mistake—even one with serious consequences—there was more involved here. Not only did the State's Attorney's Police fail to turn in their weapons for testing, the Crime Laboratory did not even request them to do so until after a mistaken report was prepared and indictments based on it and after this Grand Jury investigation was initiated. *Had the Crime Lab refused to conduct an analysis of any recovered bullets and casings without having all the weapons present in the apartment, there is every possibility that the mistake would never have occurred and been submitted as fact to the Cook County Grand Jury.*
>
> In short, the Crime Lab was responsible, in part at least, for a totally inadequate search and a grossly insufficient analysis. The testimony of the firearms examiner that he could not have refused to sign what he believed was an inadequate and preliminary report on pain of potential discharge is highly alarming. If true, it could undermine public confidence in all scientific analysis performed by this agency. [P. 121; emphasis added.]

If Sadunas's allegations are true that pressures were imposed upon him by the State's Attorney's Office to produce an erroneous report based on inadequate and incomplete evidence (and the conduct of the State's Attorney's Office throughout the history of the raid provides no reason to disbelieve those allegations), the result may be more serious than to "undermine public confidence" in the crime lab's investigation; it suggests to this Commission a deliberate attempt by the State's Attorney's Office to add credence to the official version of the raid. The overall performance of the Chicago police Crime Laboratory in this case indicates that from the beginning it followed the direction of the State's Attorney's Office, and rather than seek evidence impartially and professionally, it sought to recover and present only that evidence which would corroborate the official account of the raid.

35. Ibid.

The Indictment of the Panthers by the Cook County Grand Jury

On January 30, 1970, a Cook County grand jury indicted the seven survivors on a total of thirty-one counts, ranging from attempt to commit murder to unlawful possession of firearms. The indictments, according to the federal grand jury *Report,* were based in part on (1) the police crime lab firearms report, and (2) the same police testimony as that given at the coroner's inquest, and were therefore based at least in part on erroneous scientific evidence and contradictory police testimony. As set out in pages 71 and 72 of the *Report,* the indictments were as follows:

Brenda Harris
1. Attempt to commit murder
2. Armed violence
3. Possession of firearms or firearm ammunition without having in their possession a firearm owner's identification card

Verlina Brewer
1. Attempt to commit murder
2. Armed violence
3. Aggravated battery on Ciszewski
4. Unlawful use of weapons
5. Possession of firearms or firearm ammunition without having in their possession a firearm owner's identification card
6. Unlawful possession of firearms and firearm ammunition (being under age 18)

Blair Anderson
1. Attempt to commit murder
2. Armed violence
3. Aggravated battery on Ciszewski
4. Unlawful use of weapons
5. Possession of firearms or firearm ammunition without having in their possession a firearm owner's identification card
6. Theft of a shotgun
7. Unlawful possession of firearms

and firearm ammunition (under age 21 and convicted of a misdemeanor)

Ronald Satchel

1. Attempt to commit murder
2. Armed violence
3. Aggravated battery on Ciszewski
4. Unlawful use of weapons
5. Possession of firearms or firearm ammunition without having in their possession a firearm owner's identification card
6. Unlawful possession of firearms and firearm ammunition (under age 21 and convicted of a misdemeanor)

Harold Bell

1. Attempt to commit murder
2. Armed violence

Deborah Johnson

1. Attempt to commit murder
2. Armed violence
3. Possession of firearms or firearm ammunition without having in their possession a firearm owner's identification card

Louis Truelock

1. Attempt to commit murder
2. Armed violence
3. Possession of firearms or firearm ammunition without having in their possession a firearm owner's identification card
4. Possession of firearms and firearm ammunition (within 5 years of release from penitentiary after a felony conviction)

On February 11, 1970, the defendants pleaded not guilty to all charges. Attorneys for the survivors filed motions to compel disclosure of all information about informants, police infiltration, and surveillance relating to the raid, on the grounds that the defense could not properly prepare its case as long as one of the survivors might be collaborating with the prosecution and police agencies. The court ordered the state to reply to the motion.

In the meantime, pursuant to a federal court order, agents of the federal grand jury informed the Cook County State's Attorney's Office of the FBI's ballistics findings: the two shotgun shells identified by the police crime lab as having been fired by the "Brenda Harris gun" had in fact been fired by Officer Ciszewski's weapon, and the FBI could confirm only one shot as having been fired at police by the occupants of the apartment. Because the survivors had been indicted on evidence which the FBI and the federal jury knew to be erroneous, representatives of the federal grand jury were authorized to request of the State's Attorney's Office that the prosecutions be re-evaluated in the interests of justice.[36] The State's Attorney's Office thereupon requested that the police crime lab technician re-examine the questioned evidence; he confirmed that he had been in error.[37] With the federal grand jury's request to dismiss the indictment still pending, State's Attorney Hanrahan asked that the seven officers principally involved in the raid be allowed to testify before the federal grand jury. Hanrahan stated that he had re-interviewed each of the seven officers, and, although the federal grand jury had advised the officers that they should "reconsider their testimony in light of the analyses of physical evidence,"[38] he believed in the truth of their statements.

After the officers testified before the federal grand jury, Hanrahan stated that he would "re-examine" the facts if the federal grand jury persisted in its request that the state indictments be dismissed. He requested and received copies of the police officers' testimony before the federal grand jury.[39]

On May 8, 1970, only one week before the federal grand jury released its *Report,* and shortly before the state was due to reply to the defendants' motions to compel disclosure of evidence of informants and other forms of surveillance, the state's attorney appeared in Cook County Court and obtained dismissal of all charges against the survivors.

The dismissal of these indictments raises serious questions about the propriety of the state's attorney's conduct in gaining the indictments, and about the relationship between the local and federal

36. Ibid., p. 114.
37. Ibid.
38. Ibid., p. 90.
39. Ibid., p. 114.

prosecutorial machineries. First, if the disclosure by the FBI that two recovered shotgun shells allegedly fired from a gun held by Brenda Harris had been misidentified collapsed the entire state case against all the survivors, the indictments must have been founded on the narrowest possible evidentiary base. Second, it is most difficult to understand how the misclassification of those shells could have affected the prosecution of several defendants upon charges of, for example, unlawful possession of firearms or theft of a shotgun. Third, the sequence of events suggests that the dismissal may have been prompted by the approaching reply date on the defendants' disclosure motion and/or the imminent release of the federal grand jury's *Report*. The inference is strong that the risk posed by the defendants' motion to disclose the names of any informants, and other evidence of surveillance, was perceived as a potential threat to the state (and perhaps federal) explanations of the incident, and thus, at least in part, occasioned the dismissals; that the dismissals were the product of federal pressure on the local prosecutor; and that the occurrence of the dismissals only one week before release of the federal grand jury *Report* was more than coincidental.

The Indictment and Trial of the Officials: The Special County Grand Jury

Amid increasing agitation in Chicago's black community over the failure of the federal grand jury and all the local official investigations to bring criminal charges against law enforcement officials for their conduct related to the raid, black leaders and several civil rights and attorneys' organizations demanded the convening of a special county grand jury to investigate official conduct. Public endorsement of this proposal grew, accompanied by the request that an independent special prosecutor be appointed to direct any such grand jury investigation.

On June 27, 1970, Chief Judge Joseph A. Power of the Cook County Criminal Court ordered the convening of a special county grand jury to investigate matters relating to the raid, and appointed Barnabas F. Sears, a prominent Chicago attorney, as special state's attorney to direct the investigation. Sears assembled a staff of four attorneys to assist him: Wayland Cedarquist, Howard Savage, Ellis Reid, and James Collins. From July through early December 1970, Sears and his staff worked over the evidence in the case, including the proceedings of previous investigations, and on December 8, 1970, a special grand jury was convened to hear the evidence.

The special county grand jury sought the testimony of the occupants of the apartment who had survived the raid. The occupants, fearing that no previous official investigation could be fair or impartial, had previously refused to testify before any official investigations of the raid; but on January 18, 1971, two of the survivors—Verlina Brewer and Blair Anderson—testified before this special county grand jury.

On January 21, 1971, the staff director of this Commission, in response to a subpoena, turned over to the special county grand jury copies of the sworn statements given to the Commission in October 1970 by Ronald Satchel, Deborah Johnson, and Harold Bell. These three survivors had refused to testify before the special county grand jury. The remaining two survivors—Brenda Harris and Louis Truelock—later testified. Thus the special county grand jury obtained statements, either in oral testimony or in the form of the statements given to the Commission, from all seven survivors.

On January 18, 1971, the Chicago *Sun-Times* reported that "police and several prosecutors who were involved in the case have hired lawyers," in response to letters inviting them to testify. On January 19, 1971, the Chicago press reported that Captain Harry Ervanian, director of the police Internal Inspections Divison at the time of the IID investigation of the raid, was called to appear.

On April 21, 1971, rumors began to circulate that the grand jury had voted on that day to indict fourteen Chicago officials, including State's Attorney Edward Hanrahan, for obstruction of justice, and that Police Superintendent James Conlisk had been named as an unindicted coconspirator. In the next three days these rumors increased and were reported widely in the Chicago area press. According to the newspaper accounts, the special county grand jury had deadlocked short of the affirmative votes required to return an indictment on charges related to police conduct in the raid itself, but had voted to indict the officials for their conduct following the raid.

On the following day, April 22, Chief Judge Power held a closed conference in his court with Special State's Attorney Sears, Sears's staff, and the twenty-three members of the grand jury. According to reports in the press, Judge Power ordered the grand jury to hear testimony from Hanrahan and certain other witnesses who had testified before the federal grand jury but had not been called to appear before the special county grand jury. He further ordered that the grand jury not deliberate on any indictment until all these witnesses had been heard. Following this meeting, Sears publicly criticized Judge Power for "exceeding his authority," and asserted the independence of the grand jury. The controversy grew when the Chicago *Sun-Times* on April 25, and national news sources shortly thereafter, published a detailed account of the rumored indictments.

On the following day, in open court, Judge Power—who just ten months earlier had appointed Sears as a special state's attorney—berated Sears in front of the grand jury and a crowded courtroom for refusing to call as witnesses all those persons who had previously appeared before the federal grand jury. Sears agreed to hear testimony from State's Attorney Hanrahan, but refused to subpoena the federal grand jury witnesses; he argued that neither a judge nor a prosecutor could order a grand jury to hear any witness, for only the grand jury could determine whom it would hear. Judge Power then cited Sears for contempt of court, and ordered a fine of fifty dollars per hour levied against Sears until such time as he would agree to hear all of the witnesses noted by Judge Power. In addition, Sears was fined one hundred dollars for his public criticism of the judge on April 22.

At this same court session on April 26, 1971, John P. Coghlan, an attorney representing Police Sergeant John P. Meade, one of the subjects of the rumored indictments, filed a petition charging that the special county grand jury had been prejudiced by press publicity of the "indictment" controversy, and requesting that Power take action to protect the interests of his client. Coghlan was later joined in his petition by Thomas P. Sullivan, representing twelve of the fourteen raiding policemen, and George J. Cotsirilos, representing three assistant state's attorneys on Hanrahan's staff. In addition, Sullivan and Cotsirilos filed petitions asking Power to investigate whether Sears had improperly pressured the grand jury into returning indictments.

On May 5, 1971, Coghlan, Sullivan, and Cotsirilos filed petitions requesting Judge Power to inquire into the proceedings of the special county grand jury. The petitions alleged that Sears had "contaminated" the grand jury by oratory demanding indictments, and that the grand jurors had been biased by news coverage. They requested that Power talk in private with each grand juror to determine (1) whether Sears did exhort and plead for indictments and (2) whether publicity had rendered any juror incapable of duty, in order to determine whether the grand jury should be discharged and any indictments voted by it be kept secret.

The arguments on the motions of the attorneys for the police and the assistant state's attorneys were originally scheduled to be heard on May 10, 1971, but that session was canceled when Judge Power learned that Robert E. Gilmartin, a member of the special county grand jury, was present in the courtroom. Judge Power ordered Sears to invite all the members of the grand jury to the argument, and rescheduled the return date for the following day. On May 11, 1971, in the presence of the grand jury, the three attorneys for the police and the assistant state's attorneys argued that Judge Power should question the grand jurors in private to determine whether any of them, as a result of newspaper reports of indictments or pressure by Sears, had been unduly prejudiced against possible defendants. Sears, in turn, argued that the plaintiffs had no standing in the case, and that no one, including a judge, had authority to interfere with a grand jury.

On May 20, 1971, the Illinois Supreme Court agreed to consider certain of the issues raised by the growing dispute between Special State's Attorney Sears and Chief Judge Power. In a brief order, the court allowed Sears to file a petition to prevent Judge Power from intervening in the grand jury proceeding. Sears also petitioned to the court for an order staying Judge Power's order that Sears deliver to him a copy of the transcript of the special county grand jury. While the court did not grant Sears's request for an immediate stay of Judge Power's order, it did agree to hear arguments as to whether Power had the authority to see the transcript and to interview grand jury members individually and in private. Sears's petition was joined by six Chicago area legal organizations, including the Chicago Bar Association.

One month later, on June 23, 1971, the State Supreme Court ruled that Judge Power had the right to examine a transcript of the grand jury proceedings. It also ruled that he had the right to interview the grand jurors as a group—but not individually—behind closed doors. The court reversed, however, the two contempt citations levied against Sears in April.

A sudden turn of events came on June 25, 1971, when the special county grand jury, in open court, presented a sealed indictment to Judge Power. Sears stated that the jurors had met and voted to "reaffirm" an April vote which Judge Power had refused to accept (after which vote Power had ordered the grand jury to hear additional witnesses). Judge Power immediately ordered the indictment to remain sealed, and suppressed it. Under authority granted him by the two-day-old State Supreme Court decision, Power said, he was ruling that any and all indictments would be suppressed until he examined the transcript of the grand jury proceedings and met with the grand jury to investigate charges that the jurors had been unduly pressured. He then set August 5 for further hearing on motions seeking to block publication of the indictments and to discharge the grand jury.

On August 5, Judge Power appointed Mitchell Ware, director of the Illinois Bureau of Investigation, to investigate the allegation that Sears had acted improperly with respect to the grand jury's voting of true bills. Ware resigned from his official post to assume the responsibility for investigating Sears's conduct.

Special State's Attorney Sears then filed a petition on August 13 requesting the Illinois Supreme Court to order Judge Power to make public the suppressed indictments. He also asked that Ware's appointment be voided, and that the court delay hearings on alleged misconduct by the special state's attorney's staff. The following day the chief justice of the Illinois Supreme Court, Robert C. Underwood, ordered that hearings on Sears's conduct be postponed indefinitely, and said that the full Supreme Court would consider the petitions seeking publication of the indictments and rescinding the appointment of Ware.

On August 23 State's Attorney Edward Hanrahan filed a petition requesting the Supreme Court to order that the indictment be kept secret indefinitely on the ground that it was unconstitutional.

On August 24, 1971, the debate and legal struggle and speculation over the indictments were suddenly ended. The seven-man Illinois Supreme Court met secretly, in emergency session. The unanimous opinion of the court, expressed in the written opinion of Judge Walter V. Schaefer, was that "the interests of justice would best be served by opening the indictment and proceeding pursuant to the law." The Supreme Court ordered that the indictment be opened and made public, and that Ware's appointment be revoked.

The suddenness of the ruling took the parties, the news media, and the public by surprise. On the afternoon of August 24 a packed courtroom saw Judge Power open the sealed indictment and read it, pursuant to the Supreme Court's ruling. The indictment, which he had suppressed for two months, charged fourteen Chicago law enforcement officials with "knowingly and wilfully, fraudulently and deceitfully conspir[ing] combin[ing], confederat[ing] and agree[ing]" to obstruct justice. Indicted were:

Edward V. Hanrahan, Cook County State's Attorney;
Richard Jalovec, Assistant State's Attorney;
John Mulchrone, Deputy Police Chief of Traffic and former Deputy Superintendent of Police;
John P. Meade, Police Sergeant and member of the IID;
John M. Sadunas, Patrolman Specialist, Crime Lab;
Charles Koludrovic, Patrolman Specialist, Crime Lab;

and eight of the fourteen policemen who conducted the raid of December 4, 1969:

Sergeant Daniel Groth;
Patrolman Raymond Broderick;
Patrolman Edward Carmody;
Patrolman John Ciszewski;
Patrolman William Corbett;
Patrolman James B. Davis;
Patrolman Joseph Gorman;
Patrolman George Jones.

Named as coconspirators, but not indicted, were:

> James B. Conlisk, Superintendent of Police;
> Harry Ervanian, Police Captain and former director of the IID;
> Earl A. Holt, Police Crime Lab firearms expert;
> James Meltreger, Assistant State's Attorney;
> Sheldon Sorosky, Assistant State's Attorney.

A portion of the indictment, which listed twenty-one overt acts, follows:

. . . from on or about December 4, 1969, and continuously thereafter, up to and including the filing of this indictment . . . [the 14] defendants herein, committed the offense of conspiracy, in that they did knowingly and wilfully, fraudulently and deceitfully conspire, combine, confederate and agree together and with each other, together with Harry Ervanian, Earl Holt, James Meltreger, Sheldon Sorosky and James B. Conlisk, Jr., named as co-conspirators but not as defendants herein, and with others to the Grand Jury unknown, to commit an offense to wit, obstructing justice, in that, with the intent to obstruct a criminal prosecution of Daniel Groth, Raymond Broderick, Edward Carmody, John Ciszewski, William Corbett, James Davis, Joseph Gorman and George Jones, with respect to their acts and conduct in the execution of a search warrant on December 4, 1969 at 2337 West Monroe Street, Chicago, Illinois, and to obstruct the defense to criminal charges then pending against Blair Anderson, Harold Bell, Verlina Brewer, Brenda Harris, Deborah Johnson, Ronald Satchel and Louis Truelock, with respect to their acts and conduct at the said time and place of the execution of said search warrant, by unlawfully, wilfully and knowingly destroying, altering, concealing and disguising physical evidence, by planting false evidence and by furnishing false information, and pursuant to said conspiracy, they did, among divers other acts and conduct, commit the following overt acts, to wit:

1. On December 4, 1969, Daniel Groth, Raymond Broderick, Edward Carmody, John Ciszewski, William Corbett, James Davis, Joseph Gorman and others, conducted a search of the first floor apartment at 2337 West Monroe Street, Chicago, Illinois, and collected certain weapons that were seized in said search, but did not tag them in order to specify the location where they were discovered, nor process them for fingerprints in order to determine who had handled them prior to their seizure, and they further caused said weapons to be taken to the State's Attorney's office for public display rather than to be processed by the Chicago Police Department Crime Laboratory as possible evidence of an alleged crime;

2. Immediately following the aforesaid events on December 4, 1969, a Mo-

bile Crime Laboratory team of the Chicago Police Department, consisting of Charles Koludrovic, Earl A. Holt, and others, were summoned by Assistant Deputy Superintendent Merle A. Nygren to go to, and they did go to, 2337 West Monroe Street, Chicago, Illinois to perform their duties, which were to photograph the scene, as they found it, draw a rough sketch thereof, search for and recover whatever evidence was available, mark said evidence and transport said evidence to the Chicago Police Department Crime Laboratory and make a report thereof. In executing these duties, said team intentionally focused on identifying shots allegedly fired at said police officers who conducted the said search, and said team knowingly conducted a totally inadequate and improper examination of the said scene, designed solely to establish the version of the officers who conducted said search, and said team further knowingly failed to search for and recover numerous material and relevant items of evidence relating to the events which occurred at the time and place aforesaid, which numerous relevant and material items of evidence were later recovered by others, including the Federal Bureau of Investigation. . . .

5. On or about December 11, 1969, and December 16, 1969, Richard Jalovec and Daniel Groth withheld from agents of the Internal Inspections Division of the Chicago Police Department written statements given by each of the State's Attorney's Police Officers concerning his participation in the events of December 4, 1969 at 2337 West Monroe Street, Chicago, Illinois. . . .

7. On December 10, 1969, in Chicago, Illinois, Edward V. Hanrahan, Richard Jalovec, Daniel Groth, Raymond Broderick, Edward Carmody, John Ciszewski, William Corbett, James Davis, Joseph Gorman, and George Jones gave false and misleading information concerning the events that occurred at 2337 West Monroe Street, Chicago, Illinois to the Chicago Tribune, which resulted in an exclusive article printed on December 11, 1969 by said Paper exclusively, which article was false and misleading;

8. On December 11, 1969, Edward V. Hanrahan and Richard Jalovec directed and arranged for, and Daniel Groth, Raymond Broderick, Edward Carmody, John Ciszewski, William Corbett, James Davis, Joseph Gorman, Robert Hughes and George Jones prepared and acted out for showing on local television an alleged re-enactment of the events that occurred on December 4, 1969 at 2337 West Monroe Street, Chicago, Illinois, which re-enactment was false and misleading and was shown on television that evening on Channel 2 in the City of Chicago. . . .

10. On or about December 16, 1969, John P. Meade and John Mulchrone, at 1121 South State Street, Chicago, Illinois, prepared a list of questions

and suggested answers which were to be shown to Sgt. Daniel Groth, which questions were conclusionary in nature and designed to elicit exculpatory answers and which answers were exculpatory and which questions and answers were designed to and did prevent a full disclosure of the true events occurring at 2337 West Monroe Street, Chicago, Illinois on December 4, 1969;

11. On December 16, 1969, John Mulchrone, John P. Meade, Richard Jalovec, Sheldon Sorosky, James Meltreger, Harry Ervanian, and Daniel Groth met at 1121 South State Street, Chicago, Illinois and discussed the aforesaid questions and answers prepared by Meade and Mulchrone, agreed to same, and then had said questions and answers read before a court reporter, as if they were an extemporaneous statement given by Groth, which was not the fact, and which Sgt. Groth thereafter signed;

12. Thereafter, also on December 16, 1969, at 1121 South State Street, Chicago, Illinois, John Mulchrone, John P. Meade, Richard Jalovec, Sheldon Sorosky, James Meltreger, Harry Ervanian and Daniel Groth further agreed to draft and use a uniform format for statements to be taken from the other State's Attorney's police officers involved in the December 4, 1969 incident, in which format said other State's Attorney's police officers were asked to affirm the Groth statement which contained reference to matters of which they had no knowledge;

13. Thereafter, also on December 16, 1969, Richard Jalovec, Sheldon Sorosky and James Meltreger counseled and advised the aforesaid other State's Attorney's police officers of each question they were to be asked and advised them to so do, and each officer knowing the question he would be asked before he was examined gave a statement;

14. On December 17, 1969, John Sadunas issued a Chicago Police Department Crime Laboratory report which included a positive identification of two shot shells allegedly fired from a 12-gauge shot gun by an occupant of 2337 West Monroe Street, Chicago, Illinois, on December 4, 1969, which identification he knew, or should have known, to be false, inaccurate and not based upon an adequate firearms examination;

15. On December 17, 1969, in Chicago, Illinois, John Mulchrone prepared or caused to be prepared a false and misleading statement for release to the Press concerning the events occurring at 2337 West Monroe Street, Chicago, Illinois, on December 4, 1969;

16. On December 19, 1969, John Mulchrone improperly and prematurely terminated the Internal Investigations Division investigation then being conducted by the Chicago Police Department into the conduct of certain police officers on December 4, 1969 at 2337 West Monroe Street, Chicago, Illinois;

17. Between January 6, 1970 and January 21, 1970, Raymond Broderick,

Edward Carmody, John Ciszewski, William Corbett, James Davis, Joseph Gorman, Daniel Groth and George Jones falsely testified before the Special Deputy Coroner of Cook County at an inquest into the deaths of Fred Hampton and Mark Clark, regarding shots that were allegedly fired at them by occupants of the first floor apartment at 2337 West Monroe Street, Chicago, Illinois;

18. Between January 8, 1970 and January 28, 1970, Daniel Groth, James Davis, George Jones, Joseph Gorman, Edward Carmody and John Ciszewski falsely testified before the January 1970 Cook County Grand Jury regarding shots allegedly fired at them by occupants of the first floor apartment at 2337 West Monroe Street, Chicago, Illinois;

19. On or about January 8, 1970, Edward V. Hanrahan caused to be presented before a Cook County Grand Jury evidence which he knew, or reasonably should have known, to be false and inflammatory in order to procure the indictment of Blair Anderson, Harold Bell, Verlina Brewer, Brenda Harris, Deborah Johnson, Ronald Satchel and Louis Truelock, on erroneous and unprovable charges;

20. On January 20, 1970, John Sadunas testified before the Special Deputy Coroner of Cook County, Illinois, at an inquest into the deaths of Mark Clark and Fred Hampton with respect to his positive identification of the two shot shells aforesaid, which testimony he knew, or should have known, to be false, inaccurate and not based upon an adequate firearms examination;

21. On or about January 20, 1970, John Sadunas had a long conversation with Thomas A. Hett, an Assistant State's Attorney of Cook County, Illinois, as a result of which he knowingly and wrongfully permitted his said December 17, 1969 report, which included a false identification of said two shot shells, to be used in evidence in a State Grand Jury proceeding then pending against the said persons against whom the said criminal charges were then pending, when he knew, or should have known, that his positive identification of the said two shot shells was false, inaccurate and not based upon an adequate firearms examination. . . .

Despite the excitement generated by the release of the indictments, attention began to focus on another aspect of the proceedings. Judge Joseph A. Power was being asked by many people to "step out of the case."[40] Indeed, Sears petitioned the Illinois Supreme Court to appoint a judge in the case from downstate Illinois, on the theory that all Chicago judges, whether Democrats or Republicans, would be somehow allied with Mayor Daley, and would therefore be prejudiced in

40. See, e.g., statement by Milton H. Gray, president of the Chicago Bar Association, quoted in *Chicago Today*, August 25, 1971.

favor of Hanrahan, who was a Democrat and close political ally of Daley.[41]

On August 31, 1971, the scheduled argument for the appointment of a new judge was somewhat deflated when Judge Power removed himself from the case and assigned it to Cook County Criminal Court Judge Philip Romiti, a Democrat who had served as dean of the DePaul University Law School. The day after the appointment of Judge Romiti, Illinois Supreme Court Justice Walter V. Schaefer denied the petition to assign a circuit court judge from outside Cook County to hear the case.[42]

Simultaneously with Judge Power's assignment of the case to Judge Romiti, he revealed to the public additional data about the activities of the special county grand jury, saying that the jury had refused to indict seven policemen with voluntary or involuntary manslaughter, and had declined to indict Hanrahan for official misconduct.

Hanrahan and the thirteen other defendants named in the indictment refused to enter pleas at their arraignment on August 31, and instead moved that the indictment be quashed. As part of the defendants' case attacking the indictment, Hanrahan introduced the signed statement of Mrs. Clara Goucher, one of the grand jurors.[43] Sears then moved to bar the further questioning of the jurors, but on September 2, 1971, Judge Romiti denied this emergency motion, relying on prior statements by Judge Power which permitted the jurors to talk with defense counsel. Also on September 2, Judge Power performed his last official act in the case, formally dismissing the grand jury. In connection with the dismissal he stated "that the jurors were not allowed to disclose private deliberations when they voted whether to indict, but were free to discuss the rest of the jury proceeding with the attorneys for the defense and prosecution."[44]

The defense attorneys obtained affidavits from various grand jurors stating that Sears and his staff had exercised excessive influence over their deliberations. Sears denied these charges, and to further counter the affidavits, he stated that "We [the prosecution] have no objection

41. Chicago *Sun-Times,* September 2, 1971.
42. Chicago *Daily News,* September 1, 1971.
43. Chicago *Sun-Times,* September 2, 1971.
44. Chicago *Tribune,* September 3, 1971.

whatsoever to their [the defense] request that the grand jury proceedings be made available as a part of the court record."[45] Since the defense attorneys had previously requested that these transcripts be made an official part of the court record, they would have found it difficult to object to their introduction. Sears also filed two motions asking that the affidavits of the grand jurors be stricken from consideration in the case and that the defense attorneys halt their "inquisition" of the grand jurors.[46]

After a month of continuing controversy, Judge Romiti ordered on October 23, 1971, that a "full and open court hearing" be given to the charges of Sears's improper conduct.[47]

Sears responded to Judge Romiti's order by moving that Romiti reverse himself and cancel the public hearings.[48] Sears's motion papers cited twelve errors by Romiti, and Sears orally added three others, "centering on the secrecy of the grand jury."[49] Romiti chastised Sears for making the motion without notice, adding that he had learned from newspapers and other news media that Sears was to appear before him.[50] On November 1, 1971, Romiti ruled that there was ample evidence to warrant hearings into Sears's conduct, and refused to reverse himself.

Sears once again appealed to the Illinois Supreme Court, arguing that the hearings scheduled by Judge Romiti would violate the secrecy of the grand jury. On November 5, 1971, just a few days before the hearings were scheduled to begin, Supreme Court Justice Daniel P. Ward ordered that the hearings be postponed until all the justices of the Illinois Supreme Court could consider the issues. On November 11, 1971, the Illinois Supreme Court agreed to hold a full hearing on the matter on November 24.

On November 19, 1971, Sears moved that Judge Romiti postpone all hearings related to the proceeding of the special county grand jury until the Illinois Supreme Court had held its hearings on November 24. Judge Romiti denied this motion, arguing that the Supreme Court

45. Chicago *Sun-Times,* September 21, 1971.
46. Ibid.
47. Ibid., October 23, 1971.
48. Chicago *Daily News,* October 28, 1971.
49. Ibid.
50. Ibid.

had agreed that he could hold hearings on November 29 on charges that Sears and his staff had pressured the grand jury into obtaining an indictment.[51] On December 17 the Illinois Supreme Court issued an order preventing Judge Romiti from holding a hearing into charges that the grand jury had been pressured by Sears. The court held that any undue publicity in the controversial case was caused, at least in part, by Hanrahan himself, and therefore could not be a basis for a dismissal of the indictments.

Although the Illinois Supreme Court had ruled on part of the controversy, certain legal questions raised by the defendants remained. Judge Romiti, who was reviewing these questions, could have quashed the indictments if he agreed with any of the five contentions of the defendants. The contentions, as summarized in an article in the Chicago *Sun-Times* on December 12, 1971, were as follows:

1. The indictments fail to accuse the raiding policemen of any crime in the killings of Hampton and Clark. Thus, the defendants argue, since there was no crime to be prosecuted, the defendants cannot be guilty of obstructing the prosecution of any crime. Their argument is basically, "Obstruction of the prosecution of WHAT?"
2. If the indictments for obstructing the prosecutions for the killings are dropped, the indictments for obstructing the defense of the seven survivors cannot remain.
3. The relevant statute of limitations expired before the return of the conspiracy indictment.
4. The defendants' rights were violated by presentation of federal testimony to the County Grand Jury.
5. There was undue delay from the date of the purported offense to the date of the return of the indictment.

On Monday, January 3, 1972, Judge Romiti announced that he would make a decision on the motions on January 7.[52] Hanrahan blocked this deadline, however, by filing a motion asking the Illinois Supreme Court to reconsider its decision of December 17, 1971.[53]

Judge Romiti finally ruled on the defendants' motions on February

51. Ibid., November 19, 1971. The article stated, however, that unnamed court sources had said that Judge Romiti would not begin hearings until the Supreme Court had disposed of the appeals.
52. Chicago *Sun-Times*, January 3, 1971.
53. *New York Times*, January 8, 1972.

2, 1972. In his decision he concluded that the indictments were valid, although he also said he thought the language of the indictments left "much to be desired"[54] in not stating a specific offense. Judge Romiti's decision exhausted the remedies of the defendants in the state courts, leaving an appeal to the United States Supreme Court as the only remaining challenge to the indictments. The defense lawyers were not immediately in agreement as to whether such an appeal should be made.[55]

Meanwhile, in an apparent effort to hinder the activities of Sears, payments for expenditures and time spent by him and his staff after March 31, 1971, were suspended. Prior to that time, Sears and his staff had been obtaining payment for their fees and expenses by submitting bills to Judge Power. Judge Power had then sent these bills to the Cook County Board, which paid them out of the county's general funds.[56] These payments ceased in April 1971. According to the *Chicago Journalism Review,* "The cessation of payments to Sears's staff coincided with the angry exchanges between the special prosecutor and Judge Power, when it became known that the grand jury had voted to indict Hanrahan for conspiracy to obstruct justice...."[57] The same article noted that while Judge Power, until March, had been ordering immediate payment of bills upon their submission, the March bill, which was submitted in April, was not ordered paid until May 14, 1971.

As of the end of October 1971, Sears admitted to having spent $7,000 out of his own pocket on the case, adding that "no one seems to care" whether he and his staff were paid.[58] As of October 26, 1971, Judge Power had refused to authorize pay vouchers totaling more than $100,000 due Sears and his four-member staff.[59]

On July 10, 1972, the state court proceeding finally went to trial before Judge Romiti, sitting without a jury. On July 25, during the presentation of the prosecution's case, the trial was abruptly inter-

54. Ibid., February 3, 1972.
55. Ibid.
56. *Chicago Journalism Review* (October 1971).
57. Ibid.
58. *Chicago Today,* October 26, 1971.
59. Ibid.

rupted when Sears announced to the court that he was submitting to the defense copies of four documents which had been discovered on the preceding Saturday by his assistant counsel, Mr. Cedarquist. Three of the documents appeared to be transcripts of tape-recorded interviews conducted several weeks after the raid with Blair Anderson, Harold Bell, and Brenda Harris. The fourth document appeared to be a copy of a forty-page transcript of an interview on December 22, 1969, between Donald Stang, a young lawyer, and Louis Truelock, to which was attached a diagram of the apartment at 2337 West Monroe Street. Each page of the transcript had apparently been signed and dated by Truelock, and an affidavit signed by Truelock had been attached, dated January 28, 1970, stating that he had read the attached transcript, that it was "complete and accurate," and that it had been read in his presence by two subscribing witnesses, Thomas A. Nolan and James Latturner. The affidavit had been notarized by Donald Stang.

The prosecution's production of the four documents created an uproar. The defendants claimed that the documents demonstrated that the Panthers had lied in their testimony to the special county grand jury about what had transpired during the raid, corroborated police accounts of the raid, and showed that the police action during the raid was justified. The prosecution responded that the documents had little relevance to the issues at trial—the defendants' conduct subsequent to the raid—but that they had been introduced in the interest of justice, in recognition of the duty of the prosecution to protect the rights of the accused as well as those of the People.

The prosecution and the defense agreed that a *voir dire* examination should be conducted to determine the authenticity of the documents. The *voir dire* lasted for seven days and produced extensive testimony relating to the circumstances under which the four statements might have been taken and their subsequent discovery by Cedarquist. The following account is a summary of pertinent portions of the proceeding.

Francis E. Andrew, a young attorney in a law office which represented the Black Panther Party of Illinois at the time of the raid, testified that he remembered having interviewed three or four of the survivors at a private home at some unspecified time after the raid, but, with the exception of Deborah Johnson, could not recall who they were. He recalled having tape-recorded the interviews and having given the tapes to someone at his law office with the request that they be transcribed. He disclaimed ever having seen the tapes or transcripts of the tapes thereafter until the *voir dire* hearing, and could not identify the statements in issue as transcripts of his interviews. Andrew did, however, have "one general recollection" about the interviews, which was that "no Panther had fired a weapon."

Andrew also recollected having seen a document "in the same form" as the transcript of the Truelock interview, which Truelock had signed in his presence in January 1970. He did not recall if he had ever read the document or if he had asked Mr. Stang, an attorney affiliated with his law office, to take the statement from Truelock, nor could he state that the affidavit produced by Sears was in fact a copy of the document he had seen.

Andrew testified that at the time of the interviews he was "formally representing" Truelock, but that he also consulted with other survivors who were clients "of sorts." He did not testify as to his reason for taping the interviews with the survivors, although he indicated that as far as he could recall he had not, either before or after the interviews in question, recorded interviews with other clients. With respect to the Truelock statement, Andrew testified that he had had Truelock sign an affidavit and had had the statement witnessed:

> Because Louis Truelock, when I interviewed him, without going into the details of it, since he is my client or was my client, seemed to contradict the general impression I had, from what else I knew about the case, and as a lawyer I wanted some statement which he said was true preserved to protect myself.

Andrew stated that he had not thought at the time Truelock's statement was witnessed about the fact that a witnessed statement could not be protected from disclosure under the attorney-client privilege, but realized it now.

Thomas Nolan, one of the witnesses to the Truelock affidavit, testified that at 11 P.M. on some date after December 4, 1969, Andrew had asked him to come to Andrew's law offices, where Nolan was introduced to Donald Stang and to a Mr. Truelock and witnessed the affidavit in question. He stated that he had read the statement to which the affidavit related before signing the affidavit, and was present when Truelock signed the affidavit, but that he had not seen Truelock himself read the statement. Nolan did not recall anyone else signing the affidavit. He stated that Andrew was present when both he and Truelock signed. He could not identify the statement in court as being the same document which he had read, but testified that to the best of his recollection the two documents seemed to be the same in substance.

James Earl Latturner, the second witness to the Truelock affidavit, testified that he had been at Andrew's law office on an unrelated matter late one evening during December 1969 or January 1970, and while there had been asked by Donald Stang if he would read and later witness a document. Latturner read the document, and a short time later was introduced by Stang to Louis Truelock, who signed the affidavit in Latturner's presence, after which Latturner witnessed it. Latturner could not identify the document shown him in court, other than the affidavit, as one which he had seen before. He also stated that he had not seen Andrew at any time during the evening.

Donald Stang was subpoenaed as a witness at the *voir dire,* but refused to answer any questions about the Truelock document on the grounds of attorney-client privilege, despite the court's ruling that the privilege did not apply to an attorney in the capacity of an attesting witness and that the privilege had in any event been lost by virtue of the fact that the statement had not been kept confidential.

Although Truelock did not testify at the *voir dire,* in his subsequent examination during the trial he testified that he had given the statement on December 22, 1969, to Andrew, his attorney, and did not recall whether Stang was present or not. He acknowledged that the signature on the January 28 affidavit was his, but said that when Andrew asked him to sign the affidavit he did not read the statement but "just thumbed through it and signed it."

With respect to the interview between Andrew and Deborah Johnson, Andrew testified that he had a vague recollection that he had given some documents to her attorney, James Montgomery. When served with a subpoena to produce any such documents before the *voir dire* hearing, Montgomery testified that he had a copy of the transcript of the interview between Andrew and Johnson but that he refused to release it on the grounds of attorney-client privilege. He also testified that at some time between December 4 and December 21, 1969, the date on which the interview apparently took place, he had, because he was involved in other matters, asked Andrew to take a statement from Johnson, and had received the statement some time in 1970. Montgomery further testified that he had never read the statement, and thus could not know whether it conflicted with Johnson's testimony earlier in the Hanrahan trial.

Most of the testimony about the circumstances under which the statements were discovered by Cedarquist was given by Flint Taylor, a recently graduated law student who had worked, as part of a legal clinic course, with Jonathan Hyman, an attorney at the Northwestern University Legal Aid office. According to Taylor, Hyman had gone to New York for the weekend of July 21, 1972, leaving Taylor the keys to the legal clinic and file cabinet and telling him that Cedarquist was going to come over "and look at some photographic evidence and other things that he had previously looked at." While Cedarquist was looking through the files at the legal clinic that Saturday, Taylor heard him say, referring to some papers, "I have never seen these before." Later in the day Cedarquist and Sears called Taylor, and Sears asked to see the documents. Taylor called Hyman in New York, who instructed him not to reopen the files, and Taylor relayed that instruction to Cedarquist. The next day Taylor received a telephone call from Andrew, asking him to meet Andrew and Sears at the legal clinic that afternoon, where the file was reopened and Sears read the documents, which Taylor gathered purported to be statements of some of the survivors of the raid. That evening Taylor met with Hyman, who had returned from New York, and who directed him to take the statements to Cedarquist's office to be Xeroxed.

Jonathan Hyman testified that he had received certain documents relating to the raid from Andrew after Hyman was retained as co-counsel in a number of civil rights actions on behalf of the survivors which were then pending in federal court. On Sunday evening, July 23, 1972, he spoke to Andrew, who agreed that certain documents should be taken to Cedarquist. Hyman stated that it was his understanding that the statements which he authorized Taylor to deliver to

Cedarquist came from the documents he had received from Andrew, though he also testified that he was unaware of their nature other than that they were supposed to be statements by certain unidentified clients of his. Hyman did not recall whether he had ever seen the statements before his appearance at the *voir dire* hearing, except for the first two pages of Brenda Harris's statement, which he had read "out of curiosity."

Following the close of the *voir dire* proceeding, the defense filed a motion for an order of acquittal, arguing that the statements showed that the indictment was based on perjured testimony and that they corroborated in material detail the defendants' account of the events of the raid. The prosecution responded by asserting that the circumstances of the raid had little to do with the subject matter of the indictment and that in any event the statements did not corroborate the defendants' story. The defendants' motion was denied, and the prosecution resumed presentation of its case.

At the close of the prosecution's case, the defense moved for acquittal, and on October 25, 1972, Judge Romiti granted the motion. The text of his ruling is as follows:

This court might normally be inclined to rule on this motion without comment. However, as has been pointed out so many times during the course of this trial—and by both sides—this is a most unusual case. Perhaps, then, this court might be permitted a few comments and observations to put this case in perspective.

This court is aware, painfully so, that this is one of those "you're damned if you do and damned if you don't" cases. The only question is which way is one going to be damned. It is a case which has been charged with a great deal of public interest and polarized feelings and opinions.

It has been a case, regretfully, which has created its own self-charging catalytic climate—not because of the nature of the offense, but because of the person or persons involved. In another time with other persons, I dare say this case would not have generated one line of print.

I must confess, human nature being what it is, that there exists the temptation to take what might appear to be a course of least resistance. However, being mindful of the strictures and duties of judges, to do so in this case would be an abrogation by this court of its duties.

Judicial cannons provide: ". . . a judge . . . should be unswayed by partisan interests, public clamor, or fear of criticism." In short, this court has a duty to all charged with crimes—whatever their position or status—to be certain that all rights are protected and that those charged individuals, whoever they may be and whatever the climate or sentiment of the times, be treated fairly and equally under the law. To do anything less than that in this case would be judicially improper and intellectually dishonest as well.

In considering the great mass of detailed, painstaking, oft repeated, frequently conflicting, sometimes confusing testimony of the events occurring in the early morning hours of December 4, 1969, it is easy to lose sight of the real issue.

It is not the issue before this court to determine precisely who fired which weapon, how many times and from what physical part of the apartment. The gut and only issue is whether there was a conspiracy by the defendants, or any of them, to obstruct justice: either by conspiring to obstruct the criminal prosecution of certain police officers and-or a conspiracy to obstruct the defenses of those occupants who were charged with crimes, either or both in manner and form charged in the indictment.

It is not, therefore, the purpose of this trial, nor is it the function of this court to attempt to assess or evaluate the work and conduct of the involved officers, nor to offer any critique thereon.

For four full days the court was on the receiving end of a great volume of rhetoric, oratory, some histrionics and emotional appeals—much of what was said was nothing more than a reiteration of what the court had already heard and to which it had been exposed during some 14 plus weeks of trial, with each side, indeed, each attorney, attaching his own nuances, connotations, and interpretations upon that testimony.

It is, of course, axiomatic, and is especially pointed up in a case such as this, that arguments of counsel are not evidence and are not to be considered by the court as evidence. The only evidence the court may properly consider is that which comes from the witnesses, together with whatever physical evidence [exhibits] may have been admitted in the trial.

The court must also note a difference between inferences about which so much has been said, and speculation and conjecture with which this case is so replete.

Further, it is true reasonable inferences may be drawn from proven facts. However, an inference drawn from another inference which in turn is drawn from an inference—inferences pyramiding inferences—amount to not much more than conjecture and speculation.

In the light of the foregoing, the court found it necessary to engage in an evidenciary striptease, so to speak, to strip away the layers of rhetoric, of oratory, the emotional appeals, the speculation and conjecture—in its search for some basic, hard evidence tending to prove the charges in the indictment.

After a thorough review and careful analysis and consideration of the totality of the evidence, including the testimony given by defendants before the various bodies before which they appeared; and also noting and considering, among other matters, the grave discrepancies and conflicts in testimony and the differing opinions, expert and nonexpert—all viewed in the context of the entire posture of the prosecution's case, and in a light most favorable to the prosecution—this court can only conclude and does conclude that that evidence is simply not sufficient to establish or prove any conspiracy against any defendant.

The court can only conclude and find, and does so conclude and find, that the prosecution has simply failed to prove the conspiracies, or either of them, as charged in this indictment.

The court, therefore, has no alternative but to allow the motion—and the court has no alternative but to find, and hereby does find, each defendant not guilty of the conspiracies, or either of them, as charged in Indictment No. 71-1781. A judgment of acquittal is entered as to each defendant and each defendant is discharged.

The operative language of the ruling was, simply, that the evidence was "not sufficient to establish any conspiracy against any defendant." The Commission, which has not analyzed the full transcript of the trial, cannot properly comment on whether such a conclusion was justified. It is, however, significant to note that the ruling fails to deal with any specifics whatever. It recites, instead, that Judge Romiti was involved in a "you're damned if you do and you're damned if you don't" case, and that the only question was which way he was going to be damned. Such a statement demonstrates a total lack of understanding of the judge's role: to decide the facts based on the testimony presented and to apply the law to those facts. In many cases the truth is hard to find; this case is one of them. But the judge's job is to determine the facts, without regard to the feelings that the litigants may have toward him. Clearly what would have been helpful here was a thorough review of the evidence rather than a mere conclusion that the evidence was insufficient.

Although the trial related only to postraid events, Hanrahan, in a press conference held moments after the trial ended, contended that his acquittal demonstrated the accuracy of the official accounts of the raid:

At the trial every Black Panther occupant of the apartment and every person who made wild charges during the press orgy following December 4,

1969, had an opportunity to come into court and prove those charges. When those charges were subjected to cross examination at the trial they were proved false and the truth was finally established.

Unfortunately, neither the trial nor any other official action has answered the basic questions concerning the raid.

CHAPTER 8

Federal Law
and the Administration of Justice

The Federal Grand Jury's Report

This Commission, in announcing its own establishment on December 15, 1969, requested that the Civil Rights Division of the Department of Justice immediately undertake an urgent investigation of incidents between the Black Panthers and law enforcement officials "in order to determine whether prosecutable violations of the civil rights of American citizens have occurred in any of them; and, if such violations have occurred, that it institute criminal prosecutions forthwith." In response to many such requests from varied sources, Attorney General John Mitchell on December 19, 1969, appointed Assistant Attorney General Jerris Leonard as special assistant to the attorney general to collect all the facts related to the raid and to present them to a special grand jury in Chicago.[1]

Normal procedure provides that a special assistant to the attorney general travels to the district in which the investigation he will conduct is to take place, is sworn in, and files his letter of appointment with the clerk of the district court. Letters of appointment are usually made public when filed with the clerk of court and specify the particular statutes into the violations of which the grand jury intends to inquire. In this case, however, the Justice Department insisted on secrecy, and the letter of appointment as well as other matters relating to this grand jury were sealed.

Because courts alone possess authority to summon grand juries,

---

1. Under authority of 28 U.S.C. §515.

special assistants request the impaneling of special grand juries, which are selected under procedures designed to ensure random selection and a representative cross-section of the community.[2] Once called and impaneled, grand juries (of sixteen to twenty-three persons) sit at the request of the United States attorney subject to the call of the court.

Historically, the purpose of grand juries has been to stand as a buffer between citizens and the government prosecutorial system. They are not part of the executive branch, but rather stand independently. As the Supreme Court explained in 1962, the grand jury

has been regarded as a primary security to the innocent against hasty, malicious and oppressive persecution; it serves the invaluable function in our society of standing between the accuser and the accused, whether the latter be an individual, minority group or other, to determine whether a charge is founded upon reason or was dictated by an intimidating power or by malice and personal ill will.[3]

Grand juries may commence their own investigation or they may judge the sufficiency of evidence which government attorneys gather and present to them. The limited extent of the grand jury's ability to conduct an independent investigation, however, is underscored by the fact that grand juries have no investigative machinery or personnel of their own: no legal experts, no investigators, no stenographers, no clerks. Their only "staff" consists of a foreman and a deputy foreman appointed by the convening court from among the jurors, and a secretary designated from among the jurors by the foreman, who keeps a record of the witnesses who appear and the number of grand jurors concurring in the jury's findings.[4] Having no power of their own to subpoena witnesses or to compel testimony, grand juries draw on the court's power for these purposes and are subject to the court's discretion in exercising that power. Whether a grand jury considers only the evidence presented by the government or conducts its own investigation within the scope of its independent authority, its ultimate function is to determine whether probable cause exists to believe that a crime has been committed. If probable cause is found, a grand

2. Jury Selection Act of 1968, 28 U.S.C. §§1861–74, *et. seq.*
3. *Wood* v. *Georgia,* 370 U.S. 375, 390 (1962).
4. Fed. R. Crim. P. 6(c).

jury returns an indictment. If probable cause is not found, it returns a "no bill" or "ignoramus."

The federal grand jury in Chicago which investigated the raid, instead of making a finding of probable cause or no probable cause and returning an indictment or no bill, chose to issue a report. This procedure was of dubious legality.[5] Senator McClellan, a senior member of the Senate Judiciary Committee, stated:

I doubt the legality of that report. I doubt they had the authority to do it. . . .
. . . I question whether they had the authority to do it. There is a conflict between practice and authority in this area.[6]

Courts also have been critical of grand jury reporting. In *Application of UEW,*[7] the court expunged a grand jury report and stated that once the grand jury had determined the evidence was insufficient to return an indictment, it could not then proceed to issue a report based upon information obtained in the course of its secret inquiry. Similarly, the court expunged the Ohio State grand jury *Report* on the Kent State University shootings because "In rendering . . . written findings in its *Report* the special grand jury takes over the duty of a petit jury, acts as a trying body and determines guilt."[8]

Since the grand jury *Report* has possibly been the most influential force in molding public opinion about the raid, and since the aura of conclusiveness surrounding the *Report* has resulted in widespread acceptance of the federal grand jury's findings, even among some who participated in the initial public outcry, this Commission considers it pertinent to ask whether, in fact, the federal grand jury resolved or even adequately addressed the major controversies presented by the

5. See R. H. Kuh, "The Grand Jury 'Presentment': Foul Blow or Fair Play?," 55 *Columbia Law Review,* 1103 (1955).
6. U.S., Congress, House, Committee of the Judiciary, Subcommittee 5, Hearings on S. 30, 91st Cong., 2d Sess., 1970, p. 121. One consequence of the federal grand jury's *Report* in this case was Senator McClellan's sponsorship of Title I of the Organized Crime Control Act of 1970, which permits special grand juries, under limited circumstances, to file reports. See 18 U.S.C. §§3331–34.
7. 111 F. Supp. 858, 864–65 (S.D.N.Y. 1953).
8. *Hammond* v. *Brown,* 323 F. Supp. 326, 342 (N.D. Ohio) *aff'd.,* 450 F. 2d 480 (6th Cir. 1971); *see also Ruiz* v. *Delgado,* 359 F. 2d 718 (1st Cir. 1966); *People* v. *McCabe,* 148 Misc. 330, 266 N.Y.S. 363 (Sup. Ct. Queens Cty. 1933).

raid. In attempting to answer those questions the Commission is hampered by the procedures followed by the grand jury. Ordinarily when an expert is called to testify, the factual hypotheses upon which his conclusions are based are explicitly stated so that it is possible to examine the soundness of the expert's reasoning and scientific methodology in assessing the persuasiveness of his conclusions. Since the *Report* did not reveal the full testimony of the experts before the grand jury, the public can judge only the grand jury's characterizations of what the experts said.

A similar problem arises with respect to the grand jury's treatment of eyewitness testimony. The *Report* refers to the Panther testimony at the People's Inquest on March 8, 1970, as "incomplete" and as "not subject to cross-examination and under no binding testimonial oath" —criticisms which are entirely valid—and summarily dismisses the Panthers' statements. In contrast, the *Report* relied heavily on the testimony of the officers, but summarized and excerpted it, ignoring inconsistencies in preparing a "most consistent version."[9] As a result of this technique, which the Commission considers highly objectionable, readers of the *Report* are not told of the inconsistencies among statements by individual officers on different occasions but are left, instead, with a composite and a mass of footnotes referring to a secret grand jury transcript which is inaccessible to the public.

The *Report*'s discussion of the cause of Fred Hampton's death is mostly a response to an independent (second) autopsy, which found that Hampton had been drugged at the time of the raid, that he had been shot from above and slightly behind, and that a bullet had been removed from his skull by the Coroner's Office. Those findings were

9. "These seven officers [Sgt. Groth and Officers Davis, Gorman, Jones, Carmody, Ciszewski and Broderick] had testified at the Coroner's Inquest; some had testified before the State Grand Jury; several testified that their testimony before this Grand Jury was *substantially the same* as that on other previous recitals. *Some discrepancies between the accounts given on different occasions were noted.* The Grand Jury has attempted to resolve the various discrepancies, taking into account the darkness and unfamiliarity of the officers with the premises. There are no absolute resolutions of all the officers' statements, because they were not in clear communication with each other throughout the action. *However, the most consistent version of their various recitals, as construed by the Grand Jury, is set forth below*" (p. 90; emphasis added).

According to the *Report*, the filmed re-enactment was essentially "the same" as the *Tribune* story; the grand jury testimony was "the same" as the coroner's inquest testimony.

inconsistent in several material respects with the first autopsy, conducted by the Cook County Coroner's Office. To "resolve the controversy" between the first and second autopsies, the federal grand jury commissioned a third autopsy. Although the findings of the third autopsy are characterized in a manner that implies that the findings of the second autopsy were rebutted, many of the discrepancies between the first and second autopsies can in fact be resolved in accordance with the findings of the second autopsy. But the *Report* criticizes the errors in the second autopsy while excusing the errors in the first autopsy. Moreover, after the rebuttal the *Report* never proceeds to attempt to explain the cause and agent of Hampton's death.

Similarly, the *Report* contains a rebuttal of a private ballistics expert's conclusion that police fired the first shot, without establishing who did fire first.

The special federal grand jury states that it "has sincerely endeavored to exhaust every reasonable means of inquiry to ascertain the facts of this case" and that its *Report* is "a full and factual report on the evidence it has heard so that the entire public will be made aware of the situation."[10] In the judgment of this Commission, however, many significant factual questions have not been answered, and controversies over important aspects of the raid have not been resolved. Indeed, if the Commission's own report does nothing else, it will hopefully raise and focus attention on some of the difficult and often unpleasant questions which the grand jury's *Report* ignored or pretended were answered.

This Commission is constrained to comment on the tone of the grand jury *Report* vis-à-vis the Black Panther Party. Panthers are described as "stridently militant," "violence oriented," almost obsessed with "firearms and military discipline," "philosophically oriented towards Asian communism," and as "violence-prone revolutionaries with a particular hostility for police."[11] Rather than concede that the legal system has often worked unfairly to the disadvantage of blacks rather than impartially for justice, the *Report* condemns the survivors for their refusal to participate in the investigation and concludes that the Panthers don't want the legal system to work:

10. *Report,* p. 126.
11. Ibid., pp. 3, 124, 4, 3, 12.

Given the political nature of the Panthers, the Grand Jury is forced to conclude that they are more interested in the issue of police persecution than they are in obtaining justice. It is a sad fact of our society that such groups can transform such issues into donations, sympathy and membership, without *ever submitting to impartial fact finding by anyone.* Perhaps the short answer is that revolutionary groups simply do not want the legal system to work. [P. 126; emphasis in original.]

All too much emotionalism, rhetoric, and recrimination had already been generated by the Chicago incident. Such political commentary by the grand jury could serve only further to polarize the community and to detract from an urgently needed reassertion of impartial and evenhanded administration of justice. Yet the *Report* urges that "in judging the facts of this case . . . the reader should keep the proper perspective"[12]—the reader should think of the police as having been on a legitimate and proper mission (although the legitimacy and propriety of the raid are both questionable), and should balance any police misconduct against the obvious danger of the Panthers. The *Report* refers to the Panther attorneys and the independent experts whose analysis they sought as "Panther agents."[13] The testimony of Mr. MacDonell, the ballistics expert retained by the Panthers, is characterized as follows:

While some of his contributions were significant, the expert's testimony revealed his defense orientation, perhaps accentuated by the limited time he had, and the briefings of counsel. [P. 51.]

Such comments, when juxtaposed with the grand jury's effort to construct a "most consistent police version," increase the chances for undercutting respect for the processes of law by some segments of the community.

Finally, while conceding that the survivors had a valid Fifth Amendment right to remain silent, the grand jury harshly criticized them for their silence and suggested that Panther Party officials might be indicted for the failure of the survivors to cooperate in the investigation.

The Grand Jury believes that the action of [the survivors] is without legal justification and is nothing more than political posturing to publicize the

12. Ibid., p. 125.
13. Ibid., p. 111.

Panthers' position on juries. Unquestionably, the Grand Jury could obtain a court order requiring the survivors to testify. The enforcement of such order could thus accord the Panther leaders the martyrdom they seek for the seven survivors. However, the interests of law enforcement would not be served by such action. The purpose of this investigation is to gather facts and make legal evaluations of them; the time for playing games is over. The Grand Jury will not permit itself to be used as an instrument of publicity and recruiting by the Panthers. Moreover, in the final analysis, there is no way to compel the survivors' testimony since they continue to have a valid Fifth Amendment claim to assert at any time.

The public should know, however, that the Panthers who were so outraged at the time of the incident, publishing daily claims of mistreatment and murder and demanding one investigation after another, have now withheld their cooperation from the only investigative body with authority to do anything.

In addition, the Grand Jury recommends that the conduct of Mr. Rush in formulating and announcing the Panther policy against cooperation, should be carefully evaluated by a subsequent Grand Jury to determine if it violates federal laws prohibiting obstruction of justice. Particular attention should be given the means used by Mr. Rush to secure compliance with his directions. [P. 105.]

The job of the grand jury was to determine whether violations of law had occurred and to vote indictments if it found sufficient cause. Its *Report*, critical of everybody but most particularly the Panthers, has had the effect—very possibly a politically intended effect—of leaving the impression that the only crimes committed were by the Panthers, and that, even if the police were overzealous, the Panthers deserved it. It is appalling enough that although people had been killed—or perhaps more accurately murdered—the grand jury was merely investigating denials of civil rights. For that grand jury then to conclude in effect that the victims deserved their fate, and not to indict any of the perpetrators, does little except to give credit to the Panthers' foresight in being unwilling to participate in the grand jury's investigation.

The Commission's Conclusions on Federal Law

The Commission cannot and should not reach a conclusion as to ultimate legal culpability. It is not the Commission's function to "find" whether or not the officials concerned were innocent or guilty of criminal misconduct. Such a determination of innocence or guilt should be made only after a proper adversary trial before judge and jury, where those accused would have full opportunity to confront their accusers and defend their actions. However, the Commission has not felt itself under the same constraint in adjudging the issue of whether sufficient cause exists for charges of criminal misconduct to have been brought and to be resolved in such a trial.

Under our Constitution, responsibility for initiating and pursuing criminal charges rests primarily with the states. Being governments of reserved and general powers, they have the major criminal jurisdiction as a function of the "police power" or the "general welfare power." The State of Illinois in this case has a broad range of statutory crimes for which it might have considered prosecuting either the Panther survivors or the police—crimes ranging from murder to other degrees of homicide to lesser offenses.

In contrast, the criminal jurisdiction of the federal government is relatively narrow. As a government of limited express powers, its criminal jurisdiction is restricted to functions "necessary and proper" to execute the explicit powers granted to it. One of those areas is the field of civil rights—an area where historically state machinery has often broken down. The vehicle has been the various Civil Rights Statutes: 18 U.S.C. §§241 and 242, and the Civil Rights Act of 1968 (18 U.S.C. §245).

Additional areas of federal criminal jurisdiction may also be relevant here. Whenever a witness before a federal grand jury knowingly gives false and misleading testimony, he may be prosecuted by the federal government for violation of his testimonial oath. Likewise, obstruction of justice in the federal machinery is cognizable by federal law.

It is in this context that the Chicago federal grand jury faced its task, limited to considerations of federal law.

In the introduction to the *Report,* the grand jury states that it was called "to determine if there had been a violation of the civil rights of the apartment occupants.[14] In its conclusions, the grand jury re-states the issue.

14. Ibid., pp. 1–2.

The question here is whether the facts establish probable cause to believe that the officers involved intentionally committed acts which deprived the occupants of federally protected rights, contrary to law. [P. 113.]

The Commission does not agree with the conclusion on that issue reached by the grand jury.

The physical evidence and the discrepancies in the officers' accounts are insufficient to establish probable cause to charge the officers with a willful violation of the occupants' civil rights. [P. 113.]

The *Report*'s conclusion also refers to the crime of perjury— a crime which it was not at all clear the grand jury was investigating. Again the Commission cannot accept the grand jury's conclusion.

The Grand Jury also is not persuaded from the evidence available to it that the officers are intentionally falsifying their stories. Accordingly, the Grand Jury is unable to determine that there is probable cause to believe there has been a violation of the testimonial oaths taken by these witnesses. The Grand Jury knows of no additional line of investigation which might develop the missing facts. [P. 113.]

The grand jury *Report* is not persuasive as to why the grand jury failed to return indictments, or as to how it concluded that there was no probable cause to believe that federal law had been violated.

In a final summarizing conclusion the *Report* states: "The most concise conclusion is that, in this case, it is impossible to determine if there is probable cause to believe an individual's civil rights have been violated without testimony and cooperation of that person."[15] This is, indeed, an extraordinary doctrine. It seems to say that there can be no determination of whether a crime may have been committed, despite substantial relevant extrinsic evidence, without the cooperation of the purported victims. It is even more extraordinary if considered in relation to the possible violation of the civil rights of the deceased, Mark Clark and Fred Hampton. It is hardly reasonable or humane to suggest that an investigation should be conducted into possible assaults and batteries on the survivors which would exclude

15. Ibid., p. 126.

and ignore the circumstances in which the lives of the deceased were taken.

Thus, to suggest the first premise, that this was an inquiry into possible violations of the civil rights only of the survivors, and then the second, that the survivors did not testify, in order to conclude that the grand jury could not establish possible violations of the civil rights of the survivors, was to ignore the two deaths entirely. Such reasoning on the part of the authors of the grand jury *Report* would imply that all previous civil rights prosecutions where death had resulted and the victim was, therefore, not present to testify, were in error—obviously an absurd result. If the deaths of Hampton and Clark were indeed a matter of concern to the grand jury and the public, then the assistance or nonassistance of the survivors would, as is usually the case in criminal prosecutions, be immaterial.

The physical and other evidence to which the federal grand jury was privy was more than sufficient, without the need for survivors' collaboration, to pose the issue: Was there probable cause to believe that the civil rights of the deceased and surviving Panthers had been abridged within the scope and meaning of the federal statutes?

The Civil Rights Statutes

The early Civil Rights Statutes, first enacted in Reconstruction days and presently contained in Sections 241 and 242 of Title 18 of the United States Code 22[16] make it a crime for two or more persons to

conspire to injure, oppress, threaten or intimidate any citizen in the free exercise or enjoyment of any right or privilege secured to him by the Constitution or laws of the United States, or because of his having so exercised the same . . . [Section 241]

or for any person under color of law "willfully" to subject any inhabitant of any state to

16. The grand jury *Report* also cited Section 245 of Title 18, the Civil Rights Act of 1968, when framing the issue for its inquiry. But that section, which aimed at violations of a number of enumerated rights, such as voting, campaigning as a candidate, serving on a federal jury, or participating in federal programs, would be applicable to the Chicago raid only if rather strained theories were used.

the deprivation of any rights, privileges or immunities secured or protected by the Constitution or laws of the United States, or to different punishments, pains or penalties, on account of such inhabitant being an alien, or by reason of his color, or race, than are prescribed for the punishment of citizen. [Section 242]

The Supreme Court has made it abundantly clear that the language of Section 241 "embraces *all* of the rights and privileges secured to citizens by *all* of the Constitution and *all* of the laws of the United States."[17] Section 242 was revised in 1874 "to include as wide a range of rights as 241 . . . did. . . ."[18] In the words of Mr. Justice Rutledge:

Sections [241] and [242] are twin sections. . . . There are important differences. Section [241] strikes at conspiracies, Section [242] at substantive offenses. The former protects "citizens," the latter "inhabitants." There are, however, no differences in the basic rights guarded. *Each protects in a different way the rights and privileges secured to individuals by the Constitution.*[19]

The constitutional rights and privileges with which the grand jury should most obviously have dealt in assessing the legality of the conduct of law enforcement officials in carrying out the raid were (1) the right to be free from unreasonable searches and seizures and (2) the right not to be summarily punished by state officials. This Commission finds that probable cause exists that the rights of the Panthers were infringed in both these respects, and that indictments should have been returned for violations of both Sections 241 (for conspiracy to injure citizens in the free exercise of protected rights) and 242 (for willful deprivation of rights).

Illegal Search and Seizure

The Fourth Amendment to the Constitution, part of the original Bill of Rights, provides:

The right of the people to be secure in their persons, houses, papers, and effects, against unreasonable searches and seizures, shall not be violated, and no warrants shall issue, but upon probable cause, supported by oath or

17. *United States* v. *Price,* 383 U.S. 787, 800 (1966).
18. Ibid. at 803.
19. *Screws* v. *United States,* 325 U.S. 91, 119 (1945) (concurring opinion) (emphasis added).

affirmation, and particularly describing the place to be searched, and the persons or things to be seized.

The deep significance which respect for this right bears to constitutional government is borne out by a legion of Supreme Court opinions. The Fourth Amendment binds federal law enforcement officials,[20] and, ever since 1949, when the Supreme Court made it clear that the Fourth Amendment is to be considered as incorporated in the Fourteenth Amendment ("due process"), it is binding on state officials as well.[21] To insure enforcement of the right, the Court has directed federal and states judges to exclude from any criminal prosecution evidence obtained directly[22] or indirectly[23] from an unlawful search. The right has been deemed to protect privacy as well as the security of home and personal possessions. In the words of Justice Frankfurter, "The security of one's privacy against arbitrary intrusion by the police—which is at the core of the Fourth Amendment—is basic to a free society.[24]

The constitutional guarantee against unreasonable searches and seizures, applied to the states through the due process clause of the Fourteenth Amendment, is one of the "rights and privileges" protected by the Civil Rights Statutes. An absolute tie-in between the Civil Rights Statutes and unreasonable searches was first suggested by Justice Jackson in *Irvine* v. *California*,[25] when he said:

> If the officials have wilfully deprived a citizen of the United States of a right or privilege secured to him by the Fourteenth Amendment, that being the right to be secure in his home against unreasonable searches, as defined in Wolf v. Colorado, supra, their conduct may constitute a federal crime under [18 U.S.C. §242].

That the guarantee against unreasonable searches falls within the scope of this language is confirmed by reference to section 1983 of Title 42 of the United States Code, a provision analogous to Section 242 of Title 18, but providing for civil, rather than criminal, liability.

20. *Weeks* v. *United States,* 232 U.S. 383 (1914).
21. *Wolf* v. *Colorado,* 338 U.S. 25 (1949).
22. *Weeks* v. *United States,* 232 U.S. 383 (1914); *Mapp* v. *Ohio,* 367 U.S. 643 (1961).
23. *Wong Sun* v. *United States,* 371 U.S. 471 (1963).
24. *Wolf* v. *Colorado,* 338 U.S. 25, 27 (1949).
25. 347 U.S. 128, 137 (1954).

In *Monroe* v. *Pape*,[26] Mr. Justice Douglas summed up the purpose of section 1983 as follows:

> Its purpose is plain from the title of legislation, "An act to enforce the Provisions of the Fourteenth Amendment to the Constitution of the United States, and for other purposes." . . . Allegation of facts constituting deprivation under color of state authority of a right guaranteed by the Fourteenth Amendment satisfies to that extent the requirement. . . . [T]he guarantee against unreasonable searches and seizures contained in the Fourth Amendment has been made applicable to the States by reason of the Due Process Clause of the Fourteenth Amendment, *Wolf v. People of State of Colorado,* 338 U.S. 25; *Elkins v. United States,* 364 U.S. 206, 213.

The December 4, 1969, search was conducted pursuant to a warrant signed by Illinois Circuit Judge Robert Collins. Whether the search was lawful under constitutional standards of reasonableness depends first on whether the warrant was issued only after probable cause was shown as required by the Constitution, and second on whether the execution of the search was reasonable.

Validity of Search Warrant

Certain preconditions must be met before a search warrant can validly be issued. The application for a warrant must set forth facts which enable the judicial officer to make an independent and objective judgment that there is probable cause to believe (a) that the items toward which the search is directed are evidence of criminal activity and (b) that the items will be found in the location to be searched. It is very questionable whether the application in this case met the Supreme Court's minimum standards for such information, particularly because conclusions based not upon the affiant's (Sergeant Groth's) personal observation, but upon hearsay (the informant's information), must be substantiated to a greater degree.[27]

When an affiant bases his conclusion completely upon information provided by an informant, as was the case with the warrant issued by Judge Collins, the application must contain sufficient detail for the judicial officer to determine independently whether probable cause

26. 365 U.S. 167, 171 (1961).
27. *Spinelli* v. *United States,* 393 U.S. 410, 415 (1969).

exists. In setting standards for judging probable cause, the Supreme Court has been careful not to impose impossible conditions on search warrant applications.[28] Certain minimum requirements have been imposed, however, to prevent the magistrate from merely relying on the applicant's conclusions, thereby relinquishing his own protective function.[29] The basic tests were set out in *Aguilar* v. *Texas*.[30] The Court in Aguilar made clear that the application must contain information showing (a) reason to believe that the informant's conclusions concerning criminal activities were valid and (b) that the informant was reliable or truthful. These tests were recently reaffirmed by the Supreme Court, although the importance of establishing the informant's reliability, particularly when the informant's information is based on his personal observation, was de-emphasized.[31]

The search warrant application in this case, prepared by Assistant State's Attorney Jalovec and signed by Sergeant Groth, read in pertinent part as follows:

A reliable informant, who has furnished reliable information to affiant on several past occasions which has led to the confiscation of 2 sawed-off shotguns in two separate raids, and has provided information that has led to several convictions, informed the affiant DANIEL GROTH that on December 2, 1969, he had occasion to enter the above described premises at 2337 W. Monroe, 1st floor apartment. During this visit, he observed numerous weapons, including three sawed-off shotguns, whose barrels appeared to be approximately 12 inches in length. Along with these weapons he observed numerous rounds of ammunition. When he left the premises the above described sawed-off shotguns were still there. Independently of this above information, DANIEL GROTH was informed by ASA Richard S. Jalovec that on December 2, 1969, Jalovec had a conversation with a reliable informant who also stated that sawed-off shotguns and other weapons were being stored in the first floor apartment at 2337 W. Monroe, Chicago, Illinois. This informant, according to Jalovec, has provided information in the past which has led to the arrest and indictment of numerous individuals.

Although Sergeant Groth attempted to provide adequate information in accordance with the Supreme Court's standards, the applica-

28. *United States* v. *Ventresca,* 380 U.S. 102, 108 (1965).
29. *Spinelli* v. *United States,* 393 U.S. 410, 415 (1969).
30. 378 U.S. 108 (1964).
31. *United States* v. *Harris,* 403 U.S. 573, 579 (1971).

tion was probably insufficient as a matter of law. The informant purported to be an eyewitness to the presence of illegal weapons (sawed-off shotguns) in the apartment, but the application describes the circumstances of the informant's visit to the apartment only sketchily. It gives no details such as the hour of the visit, the length of stay, what rooms he inspected, or where he saw the sawed-off shotguns—details which would show familiarity with the premises and tend to be self-corroborative.

The application also attempts some explanation of why the affiant concludes the informant to be reliable, in that it refers to other occasions on which the informant's reliability has been demonstrated; but there is no independent corroboration of the affiant's statements.

That portion of the application describing Jalovec's conversation with another informant does not even approach the Supreme Court's standards, as no basis is given for that second informant's conclusion.

If the warrant was, as the Commission finds probable, insufficient as a matter of law, then no evidence obtained in the search would have been usable in any legal action against any of the Panthers. It would not follow, however, that there was a criminal violation. Even if the legality of warrant would not have been sustained in a court test, its execution by an authorized police officer would not on its face seem to constitute a violation of the Civil Rights Act (Section 242) for which the officer should be indicted. The Act requires for a violation that the offender "wilfully" subject an individual to deprivation of rights—and that would be the case only if Sergeant Groth willfully distorted the facts or made false statements in his affidavit, or if the police who served the warrant knew it to be untrue.

Regardless of whether indictments of the police or the state's attorney on this ground were justifiable, it is unfortunate that the grand jury gave such scant attention to the issue. It is common police practice, supported by the courts, to use information supplied by unnamed informants as the basis for search warrant applications. It is in just such cases that the maximum verification should be demanded.

Validity of the Execution of the Search

The relationship between a deprivation of rights and a criminal violation of the Civil Rights Acts becomes more direct when one considers the validity of the execution of the warrant—whether the search was "unreasonable" in the manner in which it was carried out.

The *time* when a search warrant is to be executed, i.e., night or day, is a factor for judicial determination, since time is an essential element of reasonableness.

The time of a police search of an occupied family home may be a significant factor in determining whether, in a Fourth Amendment sense, the search is "unreasonable." [32]

Prior to 1964 the relevant Illinois law distinguished between night and day searches and required two judges or two justices of the peace to authorize a search in the nighttime. In 1964 these statutes were replaced by 38 Ill. State Ann. §§ 108–13, which provides: "The warrant may be executed at any time of any day or night." This Illinois statute would appear unconstitutional on its face if its intendment is that the police, rather than the courts, are to determine whether a search warrant is to be executed in the daytime or in the nighttime. "When the right of privacy must reasonably yield to the right of search is, as a rule, to be decided by a judicial officer, not by a policeman or government enforcement agent." [33] But even if granting the enforcing officers the discretion to decide between daytime and nighttime searches were constitutionally permissible, the determination of whether a nighttime search is valid would ultimately have to be subjected to a reasonableness test: Was it more reasonable to execute the warrant in the nighttime than in the daytime?

Chief Judge Hastie has stated the federal constitutional limitations on state nighttime searches as follows:

At common law, prior to the adoption of the Fourth Amendment, there was a strong aversion to night time searches. 2 Hale, Pleas of the Crown, Stokes & Ingersoll ed. 1847, 113; Cooley, Constitutional Limitations, 7th ed. 1903, 430; Voorhies v. Faust, 1922, 220 Mich. 155, 189 N.W. 1006, 27 A.L.R. 706; Commonwealth v. Hinds, 1887, 145 Mass. 182, 13 N.E. 397. Even the odious "writs of assistance" which outraged colonial America permitted search of dwellings only in the daytime. Lasson, *History & Development of the Fourth Amendment to the United States Constitution,* 1937, 54. The significance of this aversion of the common law to nighttime searches is

32. *United States ex. rel.; Boyance* v. *Myers,* 398 F. 2d 896, 897 (3rd Cir. 1968).
33. *Johnson* v. *United States,* 333 U.S. 10, 14 (1948).

underscored by the Supreme Court's reminder that the search and seizure clause is properly "construed in the light of what was deemed an unreasonable search and seizure when it was adopted". *Carroll v. United States,* 1925 267 U.S. 132, 149, 45 S. Ct. 280, 284, 69 L. Ed. 543.[34]

During the early years of the Republic this common law tradition was embodied in two federal statutes, passed by the first Congress, that authorized only daytime searches.[35] Thereafter, the reluctance to authorize nighttime searches except under exceptional circumstances continued as an integral part of our jurisprudence. Today, consistent with restrictions imposed by prior federal statutes, Rule 41(c) of the Federal Rules of Criminal Procedure provides:

> The warrant shall direct that it be served in the day time, but if the affidavits are positive that the property is on the person or in the place to be searched, the warrant may direct that it be served at any time.

Similar limitations have been imposed under state law.[36]

Aversion to police intrusion at night as a serious threat to ordered liberty also appears in authoritative contemporary judicial pronouncements. As Mr. Justice Frankfurter concisely stated:

> Searches of the dwelling house were the special object of this universal condemnation of official intrusion. Night-time search was the evil in its most obnoxious form.[37]

In the case in question, no compelling reason existed for conducting the search in the dead of night; indeed, the circumstances suggest that a daytime raid would have been more likely to accomplish the purpose of the warrant without risk of injury to the police or the occupants.

Sergeant Groth advised his men that they should assemble for the raid at 4:00 A.M., and told them that the early morning time had been chosen to avoid a "trap." According to Groth, "It was the ideal time to lessen the chance of injury to others and to catch occupants of the apartment unaware."[38] The grand jury *Report,* however, observed:

---

34. *United States ex. rel. Boyance* v. *Myers,* 398 F.2d 896, 897–98 (3d Cir. 1968).
35. Act of July 31, 1789, § 24, 1 Stat. 43; Act of March 3, 1791, § 29, 1 Stat. 206.
36. See *Petit* v. *Colmary,* 4 Penna. 266, 55 A. 344 (1903); *People* v. *Wittler,* 247 Mich. 656, 226 N.W. 685 (1929); *People* v. *Watson,* 39 Misc. 2d 808, 241 N.Y.S.2d 934 (Cr. Ct, New York City 1963); *State* v. *Sabo,* 198 Ohio St. 200, 140 N.E. 499 (Sup Ct. 1923).
37. *Monroe* v. *Pape,* 365 U.S. 167, 210 (1961) (concurring in part, dissenting in part).
38. Testimony at coroner's inquest, January 7, 1970.

Moreover, the whole concept of going on a raid in a high crime density area to obtain weapons from known militants—led by a convicted felon believed to be dangerous—with only fourteen men, in plainclothes, in the dead of night, with no sound equipment, no lighting equipment, no tear gas and no plan for dealing with potential resistence, seems ill-conceived. [P. 117.]

The state's attorney's police did not choose to execute the search when there was reason to believe that most or all of the occupants would be away from the apartment. Contrary to established procedure, they made no provision for the use of tear gas, in case of resistance, to force the occupants to leave the apartment and allow the search to be conducted without interference—despite the fact that in case of resistance a search could best have been achieved by flushing all occupants out of the apartment, and despite the fact that illegal weapons were not easily disposable items which could have been hidden, destroyed, burned, swallowed, or flushed down a drain. The police carried heavy weaponry—in anticipation of resistance, they said—but did not use any equipment that could have helped to avoid violence.

Summary Punishment

No element of the planning and staging of the December 4 raid supports the contention that the intent of the mission was the routine execution of a search warrant.

The character of the preparation for the raid, and the plan itself, must be considered in the light of two elements discussed earlier: the existence and escalation of virtual guerrilla warfare between Panthers and police in Chicago, including fatal shoot-outs between the two groups, and the extensive use of infiltration, surveillance, and informants by the police, State's Attorney's Office and the FBI.

Taking into account all the factors attendant upon the instigation, planning, and preparation of the raid, and the subsequent events at 2337 West Monroe Street, the Commission is convinced that the raid was not, as the grand jury *Report* puts it, merely "ill-conceived." Every indication is that the raid, contrary to its stated objectives, was conceived and planned as an armed confrontation with leaders of the Illinois chapter of the Black Panther Party under circumstances in which the planners of the raid knew—or should have known—that loss of life was almost inevitable. The events of the raid itself, and the deaths that in fact occurred, confirmed what the planning of the raid so clearly suggested.

Every analysis, private and official, of the ballistics and other related evidence—including the report of the FBI Crime Laboratory, which the grand jury accepted as conclusive and uncontroverted—established that only one shot was fired by the occupants of the Panther apartment during the entire course of the raid, and all the evidence indicates that that lone Panther shot was fired in the beginning moments of the raid. From that moment on, there was no resistance from the occupants of the apartment.

And yet, as was also substantiated by the physical evidence and the testimony of all participants, police crashed in the front and rear of the apartment, killed one occupant of the living room and wounded the other, then continued to fire into the occupied rooms of the apartment, raking the walls and interiors of the two bedrooms where six people tried only to avoid being killed.

Fred Hampton was shot through the head while he lay, probably drugged, and in any event defenseless, in his bed. The three occupants of the other bedroom suffered multiple wounds from the machine gun fire of police.

It is too obvious for extended discussion that summary punishment by law enforcement officials is a violation of the Civil Rights Statutes, Title 18, Sections 241, 242. As the court stated in *Crews* v. *United States:*[39]

An officer of the law undoubtedly knows that a person arrested by him for an offense has the constitutional right to a trial under the law, and if the jury should believe from the evidence beyond a reasonable doubt that such an officer willfully failed to accord to one arrested by him the opportunity for such a trial but substituted instead his own trial by ordeal, such jury would be justified in finding that such a denial of such constitutional right was consciously and willfully made. One is generally presumed to have intended the normal and reasonable consequences of his acts. A deprivation of the right to life is an inexorable and concomitant consequence of a willful homicide.

39. 160 F.2d 746, 750 (5th Cir. 1947).

In *United States* v. *Price*,[40] the Court upheld counts in an indictment under Title 18 Section 242 which charged denials of due process as a result of summary punishment:

The Second, Third and Fourth Counts of the indictment . . . charge all of the defendants, not with conspiracy, but with substantive violations of §242. Each of these counts charges that the defendants, acting "under color of the laws of the State of Mississippi," "did wilfully assault, shoot and kill" Schwerner, Chaney and Goodman, respectively, "for the purpose and with the intent" of punishing each of the three and that the defendants "did thereby wilfully deprive" each "of rights, privileges and immunities secured and protected by the Constitution and the laws of the United States"— namely, due process of law.

The Court continued with respect to the conspiracy count:

This is an allegation of state action which, beyond dispute, brings the conspiracy within the ambit of the Fourteenth Amendment. It is an allegation of official, state participation in murder, accomplished by and through its officers with the participation of others. It is an allegation that the State, without the semblance of due process of law as required of it by the Fourteenth Amendment, used its sovereign power and office to release the victims from jail so that they were not charged and tried as required by law, but instead could be intercepted and killed. If the Fourteenth Amendment forbids denial of counsel, it clearly denounces denial of any trial at all.

40. 383 U.S. 787, 793 (1966).

CHAPTER 9

Conclusions

The Commission is of the opinion that it would have been improper to make actual findings of guilt; such conclusions should be made only after a trial during which the accused may exercise all of his rights. Rather, where the evidence suggests that a crime has been committed, the Commission has analogized its function to that of a grand jury, and has made findings of probable cause. It may be suggested that it was improper for the Commission even to have made findings of probable cause, since it does not have the power to compel testimony or to conduct a trial at which the accused may be exonerated. However, the circumstances surrounding the incident under investigation are so extraordinary that special measures seem called for. The existence of this Commission is itself a reflection of a widespread feeling that in this instance the legal system failed.

Police-Community Relations in Chicago at the Time of the Raid

The latter part of the 1960s was a period of rapidly increasing tension between Chicago's black residents and the Chicago Police Department—much as it was for blacks and police throughout the nation. Mayor Daley's widely publicized edict to "shoot to kill arsonists, shoot to maim looters," and the apparent license which that directive gave Chicago's police in dealing with the black community, are major examples of this increasing tension.

The War on Gangs waged by the Chicago Police Department exacerbated an already tense situation, and made black youths, particularly radicals, a focus of intense police surveillance. A direct result of the War on Gangs was an increase in the number of confrontations between black youths and the police.

Throughout the country, on the national and the local level, the Black Panther Party was the subject of wide publicity and extensive surveillance. Immediately following the chartering of the Illinois chapter of the Black Panther Party, the Black Panthers became one of the most publicized of the targets of the Gang Intelligence Unit.

The creation within the Cook County State's Attorney's Office of the Special Prosecutions Unit, independent of the state's attorney's police, expanded the role of the prosecutor's office from the investigation and prosecution of crime to the surveillance of suspects and the infiltration of "suspect" groups. In addition, the existence of the Special Prosecutions Unit raises, at least in retrospect, the question: "Who polices the police?"

During the several months preceding December 4, 1969, several black youths died in violent confrontations with the police. Each of those deaths, when officially investigated, was held to be a case of justifiable or accidental homicide. Those determinations were largely disbelieved by the black community. Moreover, the determinations both heightened the tensions between the police and the black community and led to further distrust by the black community of the police and of official investigations of allegations of police misconduct.

The death and wounding of several police officers in the months immediately preceding the raid had the effect of emotionalizing the police. Once again, the Black Panther Party was the primary focus of the police, as many officers were predisposed to the view that the Panthers constituted a special and immediate risk to their physical safety.

The Plan for and Purposes of the Raid

The federal grand jury's *Report* concluded that the raid was "ill-conceived." The Commission considers that characterization of the raid to be a vast understatement, and has found that there is probable cause to believe that the predawn raid, carried out by officers with heavy armament but without tear gas, sound equipment, or lighting equipment, involved criminal acts on the part of the planners of the raid.

The infiltrator who reportedly informed the police and/or the FBI that illegal weapons were likely to be found in the Panther's apartment was also reported to have informed them that the apartment was likely to be unoccupied at 8 P.M. on the evening preceding the raid. If the object of the raid had been, as stated, to search the premises for illegal weapons, that purpose could best have been accomplished without violence when the apartment was empty. Assuming that the search had disclosed illegal weapons, appropriate arrests could have been made thereafter.

Alternatively, the police could have surrounded the apartment and, communicating with the residents either by telephone or by loudspeaker, told them that the apartment was surrounded and ordered them to come out. The residents might have surrendered if given a chance. And the firepower available to the police department was surely more than ample to have permitted such an approach with no more danger to the police than was presented by the course of action actually followed.

Instead, however, the police chose to serve the warrant at 4:45 A.M., heavily armed and dressed in plainclothes. It is probable that the method chosen to execute the search warrant not only failed to avert violence, but instead actually maximized the likelihood of violence and clearly endangered the lives of the Panthers in the apartment. Moreover, it is probable that the purpose of the raid was to conduct a surprise attack on the Panthers, and that serving the search warrant was merely a guise.

The Commission finds that there is persuasive evidence that viable alternative methods of executing the search warrant did exist, methods which could have been utilized if the police officers and state's attorney had attempted to serve process in a manner respectful of the law.

The Opening Moments of the Raid—The First Shot

An analysis of the testimony by the police and by the Panther survivors about the events of the raid cannot be conclusive. The stories told by the police and the survivors are so fundamentally inconsistent that it is impossible to determine from the testimony what actually happened. However, the various narratives together with the physical evidence which has been available to the Commission have made several conclusions probable.

The question of the first shot was raised initially by the police, who claimed they were met by gunfire as they attempted to enter the apartment. The federal grand jury seemed to accept that theory, but never adequately addressed itself to the question. The result was to leave officially unanswered a question that was widely believed to be central and to justify the police use of gunfire, and at the same time to imply that the police version of the first shot was correct.

The Commission finds that too little consideration was given by the federal grand jury, or by any other investigative body, to the ballistics report prepared by Mr. MacDonell. Although MacDonell relied on nonphysical evidence to reach his conclusion that Clark had not fired the first shot, and although that conclusion is therefore not definitive, it was a conclusion that, had a policeman rather than a Panther been the victim, would have been examined quite thoroughly by any investigative body. Instead, the federal grand jury characterized MacDonell's analysis as an "imaginative theory," a characterization which tends to discredit the analysis as sheer speculation. "Imaginative theories," however, when tested, often provide the crucial links between pieces of circumstantial evidence. MacDonell's theory was, instead, summarily dismissed.

Based on the evidence available to it, the Commission considers it probable that the first shot was fired neither by Mark Clark or Brenda Harris nor by Sergeant Groth or Officer Davis, but rather in the entrance hallway, apparently accidentally, by Officer Jones. Reference to such a shot is found both in the federal grand jury's *Report* and in the report prepared for the Commission by Mr. MacDonell, although little weight is given to it by either the federal grand jury or Mr. MacDonell.

More important, far too much weight has been given to the issue of who fired the first shot. First, there is considerable discrepancy as to the manner in which the police announced their presence at the apartment. While the Commission is of the opinion that the federal grand jury failed adequately to consider the controversy over who fired the first shot, the Commission also thinks that the significance of that issue has been highly exaggerated. Assuming, as is far from clear from the conflicting versions of the event, that the raiding officers did announce their presence and identify themselves as police, it is necessary to consider that it was 4:45 in the morning, the residents were asleep, and the police were in plainclothes. Under those circumstances, it is not unreasonable to suppose that anybody hearing an intruder entering his apartment is likely to reach for any available weapon—including a gun, if one is available—and use it. More importantly, the pattern of the shooting after the initial exchange of shots makes the question of the first shot seem relatively insignificant.

The Pattern of the Shooting

Approximately six shots were apparently fired as the police entered the living room through the front door—two by Sergeant Groth, three by Officer Davis, and one by Mark Clark. The FBI's ballistics analysis shows that during the remainder of the raid between seventy-seven and ninety-four shots were fired by the police—and none by the apartment's occupants. Accordingly, with the exception of one shot, the police testimony of gunfire directed at them from the occupants must be rejected.

The police testimony describes several orders for cease-fires, each of which was broken by shots fired by the occupants or by their shouts to "shoot it out." The evidence that no shots were fired by the occupants discredits the police testimony that they were returning fire; equally important, it discredits the police testimony that the occupants were advocating a shoot-out, for it is highly implausible that several calls to shoot it out could have been made without a shot being fired.

It was suggested to the police by the federal grand jury that police mistook the gunfire of other officers for firing by the Panthers. The fact that the police undoubtedly felt themselves endangered by the Panthers might have explained their propensity to shoot rather than to investigate. However, the police emphatically rejected the grand jury's suggestion. Moreover, that suggestion would not account for the police testimony that occupants of the apartment advocated a shoot-out. Since no shots were fired by the occupants, it is unlikely that the police testimony in that regard was true. If, however, the testimony of the officers that cries to "shoot it out" were heard is true, it seems far more likely that those cries were made by other police officers. If such was the case, those officers might well have intended the actual result—the killing and wounding of certain of the occupants.

Officer Gorman testified before the federal grand jury that as he fired his machine gun into the front bedroom, he saw one of the occupants aiming a gray shotgun at him, and the statement purportedly made by Blair Anderson shortly after the raid indicates that both he and Satchel had weapons. The Commission has been unable to establish the truth or falsity of that testimony. However, it seems likely that the occupants would have been able to fire at least one shot, if that had been their intent, while Gorman was firing into the closet. The front bedroom was a small room—approximately fourteen feet deep and seven feet wide. In it were two beds and a chest; the closet further reduced the actual space in the room. Three people were in the room; each of them was wounded several times. And while they were being wounded, not one shot was fired by any of them. Moreover, even if the occupants were armed, the Commission cannot condone the indiscriminate firing of a full round of thirty machine gun bullets into the room or the planning of a raid that would permit such an occurrence. There were other methods readily available to effect the arrests.

The Commission finds that attribution of culpability in the killing of Mark Clark and the wounding of Brenda Harris may be less clearly definable in the context of the already-begun raid. Clark apparently did fire at the police—regardless of whether his shot was the initial shot. Although Brenda Harris claims never to have touched a gun during the raid, the police testified that she did have one, and in the statement that she purportedly made to Andrew shortly after the raid she admitted that she had had, and had been attempting to fire, a shotgun. Moreover, the police knew *somebody* had fired at them, and a mistake by them as to who it had been may be understandable. The Commission is convinced, however, that both the killing of Clark and the wounding of Harris would have been avoided by proper planning, and that while no culpability is necessarily assignable to the officers who did the shooting, there is probable cause to believe that the planning of the raid was so inadequate as to constitute criminal conduct.

The Shooting of Fred Hampton

The death of Fred Hampton appears to the Commission to have been isolated from the killing of Mark Clark and the wounding of Brenda Harris on the one hand, and from the wounding of Ronald Satchel, Verlina Brewer, and Blair Anderson on the other. The Commission has concluded that there is probable cause to believe that Fred Hampton was murdered—that he was shot by an officer or officers who could see his prostrate body lying on the bed. Unfortunately, the inadequate investigation by the police and the other officials and their inadequate examination of the available evidence make it impossible to know which officer or officers actually fired the fatal bullets.

The Commission has been unable to determine whether the purpose, or a purpose, of the raid was specifically to kill Hampton. There is some evidence that Hampton was shot after the other occupants of the rear bedroom were removed. If that was not the sequence of events, it seems likely that he was the sole target of the police shooting from the doorway of the bedroom. Neither of those sequences, however, would establish that Hampton's death was an object of the raid.

On the other hand, the fact that Hampton appears from virtually all the testimony never to have moved during the raid, the fact that after the police entered the apartment all the testimony placed him in bed, and the possibility that his failure to move was caused by his having been drugged are relevant to the question of the purpose of the raid.

Whether Hampton Was Drugged

The Commission has been unable to determine whether Hampton was drugged at the time of his murder, but considers it more probable than not that he was. The blood tests performed in connection with the second autopsy reportedly showed that Hampton had been drugged with a massive dose of secobarbital. The blood test reportedly conducted by the Cook County coroner failed to show the presence of any barbiturate, but there is a substantial doubt whether that test was ever conducted. The federal grand jury accepted as conclusive the findings of an FBI blood analysis which did not show the presence of any drugs. But the experts consulted by the Commission unanimously expressed the opinion that the FBI test, because of the embalming procedure used on Hampton's body, the instability of secobarbital in solution, and the long time during which the blood was stored without having been frozen, should not have been accepted as conclusive. In addition, certain of the experts concluded affirmatively that the blood did show the presence of a barbiturate, and that the FBI results were not just inadequate but wrong. In short, although the Commission has concluded that it is probable that Hampton was drugged, a final resolution of the issue is beyond the Commission's competence.

If Hampton was drugged, it would explain why, despite specific attempts to wake him, he was not awakened. Moreover, a finding that he was drugged might suggest that his death was an objective of the raid—that the police went to the apartment knowing that Hampton would be there and that he would be incapable of defending himself.

It seems unlikely that it will ever be known whether Hampton was drugged and whether his death was the major focus of the raid. The only investigative bodies who might have made that determination either failed to do so or have had their credibility so impeached that any conclusions reached by them must be disregarded. The Commission nonetheless considers it important to raise the issue because the facts compel that it be raised. The failure to raise it would be to hide from an unanswerable question solely because the most likely answers are not easy to accept.

State and Local Investigations

The performances following the raid of the various local law enforcement bodies which investigated the incident were singularly inadequate—in some cases by the admission of those official bodies. More important, however, is that some of those investigations—again by the admission of the investigators—were designed not to determine the facts but solely to establish the innocence of the police. It has been noted earlier that large segments of the black community had grown to distrust the police, as well as internal or other official investigations of police misconduct. The investigations of this raid confirm the validity of that mistrust.

The survivors of the raid have been widely condemned for their refusal to participate in certain of the official investigations. There is, however, not one hint that the participation by the survivors would have diminished the partiality and bias of any of those investigations, while there is much to suggest that their participation would have increased the acceptability of those investigations to the public. For example, despite the lack of evidence against the survivors and the substantial evidence against the police, it was the survivors and not the police who were initially indicted. And no investigation would have made available to the survivors the resources that were available to the state, or would otherwise have put the survivors and the police on equal footings. In short, the Commission has concluded that the refusal of the survivors to participate in the official investigations of the raid was understandable and justified. Until the black community at large has reason to think that blacks are being treated fairly by the police, and that police criminality will be dealt with justly by the law enforcement agencies, there is little chance of diminishing violence between police and blacks. If "the law" is designed to protect "the other side," then "the law" will inevitably be ignored.

The Commission considers that the performance by Special State's Attorney Barnabas Sears requires special comment. Mr. Sears, an established and respected lawyer, was appointed by Chief Judge Power of the Cook County Criminal Court to investigate matters relating to the raid. When the Sears investigation failed to establish the innocence of the police—and instead resulted in the indictment of State's Attorney Hanrahan and thirteen other officials on charges of conspiring to obstruct justice—Sears became himself the subject of harsh treatment by Judge Power and by other members of Chicago and Illinois officialdom. The conclusion seems inescapable that Judge Power, too, was not impartial—that he intended Mr. Sears's investigation to exonerate the police regardless of the facts. Although the trial that followed from Mr. Sears's investigation resulted in the dismissal of charges against the indicted officials, the Commission questions whether that result would have followed if the resources of the state had been made more readily available to Mr. Sears rather than having been weighted against him.

The question of "Who polices the police?" is itself difficult. When it appears that law enforcement officials are working in unison, not for justice but solely to protect some of their own, the questions become that much more difficult. Who will judge the police? Who will judge the judges? And how can society expect the oppressed, or those who believe they are oppressed, to act when society's official avenues of recourse are closed to them?

Federal Law

The Commission finds that the raid of December 4, 1969, was not executed in compliance with the Fourth Amendment guarantees against unreasonable search and seizures; that there is probable cause to believe that the Civil Rights Statutes, Title 18, Sections 241 and 242, of the United States Code, were violated in the raid by the imposition of summary punishment on the Panthers with the intent to deny them their constitutionally protected rights to due process; and that the federal grand jury, in failing to return indictments against certain Chicago and Cook County police and other officials for their raid-related conduct, failed in its duty to proceed against violations of civil liberties.

Summary

The federal grand jury *Report* found instances of official misfeasance, malfeasance, and nonfeasance related to investigations of the raid. It also established what the Commission deems to be a *prima facie* case of illegal denial of the constitutional rights of the residents of the apartment. Nonetheless, the federal grand jury and the first state grand jury failed to return any indictments against the officials, and, instead, the first state grand jury indicted the survivors. The attitude of both grand juries appears to have been that the Panthers were dangerous, and, consequently, that any excesses by the police against them could be excused. The Commission deplores that approach.

One of the primary purposes of the criminal law is deterrence. If no attempt is made to prosecute the police in instances of apparent misconduct, such as appear to be present in this case, then it seems likely that police misconduct will continue in the future. It is perhaps too much to expect, at least until police service is thoroughly professionalized, that an officer in the course of a raid against people who he honestly believes intend to harm him would refrain from taking violent action to protect himself. To state that one understands, and perhaps is forced to accept, such a position does not, however, change the Commission's conclusion. It merely focuses attention on the culpable parties.

In other words, it would be perfectly proper to indict those officials who participated in the planning of the raid without indicting all of the participants, and if more evidence were obtained with respect to the roles of various of the officers, it might be proper to indict those police with respect to whom probable cause was found without indicting all of them. Clearly, however, it is unacceptable to conclude that because some of the police may not be guilty of any crime, none of them is. To follow such a course of action may well have the effect of increasing the number of instances of unjustified and unjustifiable police violence. The Commission is concerned, as all people must be, with the protection of police lives; it is also concerned, however, with the preservation of the lives of all persons, including those who may be suspected of having committed crimes. Summary execution is not tolerable; arbitrary punishment cannot be condoned. The best method for minimizing senseless killings and injuries seems to lie in establishing a situation where all people can expect justice; the Chicago incident seems calculated to foster a different result.

APPENDICES

I. Report on the Investigation of the Premises at 2337 West Monroe Street, Chicago, Illinois, and the Examination of Evidence Removed Therefrom

by Herbert Leon MacDonell,
Consulting Criminalist

*(Edited by the Commission of Inquiry
to Delete References
to Illustrations, Photographs, or
Exhibits Not Included in the Text)*

I. Introduction

At approximately 11:35 A.M. on Saturday 6 December 1969 I received a telephone call from Mr. Gerald Lefcourt during which he described the shooting at 2337 West Monroe Street, Chicago, Illinois. This was the first I became aware of the incident as it was not reported in our local newspaper. At 11:55 A.M. Mr. William Kunstler called regarding the same matter. During the afternoon at about 3:45 P.M. Mr. Dennis Cunningham and Mr. Francis Andrew also called me. Later that same evening at about 8:45 P.M. Mr. Andrew called a second time. The purpose of these telephone calls was to locate someone who was knowledgeable in physical evidence and who would come to Chicago to conduct an independent examination of the premises at 2337 West Monroe Street.

During our conversation I advised Mr. Andrew that my examination would be impartial and it made no difference to me as to whether I was retained by the defense or the prosecution, my conclusions would be the same. I further informed him that I would seek the truth of the matter and that if he didn't want the truth then he should not request me to conduct an investigation. Finally, I told him I would not suppress any evidence that I might uncover during, or as a result of, my examination if, and when, questioned about it by anyone in authority. Mr. Andrew agreed to all of these remarks and asked that I fly to Chicago as soon as possible.

On Sunday 7 December 1969 I flew to Chicago and met that evening with Mr. Andrew and his associate Mr. Ray McClain. At that meeting I was shown several photographs of the apartment where Fred Hampton and Mark Clark had been shot three days earlier. No attempt was made to prejudice me regarding the scene, the events that had transpired, nor what I should do when I went there the following day. This meeting was short, perhaps an hour or so, as Mr. Andrew had another appointment.

II. Examination of the Scene

Mr. Andrew picked me up at my hotel at approximately 7:30 A.M. on Monday 8 December 1969. We drove to 2337 West Monroe Street and he went to the front door which was partially open. No one was within the apartment so he drove to two other locations in an unsuccessful attempt to find a member of the Black Panther Party. We returned to the apartment at about 8:30 A.M. and this time we both went in. No one else had arrived since our first visit a short time before.

The apartment was dark and without heat, perhaps at about 20°F. Furniture, household accessories, clothing, and personal items were strewn about throughout the entire apartment in such a manner that in places walking was difficult. Perhaps the best general description would be to say that every room looked as though it had been ransacked three times over.

After walking through the apartment a second time Mr. Andrew and I connected some lights and lit the space heater in the living room. While we were in the rear bedroom placing a door panel in front of a broken window several black men appeared in the doorway. Mr. Andrew introduced me to one or two of them and informed me that they were representatives of the Black Panther Party. I do not recall any of their names, nor did I make such a record.

Considering the vast amount of evidence that was available for examination I decided priority should be assigned to stationary walls rather than to furniture or other objects which could have been moved following the police raid of 4 December. At that time I did not know there had been "tours" through the apartment by the general public, nor was I aware they would begin again later that morning. In fact, Mr. Andrew told me very little unless I asked him a specific question. The Panthers made no comments at all and left us alone for several hours.

Fortunately, I examined, measured, and photographed the front entrance foyer and entrance hallway before anyone returned. The "tour" began sometime in the late morning and continued until approximately 8:00 P.M. Since the passage of viewers did not interfere with my examinations or photography I did not concern myself with these people at all. As many as two thousand persons could have walked through the apartment while I was there, perhaps even more. On returning from a very quick lunch I took [a photograph of people waiting to enter the apartment]. On several occasions I requested a delay of tour groups so I could take photographs without interference. In every instance the Panther guides immediately complied with my request and made no effort to rush me in my work. There was never any doubt that I was receiving assistance, cooperation, and courtesy from the Panthers, the attorneys, and the attorneys' assistants. Likewise, there were no questions asked nor information offered that could in any way be interpreted as showing me where to look, what to look for, or where not to look. In short, I was given complete freedom to conduct the investigation as I wished without interference or direction from anyone. A television crew filmed many of my activities with similar liberty throughout the apartment. They did not interrupt me nor did I interrupt them.

1. *Entrance Foyer*—Nothing significant was detected, photographed, or recovered from this area. Some leaves were removed from behind the south wall. No bullet holes were found in this area.

2. *Entrance Hall*—A shotgun had been fired just inside the entrance foyer door along the north wall striking the east wall point blank. This is indicated by the "1" on the apartment diagram on page 53. The blast was horizontal, about 50″ high, very close to the north wall. The muzzle was about 12″ from the east wall at the time of discharge.

Two shotgun wads were on the floor in the northeast corner below the point of impact on the east wall. These were photographed where they were found. Two shot pellets were recovered at the same area, one on the floor with the wads and the other in the east wall. These wads and pellets are described later in Sections III-2 through III-4.

There was a large hole about twenty inches from the ceiling at the juncture of the south and west walls. This is discussed in deatil in Section IV-1. The point of impact is erroneously placed on the apartment diagram. The "2" should be in the southwest corner, not on the west wall. No other bullet holes were found.

3. *Upstairs Stairway*—It was obvious that the hole in the southwest

corner of the entrance hall went completely through that wall. Permission was asked of and granted by the occupants of the upstairs apartment to examine their stairway. Although this stairway was very dark, looking up the stairs an exit hole could be seen on the left or east wall, and a point of impact or entrance hole slightly higher on the right or west wall. Both walls were painted with a metallic, copper or bronze colored paint. An examination of the point of impact did not reveal any projectile as the plaster covered a firm, outside wall. I concluded that a slug had struck this wall and fallen down to the steps. Because of the darkness and dirt on the stairs I was sure that if a slug had fallen from the impact point it would still be on the step below it. I simply reached down and picked up a large lead shotgun slug from the top of the tenth step. This slug is described later in Sections III-5 and IV-1.

4. *Door to the Living Room*—The door between the entrance hall and the living room had two bullet holes through it. One, the higher of the two, was fired into the door from the hall side; the second was fired from the living room side (see Figure 2, p. 79) and was much larger, over ¾ of an inch in diameter. These are indicated as "4" and "3" on the apartment diagram, respectively. I removed a large section of the panel containing both bullet holes and transported it to Corning for more detailed study.

5. *Living Room*—The south wall of the living room was covered with bullet holes. By my count there were forty-five, all entrance holes. These shots are indicated by "8" on the apartment diagram. The majority, up to twenty-seven, were noticeably larger than the rest. As an aid in understanding the trajectory of these shots I placed small wooden dowels into the holes and, in all but three cases, they could be extended completely through the wall. Care was exercised in this operation so the holes would not be disturbed. Lightweight plastic straws were delicately probed into each hole until they emerged through the wall into the north bedroom. Then a dowel was slipped through the straw which acted as a protective guide. Three slugs that struck wall studs did not completely penetrate the wall and were presumed embedded in solid wood. They were not recovered. Figure 3 shows the dowels in place in a photograph taken looking in a southeastern direction.

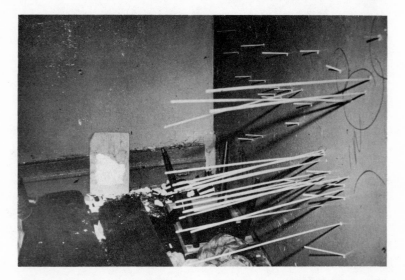

Figure 3: Living room, south wall on the right, with wooden dowels placed in the bullet holes.

One entrance hole was detected on the east wall. This is indicated as "7" on the apartment diagram. The hole was ⅞ " diameter, about 30" high and about 35½ " from the south wall.

Examination of this hole disclosed that the plaster covered a firm, outside wall. The slug had passed between wooden lath, struck the concrete, and apparently fallen behind the high baseboard. I cut an opening just above the baseboard directly below the impact hole. After bringing out several pieces of wood, nails, and concrete, I retrieved a lead slug. This slug is described later in Sections III-7 and IV-2.

An apparent bullet hole was detected high in the northwest corner of the living room. This point of impact is erroneously shown in the corner as "6" in the apartment diagram. It was on the east side of a jog in the corner, 18½ " from the ceiling and 4" from the north wall. Trajectory of this shot placed the origin in line with the space heater. I was told by one of the Panthers that this shot had occurred several weeks before the raid when "one of the brothers had an accident cleaning his 9 mm. Luger." Because of its trajectory and the cooperation I had received from the Panthers I accepted this as an honest explanation and did not recover the slug which was deeply embedded in the wall. (The federal grand jury *Report,* p. 82, identifies this slug as a .380 and not a 9 mm. Since no .380 firearm was recovered at the scene or was carried by police it must have been the result of an earlier event. Thus, while the Panther did not know firearms very well, he was apparently telling the truth as he knew it.) An expended cartridge case was recovered from near the center of the living room. See Section III-8. No other bullet holes were found.

6. *Dining Room*—One shotgun blast was evident on the east wall about 15″ from the ceiling and 22″ south of the north wall archway. Its location is indicated by "19" in the apartment schematic but is erroneously placed approximately 2′ too far south. No other bullet holes were found.

7. *North Bedroom*—Forty-two slugs entered the north bedroom from the north wall. All of these shots were fired from or through the living room. Most of the exit holes in the north wall are shown in Figure 4. The envelope at the upper left is 15″ wide. The two large holes on the right were produced by shotgun blasts. The upper hole is about 47″ from the west wall, the lower is about 52″. These shots were fired from or across the hallway at a slightly downward angle. A single lead shot pellet was removed from the lower hole. This is described in Section III-9. These shots are indicated on the apartment diagram as "12." Another view, taken looking west along the north wall, shows trajectory of the shots coming from the living room. Nine other holes were observed near the ceiling at about the center of the north wall. Their origin is discussed in Section IV-8.

When the north bedroom door was opened widely, it covered twenty-five of the exit holes on the north wall. As dowels placed in these holes were extended toward the door it was found that every dowel could be extended further through the door itself. All twenty-five holes in the door were aligned in this manner. [Two additional holes found in the edge of the door] appear to be part of a group of at least three. The third shot was fired downward, as were the other two, but it passed just in front of the door until it hit the center panel.

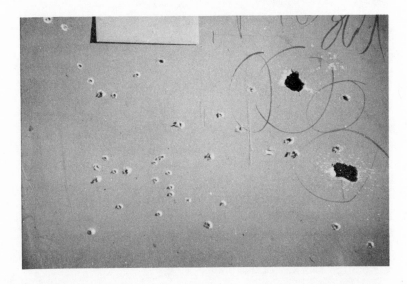

Figure 4: North wall of the north bedroom, showing bullet holes and holes from shotgun blasts.

Fine, white powder was present on the inside of the north bedroom door surrounding some of the lower bullet holes. This is explained in Section IV-7.

Six of the slugs that passed through the bedroom door entered the closet located in the southwest corner of this room. One of these was very low and struck a gallon can of white paint that was on the closet floor. Upon impact the paint can erupted and threw white paint back out of the closet.

Strings and dowels were used to trace the continuation of most shots entering the north bedroom from the living room. A copper case fragment was removed from the south wall, 15″ high and 16″ north of the closet. See Section III-10.

Three shots were fired into the north bedroom from the hallway, entered the closet, passed through its single plasterboard east wall and then entered the south wall of the bedroom. They are indicated as "13" in the apartment diagram but are erroneously placed too far west and incorrectly strike the south rather than the east wall of the closet.

Nine holes were found in the single piece of plasterboard that constituted the north wall of the closet over the opening. These holes were a nine-shot pattern and exited from the closet into the room near the ceiling.

In all, thirty-four slugs struck the south wall of the north bedroom. Six bullet holes were discovered on the east wall. These are indicated as "11" on the apartment diagram. No photographs were taken of these nor were any projectiles recovered from them. Their trajectory suggested that they were fired from the doorway. No other bullet holes were found.

8. *South Bedroom*—Twenty-six slugs entered the south bedroom from the north wall. All of these shots were fired from or through the living room. Trajectories of all but one of these shots are consistent with projections of those from the north wall of the north bedroom, or from the doorway of that room.

Several points of impact were found on the south wall. Because of the variations in their appearance it was not possible to conclude that more than eight were caused by slugs. A jacketed slug was removed from the right casing of the east window 28″ from its top. This slug is described later in Section III-11.

Three shotgun patterns were present on the east wall. Two were high, 24″ and 26″ from the ceiling, and one was very low, 15½″ from the floor. These groups are indicated by "16" and "17" in the apartment diagram. The upper left holes were about 41½″ from the south wall, the upper right 32½″, and the lower 47″. Each group consisted of nine individual holes. A fiber compression wad was removed from the upper right group. A lead shot pellet was also removed from this group. Another lead shot pellet was removed from the upper left group and a lead fragment was removed from the lower shot group. These pieces of evidence are discussed in Section III-12 through III-14.

A shotgun discharge pattern was found in the left side of the west window frame. There was no glass in the lower portion of this window; it is the one Mr. Andrew and I covered with a door panel as described earlier. No other bullet holes were found in this room of which I have records. I believe there was at least one hole in the back, or north, wall of the closet; I did not make photographs or sketches of such, however.

9. *Bathroom*—Nothing significant was detected, photographed, or recovered from this room. A hole that looked like a bullet hole was observed on the north wall, 26" high and 2" from the west wall just above the tub.

10. *Kitchen*—Nothing significant was detected, photographed, or recovered from this room. The window on the south wall was partially broken. No bullet holes were found in this room.

11. *Outside Shed*—A shotgun pattern was found on the west wall of an outside shed. This shed is located southeast of the apartment at 2337 West Monroe Street.

III. Examination of Evidence in Corning

The examination of evidence was conducted in my laboratory in Corning, New York. Because of the nature of the shootings, a considerable amount of physical evidence had been created. Both the Chicago Police and the Panthers, or their attorneys, had recovered much of this evidence prior to my investigation of December 8. Some may also have been removed by "tourists." My examination of this evidence was limited to that which I had removed on the eighth and that which was brought to me later on 9 January 1970. Little, if any, comment will be made on much of this evidence as most of it is of no value or tends only to support a conclusion that may be better drawn from other evidence. Evidence I recovered is described first in the same order as listed in the previous section.

1. *Leaves* removed from the entrance foyer were examined. They are not marijuana.

2. *Shotgun Wad* removed from the entrance hall is from a Remington Mold-tite 12-gauge shotgun shell. Weight: 0.9216 g; diameter: about 0.78"; badly deformed; thickness: 0.25-0.28"; color: purple.

3. *Shotgun Wad* removed from the entrance hall is from a 12-gauge shotgun shell. Weight: 0.6465 g; diameter: 0.730"; thickness: 0.135".

4. *Shot Pellets* removed from the entrance hallway floor and wall, respectively, are both #8 shot. Weights: 73.8 mg, 74.3 mg; diameters: 0.095", 0.098", respectively.

5. *Shotgun Slug* removed from the upstairs stairway is a 16-gauge slug. It has plaster and copper- or bronze-colored metallic paint embedded in its nose and bits of wad crimped in its base. Weight: 22.4470 g (347 grains); diameter: about 0.65″; badly deformed but apparently not broken up.

6. *Living Room Door Panel* was measured to determine angles of penetration of the two shots. The smaller hole resulted from a slug entering the outside or hall side and exiting from the living room side. It was fired at a downward angle of about 13° to horizontal and at an internal angle of about 16° to the door. The larger hole was produced by a slug that entered the living room side and exited from the hall side. It was fired at an upward angle of about 18° to horizontal and at an internal angle of about 75°. A considerable amount of unburned powder was embedded in the varnish around the larger entrance hole. Markings produced by this powder are clearly visible. Additional white smudging is evident. The overall spatial distribution pattern was most unusual and is explained later in Section IV-6.

7. *Lead Slug* removed from the living room east wall is probably a .38 Special. It had a considerable amount of wooden splinters embedded in its base. Sample fibers from these splinters were compared microscopically to wooden fibers obtained from the living room door, and lath taken from the east wall of the living room. The door fibers were the same as those on the slug, the lath fibers were not. Striations are present which should permit identification of the weapon that fired this slug. Weight: 10.1018 g (156 grains); diameter: about 0.35″; badly deformed; grove width: 0.059″; land width: 0.118″; left twist rifling.

8. *Cartridge Case* removed from the living room floor is probably a .30 M1 carbine. It is stamped WCC-52. Because of the uncertain movement of this case prior to recovery it was not considered reliable evidence.

9. *Shot Pellet* removed from the north wall of the north bedroom is either a #7-1/2 or #8 shot. Weight: 78.3 mg; diameter: 0.095″. These measurements are about midway between the two sizes. It could have been in a shotgun shell labeled either 7-1/2 or 8.

10. *Copper Case Fragment* removed from the south wall of the north bedroom was not positively identified. Weight: 0.4774 g (7.3 grains); diameter: about 0.29″; badly deformed; grove width: 0.041″;

land width: 0.035″; estimated 12 right rifling. Identification of the weapon that fired this slug should be possible.

11. *Jacketed Slug* removed from the window casing in the south bedroom is a .45 caliber. It had some wall plaster on its nose. Weight: 15.1309 g (233 grains); diameter: 0.452″; grove width: 0.075″; land width: 0.159″; six right rifling.

12. *Fiber Compression Wad* removed from the east wall of the south bedroom was badly disintegrated. It was from a 12-gauge shotgun shell. Weight: 0.7211 g; diameter: about 0.75″; badly deformed; thickness: 0.25–0.28″; color: purple-gray.

13. *Lead Shot Pellets* removed from the east wall of the south bedroom were badly deformed #00 buckshot. They both had plaster embedded to their spherical surfaces. Weights: 3.4936 g, 3.5460 g; diameters: about 0.45″, 0.45″, flattened, respectively.

14. *Lead Fragment* removed from the east wall of the south bedroom crimped several fibers. These fibers were similar to samples taken from the mattress in that room. From its point of recovery it is presumed that this fragment was broken off from a larger pellet of the lower shot group.

With the exception of the .45-caliber slug [Section III-11], all evidence that I removed from 2337 West Monroe Street was transferred to Miss Seva Dubuar on 27 December 1969 in Elmira, New York. Mr. Andrew authorized and directed this action. I had previously met Miss Dubuar in Chicago on 8 December when Mr. Andrew introduced her to me as an assistant in his law office.

On 9 January 1970 Miss Dubuar came to Corning with addition physical evidence allegedly collected at the premises by the Panthers or their attorneys. I spent two days examining this material, which, at all times, remained in Miss Dubuar's custody. My examination did not begin until 11 January as on the tenth I met with Mr. Andrew, Mr. Dennis Cunningham, Dr. Victor Levine, and Dr. Cyril H. Wecht in Pittsburgh. During that meeting Mr. Andrew gave me ten more pieces of evidence for examination. When she left on 12 January 1970, Miss Dubuar took all evidence that she had brought on the ninth, those items I had been given by Mr. Andrew, and the .45-caliber slug that I had retained earlier for comparison purposes.

There is no reason to discuss all data regarding every piece of evidence examined. To do so would only be exhaustive and repetitious. No one could question the fact that several shots were fired from a variety of weapons. Therefore, I have simply listed a summary of the firearms evidence that I personally examined in Table 1 [omitted].

The following remarks refer to evidence that is included in Table 1:

1. The identification numbers in this table are the same as those originally assigned to each item by Mr. Andrew or members of his staff.

2. All fourteen .45-caliber slugs had right-hand, or clockwise, rifling consistent in every respect with test slugs fired in a Thompson submachine gun.

3. Since no weapon was available for test firing I selected the slug I had recovered as a standard and compared all others to it. [One slug] was not compared as it was covered with white paint that obscured microscopic striations necessary for matching.

4. Because of possible weight loss upon impact, it is recognized that almost any buckshot pellet smaller than 00 could originally have been this large. Nevertheless, in consideration of the general condition of these pellets, it is believed that the classification assignments in Table 1 are correct.

In all, 101 pieces of firearms evidence were examined; or, if each pellet is considered individually, 151 total. How many additonal pieces of evidence were removed as souvenirs during the tours will never be known.

IV. Evaluation of Physical Evidence

Although there was an inordinate quantity of firearms evidence in this case, in the final analysis only three items are necessary to reconstruct the events of greatest significance. Specifically, the question of who fired the first shot is paramount. Since only one shot was fired by the Panthers, it is only necessary to determine whether or not this was the first shot. It would be academic to prove that it was the sixth rather than the seventh, for example.

Initially, we may consider three possibilities regarding the sequence of shots. First, that the Panthers shot first; second, that the police shot first; and third, that the Panthers and the police fired their initial shots simultaneously. It is fortunate that the shotgun blast fired from within the apartment and one pistol shot fired into the living room both struck the same door panel. These events resulted in permanent physical facts that allow conclusions to be drawn as to which of the two shots was fired first. Unfortunately, however, these conclusions are based, in part, upon related events that cannot be established or proven by physical evidence alone.

1. The shotgun blast fired by the Panthers penetrated the living room door, continued across the entrance hall, struck and penetrated a partition, crossed the stairway to the upper apartment, struck an outside wall and fell to the stairs where it was recovered. I was able to look through the large hole in the living room door and sight this path to the final point of impact before the door was removed. The recovered shotgun slug was undoubtedly the projectile that was fired in the living room and ultimately penetrated the stairway walls. The presence of copper- or bronze-colored metallic paint on the slug confirms this. This is the first significant factor.

2. The slug removed from the living room east wall contained wooden fibers consistent with the living room door. It is concluded that this slug was the projectile that was fired into the apartment through the living room door. This is the second significant factor.

3. Further proof of the validity of the two previous conclusions may be established by geometry. Angles of penetration through the living room door panel have been described in detail in Section III-6. Using a scale model or diagram it will be found that projection of two lines through the door panel at their reported vertical angles will result in trajectories for each shot consistent with their respective points of impact. A tolerance of $\pm 5°$ was assigned to these angles of penetration from overhead and, further, to incorporate them into a scale diagram of the apartment. This has been accomplished as illustrated [on page 79.] From these diagrams it is evident, that since the living room door has to be moved 16″ to satisfy the two trajectories, then these two shots could not have been fired simultaneously. This is the third significant factor.

4. Since the two shots through the living room door could not have

been fired simultaneously the obvious question is: Which shot was fired first? The answer to this is simple provided two additional facts are known. First, were the two shots fired at nearly the same time? Second, was the door opening or closing when the shots were fired? Physical evidence cannot establish either of these; however, there has been considerable testimony reporting that these shots occurred close together as the police were breaking in. If this is true then there is no question regarding sequence of shots, the police fired first! A study of the diagrams [on page 79] clearly demonstrates why this must be so; it is elementary geometry. If, however, the living room door was being closed at the time of the shooting, it is just as conclusive that the Panther's shot was fired first. Therefore, the final proof of sequence must rest with the confidence assigned to the direction the door was traveling and the interval between shots. A liberal tolerance of $+10°$ would not change this conclusion.

One highly unusual, but seemingly unimportant aspect of this case is the identity of the Panther shotgun slug. This slug did not appear fragmented when I examined it. It weighed 22.4470 g or 347 grains, the exact weight of a Federal or Winchester 16-gauge shotgun slug.* Remington 16-gauge slugs weight 355 grains.* The next larger slug, a 12-gauge, weighs 401 grains.* Upon this basis I conclude that the Panther slug was a 16-gauge slug. Naturally, a 12-gauge slug could break up and lose weight if it struck something solid. The chance of losing just enough weight to result in the exact weight of a 16-gauge slug seems unlikely—but of course it is possible, I found no obstruction in the flight path at the scene sufficiently solid to cause fragmentation; the door panel and plaster would not cause the slug to have lost weight. Thus the slug must be a 16-gauge slug.

6. The powder pattern on the inside of the living room door was also most unusual as described earlier. This pattern could not be reproduced by test firings of standard 12-gauge slugs in a variety of 12-gauge shotguns at several distances. For this reason some unconventional test shots were made. Specifically, 16-gauge slugs were enlarged by taping and fired in 12-gauge shotguns, and 16-gauge slugs were reloaded into 12-gauge shells and fired in 12-gauge shotguns, and 16-gauge slugs were reloaded into 12-gauge shells and fired in 12-

*These weights are actual weights, which are lower in all cases than rated weights.

gauge shotguns. When either of these combinations were fired into varnished door panels, powder patterns resulted that were identical to the one on the inside of the living room door. Diameters of the holes produced from these test firings were consistently just over ¾", the same as the hole in the living room door panel. The federal grand jury *Report* makes no reference to a 16-gauge shotgun being available to either the police or the Panthers. This fact supports the theory that the one shot fired by the Panthers was a 16-gauge slug that had been reloaded into a 12-gauge shotgun shell. The weight of the slug and the powder pattern together confirm this hypothesis. There is no apparent significance to the reloaded shell as such, however.

7. Section II-7 described the trajectory alignments of shots fired through the wall between the living room and the north bedroom. Twenty-five of these shots penetrated the door to the north bedroom while it was wide open. Additional physical evidence supports the open position of this door during the shooting. In particular, plaster from the north wall of the north bedroom was blown against the back of the bedroom door. These deposits only occurred on the lower portion of the door because of garments that were hanging higher on the wall at the time of shooting. In addition, paint was spattered from the closet in the north bedroom to the lower left corner of the outside of the bedroom door. Had the door been closed at the time of shooting this condition could not have been produced.

8. The shotgun blast that struck the east wall of the dining room was fired from the archway leading into the kitchen. This shot was a single shot of #00 buckshot from a 12-gauge shotgun. It went through the top of the north bedroom closet and terminated on the north wall.

9. The anomalous trajectory of one shot entering the south bedroom was [mentioned above]. The reason this slug entered traveling slightly west is that it struck a bureau in the north bedroom and ricocheted on into the south wall. This shot is indicated by "15" in the apartment diagram.

V. Federal Grand Jury

The report issued by the federal grand jury is not accurate in several respects regarding my participation in this case. While the following comments on their report are not directly associated with physical evidence, I feel the reader can judge the issues for himself. The following quotes are from the *Report of the January 1970 Grand Jury,* United States District Court, Northern District of Illinois, Eastern Division.

Item 1: Page 51. "After being briefed on Andrew's view of the case, the expert spent approximately fourteen hours in examination of the premises on December 8. During portions of this time, the Black Panther Party was conducting tours of the premises. The expert retrieved various items of physical evidence, including the projectile which was fired from within the apartment through the living room door. This projectile was found on the staircase to the upstairs apartment, just below an apparent impact point on the west wall of the staircase. The expert also found a projectile which had struck the southeast wall of the living room and could have been fired through the living room door, partially open."

Comment: I was not given Mr. Andrew's view of the case at any time. This is pure speculation on the part of the grand jury, based neither upon fact nor testimony. It is stated very factually and suggests that I was brainwashed. It is incorrect. Perhaps item three of the agreement drawn by Mr. Andrew between ourselves will express our mutual feelings on this point better. It states: "The expert is to perform his services according to the most recent scientific methods and skills, and he is to testify in court according to the truth which he discovers through those scientific methods, but he is not to volunteer unsolicited information or conclusions during that testimony. In other words, the expert's testimony is to be influenced in no way by the fact that he is retained by the clients." This agreement was made between Mr. Andrew and myself on 8 December 1969.

Item 2: Page 51. "While some of his contributions were significant, the expert's testimony revealed his defense orientation, perhaps accentuated by the limited time he had and the briefings of counsel."

Comment: The references to "defense orientation" and "briefings of counsel" are again stated very factually when they could not possibly be more than opinion. This conclusion is unfounded and inaccurate. I was, am, and always shall be "truth orientated." If the truth helps the prosecution, it does not follow that the witness is prosecution orientated; likewise, if it helps the defense, it should not suggest that the witness is defense orientated.

Item 3: Page 51. "For example, he proposed an imaginative theory as to who fired the first shot based upon the position of the living room door and the assumed trajectories of the incoming and outgoing rounds. He illustrated that if the door was opening at the time of the first of two closely spaced shots, the incoming shot would have to be fired before the shotgun blast from within the apartment. However, if the door was closing, then the shotgun blast from within the apartment preceded the shot from outside the door. The expert stated that his opinion on who fired the first shot would be based on prior testimony establishing whether the door was opening or closing at the time."

Comment: The suggestion that my theory explaining the sequence of shots is "imaginative" is technically sound, but it implies a greater degree of uncertainty than is warranted. All theories are imaginative because they cannot be absolutely proven. Many such theories are well accepted, however, because they have been subjected to repeated challange, and because they cannot be disproven. My theory is based upon the science of mathematics, specifically geometry, but as previously reported, it also required two additional facts. These facts, that the door was opening and that several shots were fired close together, were established by testimony of the officers who conducted the raid. There is no imagination on my part regarding any of these facts. The grand jury either did not listen, did not comprehend, or did not have the desire to comprehend, when so simple a point was overlooked.

Item 4: Page 51. "His theory excluded any other movements of the door, i.e. it could have been kicked open and bounced back. In addition, his opinion that a deer slug shotgun blast through a door at close range would not cause it to move seemed strained to the Jury and was later contradicted by FBI tests on a similar door."

Comment: I did not testify that a shotgun blast fired through a door at close range would "not cause it to move." I stated that its effect to a swinging door would be negligible, especially when the shot strikes nearer the hinged side as it did in this case. The powder pattern on the inside of the living room door contained many granules of unburned powder. Firing a 16-gauge slug in a 12-gauge shotgun reduces the burning efficiency of the powder and the overall energy produced. Any testing that was not conducted with this type of unconventional load would not, therefore, be relevant to this case. Although it may have seemed "strained" to the grand jury to believe that a shot can penetrate a door and not cause it to move, I submit that twenty-five shots penetrated the north bedroom door and it did not move! Twenty-one were on the outer half of the door, away from the hinges, and nine of these penetrated the thicker outside edge. Certainly the energy transferred to this door by twenty-five slugs was greater than that of one slug striking the thin panel of the living room door. Had the bedroom door moved, the trajectories could not align. It did not, and that is relevant to this case.

Item 5: Page 52. "Any investigation that is designed to prove a theory rather than establish the facts has to be thoughtfully scrutinized and should not be accepted as objective without such scrutiny."

Comment: Since this statement closes the section titled "The Panther Investigation" it implies that the purpose of the investigation was to prove some theory. While I cannot speak for Mr. Andrew or Dr. Levine, I personally was attempting no such thing. In fact I testified that I have lectured and published on this subject many times, stating that an investigator should "never look for evidence to support a theory, but develop your theory from the evidence. . . . All evidence must be consistent with a theory or the theory must be modified to accept it."* The similarity between this quotation and that of the grand jury is somewhat remarkable.

VI. Rumors and Facts

There have been two rumors concerning my participation in this case that I should like to comment on. There may be others I have not heard, but for obvious reasons rumors will always be generated in any case of this kind.

Rumor 1: "MacDonell fired the shotgun blast in the entrance hall" (that struck impact point 1).

---

*"Ballistics—A Case Example of Deductive Reasoning from Unusual Physical Facts," *Law Enforcement Science and Technology,* Port City, 1969, vol. 11, 365–371.

Comment: This rumor was probably started because the State's Attorney's Police and the Chicago Police Department Crime Lab failed to observe the impact point on 4 December. I did not fire this, or any other, shot in Chicago during this investigation. The rumor was disproven completely when photographs taken on 4 December showed this impact point. I didn't get to the apartment until 8 December, four days later. See grand jury *Report,* page 81.

Rumor 2: "MacDonell fired the smaller hole through the door panel after he took it back to Corning."

Comment: The police did not believe the smaller hole went through the door. It did, at 16°. I did not fire any shot through this panel or alter it in any way while it was in my custody. Again, photographs taken on 4 December show this hole and absolutely disprove the rumor. See grand jury *Report,* page 45.

VII. Discussion

It is interesting that several persons have asked why I became involved in this case. The answer to this has been clearly expressed in the introduction; I was asked to make an impartial investigation. To the best of my ability I have achieved this objective.

The fact that considerable evidence was left at the scene is completely understandable. Unless something approaching a small army had been available, I think anyone remaining very long at 2337 West Monroe Street following the shooting of 4 December 1969 would have been a damn fool. May all who disagree visit that area at night, as I have, and test the strength of their convictions. Personally, I do not blame any officer, white or black, for leaving the scene posthaste. It was unfortunate from the security standpoint, but undoubtedly the best decision under the circumstances.

For the record, I am not a member of the Black Panther Party. I do not accept their philosophy nor support their programs. They have made no effort to recruit me and I have not attempted to discuss politics with them. I am a criminalist concerned with physical evidence, not a politician delving into sociology.

VIII. Conclusion

Conclusions have been drawn throughout this report. The two significant facts that have been revealed as a result of this investigation are reported as follows:

1. There is no evidence that more than one shot was fired at the police from within the apartment.

2. The one shot fired out was not the first shot; the first shot was fired by the police. This conclusion is based upon previous testimony that the living room door was opening at the time of the shooting.

4 December 1970
Corning, New York

II. The Commission Staff

(June 1, 1970–September 30, 1971)

Staff Director:
Herbert O. Reid

Deputy Staff Director:
Raymond Baxter

General Counsel
Barbara Morris

*Administrative Assistants
to Director:*
John Brittain
Jacqueline Rothschild

Coordinators of Task Forces:
Philip Ryan (West Coast)
Thomas Todd (Midwest)
Paul Diggs (Eastern Seaboard)

Senior Researchers:
Mark Abramson
Carolyn Durway
Perry Faithorn
Steven Zalkind
David Helms
Donald Mosby
Beryl Bernay
Michael Morehead

Student Researchers:
Larry Dillard
Sharon Laufer
Lewis Myers
Don Porter
Steven Raison
Herbert O. Reid, Jr.
Steven Smith
Jesse Zachary

Executive Secretaries:
Margot Donahue
Maureen Ikeda
Hale Wingfield
Joyce Arnold

Supporting Office Staff:
Frank Colon
Annette O'Neal
Michael Smith
Barbara Harris

FOR THE CHICAGO REPORT:
Raymond Baxter, Supervisor of Research
Thomas Todd, Coordinator of Field Investigation
Charles Fishman, Special Coordinator

Special Consultants:
Walter Booker
Bernard Davidow
Jameson Doig
Dr. Leo Goldbaum
Walter Levine
Herbert MacDonell
Richard Newhouse
John Spiegal
Janeus Park
Frank Reeves
Hylan Lewis
Nathaniel Jones
Harry Kalven, Jr.
Jon Waltz

Index